Education and Democracy
In the 21st Century

Education and Democracy
In the 21st Century

Nel Noddings

Teachers College
Columbia University
New York and London

Published by Teachers College Press, 1234 Amsterdam Avenue,
New York, NY 10027

Library of Congress Cataloging-in-Publication Data

Noddings, Nel.
  Education and democracy in the 21st century / Nel Noddings.
    pages cm
  Includes bibliographical references and index.
  ISBN 978-0-8077-5396-5 (pbk. : alk. paper) — ISBN 978-0-8077-5397-2
(hardcover : alk. paper)
  1. Education. 2. Democracy and education. I. Title.
  LB1025.3.N63 2012
  370.11'5—dc23

                                                    2012042072

ISBN 978-0-8077-5396-5 (paperback)
ISBN 978-0-8077-5397-2 (hardcover)

Printed on acid-free paper
Manufactured in the United States of America

20 19 18 17 16 15 14   8 7 6 5 4 3 2

Contents

Preface

Several major themes will guide our thinking throughout this book. The first is the need to accept and appreciate interdependence at every level as we work toward global democracy. The second is to recognize that education is an enterprise with multiple aims and to explore ways in which these many aims can guide choices in organizational structure, curriculum, and pedagogy. A third is to bring critical, analytical thinking to our work as educators. Some old ideas should be abandoned, but others should be resurrected. Why and for what purposes? As we engage in such analysis, a fourth theme will emerge with some urgency: We should give up the hopeless search for panaceas and instead ask of each idea suggested: Are there moral objections to it? If not, where might this be useful? For whom? Under what conditions?

Education in the 21st century must put away some 20th-century thinking. All over the world today, many educators and policymakers believe that cooperation must displace competition as a primary form of relating. Competition is not to be abandoned—some competition is healthy and necessary—but it should no longer be the defining characteristic of relationships in an era of growing globalization. If we agree with this judgment, then we must consider how to prepare students for a cooperative world, not solely for one of competition.

Another significant change in our thinking involves our dependency on bureaucracy. We all complain about *bureaucracy* in the pejorative sense of the word and have little respect for "bureaucrats." However, the change in thinking must probe critically into the basic notion that defined bureaucracy as an efficient mode of governmental management—the assignment of specific tasks and problems to specific bureaus or agencies. We have learned that this way of thinking often impedes the resolution of problems instead of assisting it. The bureaucratic way of thinking has been pervasive and has too often dominated educational thought. Many prominent educational thinkers, for example, have insisted that the school's job is to promote intellectual growth; other aspects of children's development should be handled by the family, religious institutions, or some other special agency.

This thinking has infected everything we do in schools. The disciplines have been sharply separated: Science teachers teach *science*; they do not correct oral language or even teach the mathematics required in science (that is the job of math teachers); English teachers teach literature, not the social roots and effects of the works taught (that is the job of history teachers); math teachers teach specific mathematical skills and concepts, not the religious beliefs of the Pythagoreans or the biological manifestations of Φ or π (is that anyone's job?). Everything from moral education to self-understanding, grief management, and sex must be taught (separately) by experts. I will argue strongly that such thinking must be modified, preferably abandoned. Cooperation and connection must displace competition and overspecialization. The approach I take here might well be called *ecological*. It concentrates on connections, balance, and whole communities of persons and ideas.

While some 20th-century ideas should be abandoned, others should be revived, analyzed carefully, and reevaluated. Critical thinking, for example, was mentioned as an educational aim throughout the 20th century, and it still appears prominently on lists all over the world. Indeed, it is more important today than ever, not only because of the increasing sophistication of technology but because we are trying to move toward a participatory democracy that is capable of deliberation. But again, the topic has too often been treated (if at all) as a separate, special skill, and we rarely look at all the things we are doing in schools that may advance or impede its development. We talk about it, but we rarely exercise it in our own debates about curriculum and pedagogy. Consider, for example, the possible effects of standardization—the increasingly narrow specification of the entire curriculum. Is this likely to encourage critical thinking in either students or teachers? We have to *think* about this.

In the same vein, muse a bit on another widely stated aim—creativity. The United States was rightly regarded as a mine of creative output in the 20th century. Now Asia is awakening and, determined to encourage creativity, Asian countries are trying to move away from test-driven curricula. We are doing just the opposite. Should this move worry us? Not only might standardization cramp creativity; it might also undermine our exercise of democracy. In the view of democracy advanced by Dewey, Whitman, and Emerson, participants work together with an abiding sense of interdependence and appreciation for the great variety of talents and interests that produce a vibrant democratic society. Standardization as it is now promoted may threaten the fabric of that democracy.

Education is not simply one agency with a specific purpose within an enormous bureaucracy. Education is a multi-aim enterprise, and it is time that we recognize that fact and build on it. Schools must address the needs of students for satisfying lives in all three great dimensions of contemporary life: home and family, occupational, and civic, both domestic and global. In several of the following chapters, I will make suggestions for possible ways to incorporate aims from these domains into the traditional curriculum.

Why not throw out the traditional curriculum? It is in many ways obsolete, boring, and disconnected from real life. But discarding it and starting over is not an option; it simply cannot be done. We have to work within reality. It is lovely to think about ideals and ideal communities but, as we do so, we should continually return to the world as it is and ask how those ideals might guide and improve the current situation. Social reproduction theorists and critical theorists are right to point out that the prevailing culture controls the schools and has the power to use them for its own reproduction. This does not mean, however, that we can do nothing to effect changes in schooling that should lead to a more democratic, sustainable, and socially just society. We may have to be quietly persistent in doing things the way we know they should be done, adopting a form of nonviolent resistance.

Throughout this book, I will advise again and again against the search for panaceas, for "what works" on a grand scale. No whole-hog approaches! So many wonderful ideas have appeared in the history of education, and many of them have been lost because they were pushed too far and, predictably, failed as universal prescriptions. As the book progresses, I will remind readers of some of these ideas and encourage renewed appreciation of them. We should put labels and ideologies aside and try to learn from one another.

We'll begin with a critical exploration of current problems in education and then proceed to a discussion of democracy, equality, and choice. In Chapter 4, we'll take a closer look at the aims of education and why we should revitalize aims-talk. Then, in Chapter 5, we'll consider the place of the liberal arts in contemporary education. In keeping with the themes suggested above, I will urge neither total acceptance nor rejection of the traditional program in liberal arts. Rather, I will ask what we should retain, why, and in what form.

In Chapters 6, 7, and 8, we will explore some possibilities for including aims from the personal, civic, and occupational domains in the curriculum. In doing this, I will make a plea for connecting the disciplines to each other and to life itself.

In Chapter 6, we will discuss educating for home life and parenting. Considering how important the domain of home life is for most of us, it is astonishing that we do so little to prepare students for it. There are historical reasons for this neglect, of course. The curriculum, from the time of classical Greece, was designed by *men* to prepare *men* for public life. This purpose has been reinforced by the continuing emphasis on separation of private and public life, and it has been further strengthened by bureaucratic thinking. The school, it has been contended, should develop the intellect. Other matters, such as parenting, should be learned at home. Today, we recognize the importance of home life in facilitating or retarding the school success of children, and we even (ineffectually) invite parent participation in school matters. Why, then, do we not include home life and parenting in our curriculum?

Similarly, in Chapter 7, we will consider the changes that will be required if we begin to look at Earth as our home, not simply as a world of nations. In that chapter, we will look carefully at ecological cosmopolitanism—a way of moving toward world citizenship that starts with cooperative study of Earth as the home of all life.

In Chapter 8, I'll argue for renewed attention to vocational education. The odd notion that one form of secondary education can prepare all students for whatever comes next—college or any occupation—is highly questionable; it is also deceptively undemocratic. Claiming to promote equality, we ignore significant differences in aptitude, talent, and interests. Claiming to support democracy, we allow students fewer and fewer choices in their schooling. We should guide them in making intelligent choices, not "protect" them by specifying everything they must learn.

As we educate for satisfying participation in home, occupational, and civic domains, we must always be aware that it is *persons* who move about in these domains and, as persons, we carry with us our character, personality, and spirit. These matters are, then, central to the task of educating. In Chapter 9, we will discuss what we might do to educate for self-knowledge and for moral and spiritual development.

Although this whole book is, in an important sense, about the education of citizens, Chapter 10 will look briefly at some of the topics and problems that beset citizenship education today. Our concentration in that discussion will be on the development and application of critical thinking.

Finally, in Chapter 11, we'll return to the problems mentioned in Chapter 1 and, given the intervening chapters, exercise some critical thinking in revisiting them.

Acknowledgments

Thanks are owed to students in many parts of the world whose conversations and questions over the years have contributed to the present work—students at Stanford, Teachers College, Colgate, University of Miami, Beijing Normal University, Tokyo, and many others.

Sincere thanks to Lynda Stone for continuing discussion on democratic education, to Denis Phillips for ideas that emerged when we co-taught the Dewey Seminar at Stanford, to Elliot Eisner for his artistic persistence in promoting humanistic education, to Dan De Nicola for the questions he has raised about my ideas on the liberal arts, to Michael Slote for ongoing discussion of ethics, to Vera John-Steiner for her persuasive essays on intellectual cooperation, and to John Goodlad and a host of educational thinkers who have greatly influenced my views on democratic education. Hearty thanks also to my editor, Brian Ellerbeck, who shared highly useful "musings" as the manuscript proceeded.

Finally, I want to express very special thanks to Steve Thornton with whom I have discussed the ideas here for more than a decade.

The Problems of Education Through Two Lenses

The dominant view today, seen through the lens of popular news articles and political speeches, is that our public schools are failing. This lament is heard repeatedly, and it is rarely modified to make clear that the complaint should properly be directed at *some* schools, not all schools. When we hear that our schools are failing, there is an understandable temptation to seek sweeping, universal change—"school reform." Critics of current school reform, some influenced by a century of thinking on progressive education, raise a finger of caution and urge a more careful analysis of the problems. If the problems have been misdiagnosed, the solutions triggered by the faulty diagnosis may actually harm schools that have been doing well and fail to help those that really are doing badly.

The charge that our schools are failing is usually based on test scores. American students do not do as well on international reading and math tests as students from Singapore, Korea, Japan, and Finland. What does this mean and how much should it worry us? First, the countries recording higher scores may not be comparable to the United States in important ways. Some may have homogeneous populations. In some, children are separated into different educational programs at an early age, and many drop out before the age of 15. While visiting in one Asian country, I asked a prominent educator about the high school dropout rate in his country. He said with some pride that few drop out. However, he added that many children simply do not make it to high school; these children have already dropped out. If we look at the Western European countries with which we share so much of our culture, we find most of us clustered closely in the upper mid-range of scores. Thus, worry over international test scores may be misguided. If we should worry, so should England, Germany, France, Netherlands, and most of Western Europe.

There is a second reason why we should not obsess over international test scores. We are now in the 21st century, and it is time to reduce the emphasis on competition. Cooperation will be a major theme throughout this book. We are living in a global community—that is, we are trying to build such a community—and the keywords now are collaboration, dialogue, interdependence, and creativity. This does not mean that there should be no more competition; some competition is both necessary and healthy, and it often promotes better products and performances. But in the 21st-century world, collaboration is the new watchword. People must work together to preserve the Earth and to promote the welfare of all its inhabitants.

Recently, President Obama advised—to considerable applause—that we (the United States) must out-innovate, out-educate, and out-build the rest of the world. This is an example of 20th-century thinking that many of us believe must be put behind us. From one perspective, we are urged to reclaim the ways that, in the 20th century, made us great. From a second perspective, those ways are thought to be dangerous. Habits of domination, insistence on being "number one," evangelical zeal to convert the world to our form of democracy, all belong to the days of empire. In the 21st century, without deriding the accomplishments of the 20th century, we must vow not to repeat the horrors of war that accompanied our rise to world power; it is time to recover from the harm done by such thinking and look ahead to an age of cooperation, communication (genuine dialogue), and critical open-mindedness.

STANDARDS

Another idea prominent in today's discussion of education is a professed need for standards. The drive for national standards is, of course, closely connected to the perceived failure of our schools. It is supposed that, if all schools had the same high standards, all would do better. In her 1995 book, Diane Ravitch made the connection explicit. Looking at the results of the 1994 NAEP (National Assessment of Educational Progress), tests she wrote: "Nationally, 40 percent of fourth graders performed below the basic level on the reading assessment, as did 30 percent of eighth graders and 25 percent of twelfth graders" (p. xxii). She then explained that "standards are essential for the improvement of education" (p. xxiii). It is much to her credit that she has since decided that the school reform movement based on standards and testing has done enormous harm to our schools (Ravitch, 2010).

The reasoning offered on the necessity of narrowly specified standards has baffled many of us. Have teachers been unaware of what they are supposed to teach? Have they deliberately aimed low? If, in fact, teachers cannot accomplish what is already expected of them, how will a new, carefully worded set of expectations (standards) help them to do so? This is a complex problem, and I will return to it throughout this book. At this point, I simply want to make clear some of the reasons why the matter is so contentious.

First, what do we mean by *standards*? In one everyday use of the word, we mean simply a respectable set of expectations for the quality of a product or the conduct of workers to which all will be held. We say things such as "She has very high moral standards," "He meets the standard in his work," and "Their cars do not meet safety standards." As Ravitch rightly points out, none of us would advocate low standards or no standards in this ordinary sense of assessing the quality of products or performances. But notice that a *standard* is associated with a particular field of endeavor and with the people engaged in that field. When people vary greatly, as schoolchildren do, and when they are pressed into work they have not chosen, it is foolish to expect them all to meet a set of predetermined standards. Indeed, it is obvious that we do not expect everyone to meet one standard, because we persist in giving tests that rank students into quartiles, quintiles, deciles, and percentiles. For some tests, we divide students into categories labeled basic, proficient, or advanced. Why do we do this, if our objective is to be sure that all students meet a predetermined standard? How do we help students who have not met the minimal standard? And what is our reaction when, by some wonderful chance or superb effort, all or most students achieve the standard? Why, of course, we raise it.

A true story may help here. Some years ago, when I was teaching high school mathematics, our department faced a challenge. The state university had decided to require 3 years of academic mathematics rather than the 2 years previously demanded for admission. The third year of math, second-year algebra, was difficult even for many good students—students who had in the past *chosen* to take it. How were we to manage putting all college-bound students through this course? We decided to design a course for which students could choose a minimal course, a standard course, or an enriched course. Students completing the minimum course would receive high school credit, but they would not be fully prepared for a fourth year of mathematics; those completing the standard course would be ready for the next year, and those choosing the enriched course would be well along in their study of mathematics. We (a team of teachers) met the full range of students in two large sessions in one huge room (the school cafeteria, periods one and two), and students could move from one course choice to another, if they changed their minds. The essential feature of our design was this: A student had to pass each chapter (or unit) before going on to the next. We spent time deciding what students needed to know in a chapter in order to succeed at the next, and we designed our tests accordingly. Students in the minimum course had to pass six units in the year (one chapter per marking period). Notice that this represented a well-defined standard, and we worked intensively with students who needed help getting through one chapter each marking period. We not only had a standard; we had a working plan in place to be sure that all students met it. But we respected the choices students made. Kids who chose the minimal course were not pressed to do more. Many of them were bright—a few even highly creative—but they did not like math and found it onerous. One of our stated aims was to help students take control of their own educational lives, and we honored this commitment. With this plan in place, none of our students scored in the bottom decile on a national test, and only five (out of 134) placed in the last quartile.

This sounds like a remarkable achievement, and by today's main measure (scores on a standardized test) it was. However, I still believe that the kids who struggled valiantly or half-heartedly to get through the minimum material would have been better served by a course consonant with their interests. Moreover, we did *not* reduce the achievement gap in any real sense. Those students deeply interested in mathematics sometimes completed 16 chapters (or more), contrasted with the six chapters completed by minimum course takers.

In order to create and implement this plan, we had to consider the external demand (that of the state university), the interests and aptitudes of our students, the content of the subject matter and what constitutes a respectable course of study, our commitment to democratic aims, and the space available for a large group to break into smaller, constantly changing groups. These concerns were intertwined; each had to be studied for itself, and then the whole set had to be reconsidered as a system. Standard setting is a complex process. There is some doubt that it can be done across all states, all schools, all classes, and all children. I'll say more about this process in Chapter 4, when we discuss aims and standards.

Performance Standards

When we think of standards in education, we usually have performance or achievement in mind. When a teacher is said to have high standards, we assume that she expects good work from her students, but that "good work" is not properly defined as the same for all students. She probably expects more from some students than from others, and we should require that she justify this difference in her demands. We do not and should not accept a difference based on race or gender—"these kids can't read Shakespeare" or "girls aren't good at math." But our long-overdue rejection of racial and gender bias does not mean that there are no legitimate differences on which to base our expectations. For us, in the third-year math course, we justified the different standards on the basis of student aptitude, interest, and guided choice. We were thinking not only of mathematics but of participatory, deliberative democracy.

Performance standards have long been a topic of controversy for teachers. How do we decide what is required for an A? Where do we set the mark for passing? If all of our students make the required score for passing, should we celebrate or, as administrators in New York City decided recently, declare that the test must be too easy? When tremendous emphasis is placed on the scores demanded by performance standards, all sorts of new problems arise. Are the designated scores for *basic, proficient*, and *advanced* carefully researched and justified? On what basis? I'll return to this topic in the next two chapters.

Content Standards and Opportunity to Learn Standards

In addition to performance standards, Ravitch (1995) discusses *content standards* and *opportunity-to-learn standards*. Content standards state what is to be taught and learned. Why call this material "content standards"? Why not simply "content"? Although advocates of national standards claim that standards should not be confused with standardization, the objective is certainly to prescribe (or standardize) what all students should learn in certain subjects and, further, what subjects all students should be required to study. In the example of our third-year math course, the state university issued what might be called a *content standard*, but the actual content and scope were decided by individual schools. This is another important feature of standard setting, and I'll return to the topic in some detail. For now, let's stay open to the possibility that content standards stated at a general, even vague, level designed for a stated purpose may be acceptable. Most of us would agree, for example, that all or nearly all children should be able to read and to use the four fundamental processes of arithmetic on whole numbers.

What is to be gained by establishing national content standards at this somewhat vague level? The content of the traditional academic curriculum has long been standardized in this way by textbook publishers, colleges, and the testing industries (SATs, ACTs). But, at the secondary school level, not all students have participated in the standard academic curriculum. Should all students now be required to take this program of study? When we consider opportunity-to-learn standards, we can agree that all students should have an opportunity to prepare for college, if they want to do so. But what of those whose talents lie elsewhere? In the next two chapters, and later in a chapter on vocational education, we'll explore this issue in some depth. The notion of opportunity to learn has not been fully or generously studied. It has deteriorated into a simplistic decision to force everyone into the same course of study.

We do not need a host of test scores to tell us that our schools have not provided equal opportunities for children to learn. Jonathan Kozol (1988, 1991, 2005) has been telling us for 4 decades—in troubling detail—how our schools neglect and deprive poor kids not only of opportunity to learn but of the opportunity to live in safe, attractive school buildings, to be fed, to move about in communities where health care and recreation are available. A just, caring community does not feed children simply so that they can learn; it feeds them because they are hungry. We have to get our priorities right. This observation leads to another concern about 20th-century thinking. Through most of that century, policymakers depended heavily on the theoretical notion of bureaucracy. Institutions and agencies have been established to manage particular problems and tasks. When a social problem arises, the appropriate institution (bureau or agency) must be identified and charged with its analysis and solution. We are beginning to realize that many human problems require the cooperative work of several agencies. Many of the problems observed in our schools are acute social problems that cannot be solved by schools—or any one agency—working alone. Collaboration has become a necessity.

As we consider opportunity-to-learn standards, we will again encounter two very different views. From the one most popular at the moment, it is thought that every child should have an opportunity to learn the material long held to be best for academically privileged students. From another perspective, there is concern that being forced into studies one dislikes may not constitute an opportunity to learn. This discussion will be embedded in a more fundamental one about the general purpose of education in a democracy. Is it to supply every child with a prespecified body of knowledge and skills, or is it to help each child find out what he or she is good at and would like to know and do? Or is it both of these, and our task is to find an optimal balance between the two aims?

There is an important point to be emphasized in connection with content or content standards. Content in each subject should be regularly reviewed by content experts. In the 1960s and 1970s, new highly creative curricula appeared in mathematics, science, social studies, and language arts. These curricula were largely financed by national agencies such as the National Science Foundation, but they were not endorsed by the national government; that is, the government did not require or even strongly recommend that the curricula be adopted. Despite repeated assurances that the federal government would not prescribe courses of study (or content standards), there was widespread and sometimes angrily expressed concern that the government would tell states what their schools should teach (see Schaffarzick & Sykes, 1979). The paradox here is that curricula produced during this era of government support have never been surpassed in creative quality; they were more varied and exciting than anything produced before or since. Still, the political clamor against government involvement was enough to close down productive activity. In an astonishing turnabout, today many people accept the idea of national content standards, often narrowly and specifically defined, and the impetus for creative variety has been lost. This change of attitude and the loss of creativity should worry us. What could account for such a dramatic change in thinking?

In later chapters, considerable time will be given to the content of curriculum, particularly that of the high school. Many people now apparently feel that one standard academic curriculum serves the best interest of both schools and students. Years ago, Robert Maynard Hutchins delivered an aphorism that has often been quoted: "The best education for the best is the best education for all" (quoted in Adler, 1982, p. 6). Years later, Mortimer Adler repeated it in an argument for democratic schooling. Careful thinkers should challenge all three of the "bests" in Hutchins's aphorism. Who are the "best" for whom the "best" education was designed? Generally, the "best" were drawn from the economically well-to-do with a few academically talented students invited to join the circle. We could spend useful hours exploring and analyzing the curriculum that was constructed for this privileged group. Indeed, many thoughtful observers call it simply "privileged knowledge." What was it designed to do? Was it designed to increase democratic participation or to ensure that power was retained by the "best"? What exactly did it comprise? How much variation did it exhibit? We cannot launch the needed investigation here, but take note that such an investigation is needed. Adler (1982) was simply wrong when he claimed that the "shape of the best education for the best is not unknown to us" (p. 7). Living in a world where the best and brightest have led us into war in generation after generation, where corporate greed is once again rampant, where religion has not weeded out its fundamentalist irrationalities, where poverty persists in the midst of riches, and the Earth itself suffers from human abuse, we can hardly claim to know the shape of the best education. On the contrary, we have only an outline, and it is a problem we should be working on diligently. I will argue that this "best" curriculum is badly out of date and that it fails to serve the purposes for which it was supposedly designed.

TEACHER ACCOUNTABILITY

If one believes that our schools are failing and that national standards will improve achievement, it is reasonable to demand that teachers be held accountable for the stated learning outcomes. (Keep in mind that three serious questions are implied in this one sentence: If our schools are failing, how should this failure be described? Why should we expect that a careful statement of standards will improve the situation? What do we mean by accountability?) Just as none of us would argue against establishing and maintaining defensible standards, no one would argue that teachers should not be accountable for what they do as professionals. But we can reasonably argue that teachers deserve neither sole credit nor sole blame for what their students learn or fail to learn. Native ability, home environment, community resources, and personal effort all contribute to students' success or failure in learning. Clearly, teachers should know their subject matter, plan their lessons, show up on time for classes, conduct themselves professionally, treat students with care, and cooperate with colleagues in professional activities, and there are ways to evaluate all of these responsibilities. Basic to accountability in any profession is the expectation that a practitioner should be able to *account for*, to justify, his or her professional decisions and acts. Notice that this is very different from being held accountable for the outcome itself. Lawyers do not win all of their cases and physicians do not save all of their patients from death, but they are asked to explain what they did and why to the satisfaction of professional peers. Defining accountability entirely in terms of student test scores is a distortion of the concept.

Even at its best, however, the concept of accountability has weaknesses. It puts too much emphasis on compliance, on answering to a higher authority. As I have argued elsewhere, *responsibility* is a much more powerful concept for teachers. Whereas accountability points upward in the hierarchy and tends to direct teachers' attention to their own vulnerability for rewards or penalties, responsibility points downward in the chain of power to those dependent on our care and competence. Teachers are responsible, at least in part, for the physical and emotional safety of their students and for their moral, aesthetic, and social growth, as well as their intellectual development. Their responsibility for student learning cannot be described wholly in terms of test scores:

> In addition to preparing students for the next grade or courses, they must be concerned with permanent or long-lasting learning. Over the years, students forget much of what they are taught in school. Indeed, all of us forget a mass of details we once learned in order to pass classroom tests. But responsible teachers hope students will retain certain habits of mind, intellectual curiosity, and eagerness (or at least willingness) to go on learning. When a teacher sees that a set of lessons is killing the joy of learning, she reasonably creates new, worthwhile activities that may restore the desire to learn. (Noddings, 2009, p. 20)

Teachers should not be held accountable, then, for adhering strictly to the prescribed curriculum. Rather, as professionals, they should expect to justify what they do when they depart from it in recognition of their deeper responsibility to students.

CHOICE

Still another current idea in education is that of *choice*. Again, we encounter two very different perspectives on the topic. Those who see schools as failing, who recommend national standards, and demand accountability, may also advocate school choice; that is, they argue that parents should be allowed to choose their child's school. Some argue for vouchers that would permit parents to choose a private school instead of a public school. Others argue for an increase in charter schools—schools that are publicly funded but free to operate without all of the rules and restrictions that govern the regular public schools. This is another complex topic to which we'll give more attention in the next chapters. And again, most of us would not argue against the notion of choice in our schools. Choice is fundamental in a democracy. But it can be argued that the public school, the local school that accepts all of a community's children, acts as a cradle of democracy. If we take that idea seriously, we will be more interested in providing age-appropriate choices for *students* in all of the school's activities than in encouraging a parental choice of school that might contribute to social divisions and unhealthy competition. An argument for providing greater choice for *students* is an important argument against standardization. We will see that reasonable people may differ on this difficult problem.

In these introductory comments about the current perception of problems, something should be said about the so-called achievement gap. The considerable gap between the test scores of White and Asian students and those of Black and Hispanic students is persistent and troubling, as is the growing gap between well-to-do and poor students. Again, there are at least two different perspectives on the problem. Some argue that schools and teachers are at fault; they either expect too little of their minority students or lack the competence to teach them successfully. Most of us agree that "low expectations" have been a source of poor minority achievement in the past, but the problem persists even though expectations have been raised for all of our students. Are teachers simply incompetent to teach minority and poor children? Why? And in what ways are they incompetent? Programs to remedy this incompetence abound. How should we choose among them? Or should we rethink the whole problem? Constantly emphasizing the gap may actually harm our minority students by drawing attention to their supposed inadequacy and increasing the occurrence of stereotype threat. Is there a better way to describe the problem and create a path to its solution?

SCHOOLING IN THE 21ST CENTURY

I have so far considered briefly two different perspectives on the problems in today's schools. We will revisit them in some depth in later chapters. Now I want to outline some important differences between 20th-century and 21st-century thinking; the topics on this outline will serve as a preview of sorts and provide material for analysis in the rest of the book. As we move along in the 21st century, new or revised values, attitudes, and aims may displace those characteristic of 20th-century thinking, and I will argue that we should consider them seriously. Many of these ideas already appear as aims on international lists.

Collaboration should be more important than competition. Forty years ago, Jean Piaget (1971) urged us to recognize the collaborative nature of creative work:

> The great man who at any time seems to be launching some new line of thought is simply the point of intersection or synthesis of ideas which have been elaborated by a continuous process of cooperation, and, even if he is opposed to current opinions, he represents a response to underlying needs which arise outside himself. (p. 368)

Today, this theme is addressed in stimulating accounts of working mathematicians (Hersh & John-Steiner, 2011) and, more broadly, of work across science, philosophy, music, art, anthropology, and literature (John-Steiner, 2000). Such impressive historical/biographical accounts should encourage us to promote cooperation in our schools and reduce the current craze for GPAs, rankings, and test scores. This in no way entails a reduction in the commitment to excellence.

Emphasis on collaboration suggests a corresponding emphasis on communication in the form of dialogue, and dialogue requires both listening and speaking. This emphasis is important at a basic level. If we want students to succeed both as students and as productive citizens, we must help them to master standard oral English. At present, we worry and fuss about scores on multiple-choice tests and yet allow students to graduate from high school without acquiring standard oral English. Possibly the best way to learn it is to engage in regular dialogue with people who can model that standard, and all teachers—not just English teachers—should be involved in this task. On a deeper level, learning to engage in dialogue is essential in developing the capacity to think critically. To avoid what Cass Sunstein (2009) has called "group polarization," we must learn to listen receptively to people both "inside" and "outside" the groups with which we identify. This is important at every level of human activity—personal, occupational, political, and global.

The 19th and 20th centuries in the United States were marked by an almost fanatical admiration for autonomy in the form of individualism and self-sufficiency. In the complex 21st-century world, there should be a healthy recognition of interdependence at every level. Recognizing that all of us need a caregiver at some stage of our lives, we should encourage greater appreciation of those who provide that caregiving (Fineman, 2004). More generally, appreciation of interdependence is vital in identifying and solving our social problems. We have to get past our faith in the bureaucratic system and encourage interagency cooperation at the level of families, agencies, and nations.

Critical thinking is now widely recognized as important for both effective occupational life and enlightened citizenship. Too often, however, we suppose that critical thinking is an intellectual skill that can be taught in isolation from critical issues. Although there are still advocates of this view, most people today believe that critical thinking is at least to some degree field- or topic-bound (Noddings, 2012b). A person unfamiliar with quantum physics is not likely to be able to think critically about that subject. This recognition that if we want students to think critically about social issues, we should provide them with some practical experience. For example, people are more likely to think critically and appreciatively about interdependence if they are occasionally involved in caregiving activities. In Chapter 6, I will discuss ways in which we might profitably expand the curriculum by drawing on women's experience—experience that, historically, has been rich in caregiving.

Worldwide, there has also been increasing interest in creativity as an educational aim. The growth of interest shown by Asian educators is especially impressive. It is paradoxical that America—a center of innovation and creative endeavor for 2 centuries—seems to be retreating to a standard, narrowly defined, test-centered curriculum, just as China and Japan have decided to move away from test-driven curricula. As I discuss creativity in this book, I will emphasize providing opportunities for creative activity; I will not suggest that we design a step-by-step course that will make everyone measurably creative.

As we'll see throughout this book, particular educational aims are, as Dewey pointed out, rightly products of the current time. Of necessity, then, we must ask what schools should do to accomplish the larger aims of 21st-century global democracy: preservation of the Earth, continuing evaluation of technology and its effects on social life, thoughtful analysis of what it means for individuals to live a full life, and how we might induce a renewed commitment to personal integrity and moral concern for the welfare of others.

As an organizing principle, we will consider how schools can help students to achieve satisfying lives in three great domains: home, occupation, and civic life. Throughout the book, I will argue that it is a major mistake to reduce our educational efforts to just one of these domains.

Obviously, then, we need to say something about the nature of life and democracy in the 21st century. Before turning to that topic, however, I want to make it clear that I do not foresee dramatic changes in the basic structure of curriculum in America. We have to work within that basic structure. Sadly, I think we will go right on with English, mathematics, social studies, science, and foreign languages as the backbone of our curriculum. Indeed, if we continue in the direction we are now headed, the curriculum will become even more isolated from real life and its subjects more carefully separated from one another. It is this tendency that we should resist, and effective resistance will require collaboration, critical thinking, and creativity.

2

Democracy

It is almost a century since the publication of John Dewey's (1916) *Democracy and Education*. In that book, he wrote:

> A democracy is more than a form of government; it is primarily a mode of associated living, of conjoint communicated experience. The extension in space of the number of individuals who participate in an interest so that each has to refer his own action to that of others, and to consider the action of others to give point to his own, is equivalent to the breaking down of those barriers of class, race, and national territory which have kept men from perceiving the full import of their activity. (p. 87)

But, as Dewey recognized, there are many forms or modes of associated living. What, beyond the number of participating individuals, distinguishes the mode characteristic of democracy? Dewey (1916) identified two central characteristic traits: First, members of a democratic social group share "numerous and varied interests" and second, the group engages in a healthy "amount of interaction and cooperative intercourse with other groups" (p. 87). Most members of a democratic group share activities and interests within the group, and the group itself is not isolated from other groups.

Dewey (1916) insisted that there must be "free and equitable" exchanges across groups and individuals expressing different viewpoints. "Diversity of stimulation means novelty, and novelty means challenge to thought" (p. 85). We can see immediately that his description of democratic groups embodies or implies several of the values identified with 21st-century thinking: cooperation, communication (dialogue), and creativity. Dewey recommended building a democratic society from characteristics already present in at least some rudimentary form. He argued against constructing a wholly theoretical ideal and against getting stuck in ineffective patterns of conduct that might have worked if the theoretical ideal had been in place. The thinking of both Plato and Rousseau, Dewey argued, was weakened by this tendency. Dewey put his trust in the communicative interaction of actual groups working together for both improved education and an improved society. If Dewey were alive today, he might well disagree with some of what I will say in this book, but he would agree enthusiastically with the project—starting with a realistic view of where we are and looking ahead to a society more appreciative of interdependence, to a fuller recognition of individual differences and diversity, to education for fuller, more satisfying relational lives, as well as a society made stronger by individual fulfillment.

In Chapter 3, on equality, we will consider in some depth the ways in which Dewey's conception of education differs fundamentally from that of Robert Maynard Hutchins (1936/1999), Mortimer Adler (1982), E. D. Hirsch (1987), and others who insist that all children in a democratic society should be provided with the same curriculum throughout their pre-college schooling. At this point, I want to discuss briefly a fundamental difference in their conceptions of democracy. Both Hutchins and Adler believed that effective communication in a democracy depends on a base of values and common knowledge shared widely by most (ideally all) citizens. For them, democracy—its ideas and practices—precedes and supports public conversation. In contrast, Dewey believed that communication precedes and is instrumental in the construction of democracy. In the first chapter of *Democracy and Education,* Dewey (1916) emphasizes the role of communication in the process of constructing shared values:

> Men live in a community in virtue of the things which they have in common; and communication is the way in which they come to possess things in common. (p. 4)

Both Hutchins/Adler and Dewey believed in the necessity of shared values and interests, but Hutchins and Adler took the ideals of democracy and education as already known, more or less fixed and ready to transmit to new generations. In contrast, Dewey saw democracy as an ideal under construction, one into which the young are inducted through participation, especially participatory communication. Communication, as Dewey described it, is stressed in 21st-century educational thinking as dialogue. Communication affects changes in both speaker and listener. The speaker must find a way to express his or her own experience so that it means something in the listener's world of experience. Dewey (1916) wrote:

> It may fairly be said that any social arrangement that remains vitally social, or vitally shared, is educative to those who participate in it. Only when it becomes cast in a mold and runs in a routine way does it lose its educative power. (p. 6)

Hutchins and Adler were certainly not advocating a routine and boring curriculum. They believed that a current society has much to learn from the ways in which thinkers and leaders in past societies addressed their problems. Dewey did not disagree with this, but he believed that effective thinking on today's social problems must start with the experience of those living with and addressing the problems. Indeed, he accused Hutchins of divorcing education from the actual problems of living (Johnston, 2011). In education, that divorce is illustrated in Hutchins's sharp separation between vocationalism and intellectualism. Removing that separation is an important aim of the present work; it will be the focus of a later chapter. I will argue that much of the traditional (and admittedly quite wonderful) material recommended by Hutchins and Adler can be worked into courses centered on current issues and interests, into vocational as well as academic courses.

For Dewey, shared interests among diverse groups and among individuals with different talents form the basis of novelty and allow for progress in the continual project of constructing democracy. Values are not simply handed down; they are cooperatively constructed in dialogue and working together on common projects.

We should be careful, however, not to caricature these opposing views. Both recognize the need for common knowledge as well as common interests. Is the difference, then, merely a matter of pedagogy? I think it is more than that. Hutchins put great emphasis on teaching the treasured knowledge of the past. Dewey noted that such knowledge is deeply flawed. While expressing admiration for Plato's attempts to address differences of talent and interest in students, he pointed out that the only solutions available for social issues depended on the prior creation of an ideal state. Plato was unable to identify and work with promising elements in his own society. One can easily get stuck in past visions of the ideal, supposing them to be real possibilities. Dewey did not ignore the past, but he looked to an analysis of present experience to build a future. What should we select from the past and why?

Something like the Dewey-Hutchins debate continues today. There are those who insist that a broad base of common knowledge of national history and Western literature is a prerequisite for participation in a democratic conversation, and there are those, in opposition, who favor the cultivation of diversity, building democracy from a variety of viewpoints. The two positions are still at odds, and some advocates of a standard view of cultural literacy (E. D. Hirsch, for example) admit that cultural diversity would be reduced by an emphasis on cultural literacy as defined by what every *American* should know (Wilhelm & Novak, 2011). Arthur Schlesinger Jr. (1992) has also argued that the public schools have a responsibility to maintain the "historic idea of a unifying American identity" and that their failure to do so is contributing to the disunity of America (p. 17). I don't think we should brush these criticisms aside as products of intolerance. We should, instead, think about a healthy balance of diversity and unity. The direction in the 21st century should be toward global unity—a commitment beyond the national and forms of multiculturalism that may be divisive. One way to move in this direction is through what I will call "ecological cosmopolitanism," to be discussed in Chapter 7.

All political philosophers recognize the importance of education in preparing the young for citizenship. Are there political theories that provide special guidance with respect to democratic education?

TOWARD A DEMOCRATIC THEORY OF EDUCATION

Amy Gutmann (1987) starts her search for a democratic theory of education with a brief discussion of the weaknesses in the best-known political theories—conservative, liberal, and functionalist. Conservative theories, she suggests, insist on a separation of the public and private that is no longer viable in an age of changing family and gender relations. Conservative views must be given a hearing, but they cannot be used to guide the whole system of public education. Similarly, liberal theories, with their emphasis on individual autonomy, would advocate government enforcement of practices and curricular content that meet liberal standards of political rightness, but these standards would be offensive to conservatives. Her treatment is far too brief, but her main objections can be sustained by more extensive arguments. From the perspective I am taking, it is right to reject idealized, fixed political theories as guides to democratic education, but it makes sense to listen to the recommendations of their proponents.

Gutmann then considers a set of theories she calls "functionalist," those theories claiming that schools in a capitalist society function to maintain capitalism. In education, we usually refer to these theories as "social reproduction" theories. These theorists might better be called anti-functionalist. They agree with the functionalists that the schools in a capitalist state function to maintain capitalism, but they do not conclude that nothing can be done about the situation. Their remedy is to replace capitalism with some form of socialism. Bowles and Gintis (1976), for example, call for a socialist revolution. They critique the ways in which schools and educational theories function to maintain order in the hierarchy of power and privilege. I think Gutmann brushes these critiques aside too quickly. Consider what is happening in our schools today. In the interest of equality (much more will be said about this in the next chapter), many schools now force all students into college preparatory mathematics courses. The stated intention is to eliminate the invidious distinctions that have accompanied curricular tracking. There should be no more college prep, commercial, vocational, and general tracks. Democracy, it is contended, demands that all students have the same secondary school curriculum.

But what is actually happening? Algebra courses—which everyone must now take—are labeled *basic, remedial, standard, advanced, accelerated, honors,* and the like. Further, some students start algebra in the 7th or 8th grades, while others wait until they are forced into it in 9th grade. The distinctions are clearer than ever. People do not give up positions of power and status easily, and as we will see, putting all students into the "same" program may actually make it easier to rank and separate them. The desire to achieve and maintain high status may be innate in human beings. I have sometimes used as an example Dr. Seuss's story of the Sneetches. In their society, one relatively small group was largely in control. The larger subordinate group figured out that the ruling group had stars on their bellies; that was their distinction. Aha! The subordinate group submitted to having stars applied to their bellies. Now, for a time, all were equal, all were star-bellied Sneetches. Then, the original star-bellied Sneetches, unhappy with the new equality, had their stars surgically removed. The two groups went through a mad series of procedures—on and off with the stars. In Dr. Seuss's tale everything ended blissfully in a total inability to judge who was who. In real life, power relations are likely to be preserved. We will return to this problem more than once in later chapters.

Gutmann also neglects to discuss the socialism espoused by the theorists she calls functionalists. This is important, because those writers insist that socialism *is* the democratic theory sought by Gutmann. Bowles and Gintis (1976), for example, claim that "socialism is the progressive strengthening and extending of the process of economic democracy, with its attendant continual transformation of the process of interpersonal relationships in work, community, education, and cultural life" (pp. 282–283). One cannot set this claim aside so easily, and it should be especially difficult for Gutmann, who asserts that her democratic theory has been inspired by Dewey. Dewey was clearly influenced by socialism, and he voted the socialist ticket in five presidential elections. However, in Dewey's time, as in our own, it seemed impractical to use the term *socialism*.

Dewey wrote:

> A new party will have to adopt many measures which are now labeled socialistic—measures which are discounted and condemned because of the tag. . . . The greatest handicap from which special measures favored by the Socialists suffer is that they are advanced by the Socialist party as Socialism. The prejudice against the name may be a regrettable prejudice but its influence is so powerful that it is much more reasonable to imagine all but the most dogmatic Socialists joining a new party than to imagine any considerable part of the American people going over to them. (quoted in Westbrook, 1991, pp. 444–445)

Dewey's comment could have been written today. The word *socialism* is still a pejorative in America.

The heart of Gutmann's democratic theory is deliberation, a political process of analyzing, debating, and evaluating social/political practices that gives voice to a wide range of ideals without fastening on any one. Gutmann distinguishes her democratic theory from the direct teaching of moral ideals, no one of which can be fully implemented without incurring the resistance—even wrath—of those holding a different moral ideal.

"Deliberative democracy" is a relatively new category of democracy (see Held, 2006). It recognizes the legitimacy of the concern expressed by Plato and many others that participatory democracy can deteriorate to the emotional and ignorant rule of unreasonable masses. The solution, advocates of deliberative democracy suggest, is an insistence that all sides be heard on problematic issues and that every argument be logically defensible. Within the group of deliberative democrats, at least two groups may be identified—impartialists and their critics who argue that the impartialist approach can only work under ideal conditions. (This criticism is reminiscent of the one Dewey directed at Plato and Rousseau.) The critics, including Gutmann, seek a pattern of deliberation actually workable in the real world. On this, Gutmann agrees with Dewey, and so do I. (See also the essays in Soder, Goodlad, and McMannon, 2001.) I'll say more about this as we examine the role of schools in educating for deliberation.

In developing her new democratic theory of education, Gutmann (1987) writes: "The most influential theory of this century—John Dewey's—is itself explicitly democratic. The democratic theory that I develop is inspired by Dewey, but it also diverges from Dewey in at least one way" (p. 13). She agrees with Dewey that there is a need to enlarge our educational thinking beyond considerations of teacher-pupil, teacher-parent standpoints. "But," she adds, "what should that broader, presumptively democratic standpoint be?" (p. 13)

In what follows, however, she misunderstands Dewey. Using Dewey's (1900) line from *The School and Society*, "What the best and wisest parent wants for his own child, that must the community want for all its children," (p. 3), Gutmann supposes that Dewey had some particular set of knowledge, skills, and attitudes in mind that, this set being truly the "best," should be the curriculum offered to all children. Perhaps Dewey should have used different language. (He does sound rather like Hutchins in this passage.) But if we read more of Dewey's work on education, we know he meant that the best and wisest parent would want for *each* of his children what was best for that particular child. Far from describing a uniform course of study for all children, Dewey wanted a curriculum rich enough, flexible enough, to help each child find what he or she needs to build a satisfying and satisfactory life. In agreement with Dewey, I will look at the curriculum, pedagogical methods, and social arrangements in schools from the perspective of where we are now and where we should be headed in the 21st century if we take this aim seriously.

Gutmann gives little attention to the school curriculum, but she gives us two potentially valuable principles by which to judge educational policy—nonrepression and nondiscrimination. Adherence to these principles in an atmosphere of deliberation should make it possible for individuals and groups to follow their own rational moral ideals and also prevent the exclusion of future citizens from receiving an education that will permit their full participation in a deliberative democracy.

But these principles are easier to state than to apply. (On this, see the discussion in Callan, 1997.) If, for example, some of us want students to be aware that major religious groups have often supported war, and others object to including such material in the curriculum, what should we do? It isn't merely a matter of finding a reasonable, balanced way to treat the topic. Some people object to the subject appearing at all in the school curriculum. Under Gutmann's nonrepression principle, the issue should be addressed honestly, but powerful groups act again and again to repress discussion of a host of issues. Consider, for example, past and current topics that some find it objectionable to discuss critically: American exceptionalism, parenting, patriotic exercises, the use of propaganda (by our side), the downside of capitalism, same-sex marriage, hunting for sport, the existence of hell, spirituality, economic disparities, hedonism in advertising, even the ecological harm done by maintaining large lawns. The list could easily be extended (Noddings, 2006, 2012a). Recall the Texans who wanted to omit Jefferson from American history courses because of his stand on the separation of church and state. Some thinkers believe that we cannot put aside our moral ideals and simply hope that children will encounter a host of competing views outside of school. Who will see to it that disadvantaged youngsters will hear balanced accounts of the various views? Who will inform youngsters who have been indoctrinated to questionable moral ideals that there are other ways to look at things? And who is to pronounce that "these kids" and not "those" have been indoctrinated? Deliberative thinkers can embrace "nonrepression," but how do we overcome continual repression from those who reject the concept?

The problem is so difficult that some conscientious thinkers recommend abandoning the overly idealistic insistence on balance and just explicitly teaching defensible views on social justice. Bowles and Gintis call frankly for a socialist revolution, and before them George Counts wrote eloquently about the economic evils of unrestricted capitalism. A democratic socialized economy would not allow any individual to exploit the environment and fellow citizens:

> He would not be permitted to carve a fortune out of the natural resources of the nation, to organize a business purely for the purpose of making money, to build a new factory or railroad whenever or wherever he pleased, to throw the economic system out of gear for the protection of his own private interests, to amass or to attempt to amass great riches by the corruption of the political life, the control of the organs of opinion, the manipulation of the financial machinery, the purchase of brains and knowledge, or the exploitation of ignorance, frailty, and misfortune. (Counts, 1932/1969, pp. 46–47)

Counts wrote this in the early 1930s. Readers might respond with some sadness that the lament (if not the implied solution) might have been written today.

Describing how different the society would be if such practices were not allowed, Counts (1932/1969) called on teachers to take responsibility to promote the new vision of society:

> Such a vision of what America might become in the industrial age I would introduce into our schools as the supreme imposition, but one to which our children are entitled—a priceless legacy which it should be the first concern of our profession to fashion and bequeath. (pp. 50–51)

Dewey largely agreed with Counts on a democratic socialist view of the future, but he could not advocate indoctrination (or "imposition"); he insisted that the means as well as the ends must be morally acceptable. Clearly, Gutmann agrees on this, and I do, too. Indoctrination—even in the name of a great good—too easily leads to domination, authoritarianism, and even totalitarianism. Dewey put his trust in the "method of intelligence;" through dialogue, responsible experimentation, and the evaluation of current experience, students should come to the conclusions embraced by social revisionists or to well-argued alternatives. But a serious problem remains today: How will students come to rational, moral conclusions on serious social/political issues if we cannot even discuss them? (See Apple, 1996; Leahey, 2010; Macedo, 1994; Spring, 1997.) That is a problem we still face in the 21st century. When we adopt a principle of nonrepression, it becomes easier to simply omit discussion of a controversial issue entirely rather than be accused of promoting one idea over another.

Perhaps we do not need an elaborate, detailed theory of democracy, replete with principles to guide every decision. Dewey's emphasis on free and extensive communication within and across groups gives us a good start. Perhaps we should accept his advice and build our theoretical position as we go.

Consider a current, local example. The village, Ocean Grove, in which I now live is part of a larger township, Neptune, New Jersey. The village was organized years ago by the Methodist church, and the Camp Meeting Association still exercises considerable control over activities in Ocean Grove. At the center of the village stands the Great Auditorium at which a variety of lectures and musical events take place every summer. Church services are also held at the Auditorium, and a large cross, facing the ocean, is mounted on its exterior. The Auditorium is clearly a Christian establishment.

Because the Auditorium has enormous seating capacity (over 3,000) and a magnificent pipe organ, it has been an ideal site for Neptune High School graduations. This year, a complaint was filed with the American

Civil Liberties Union (ACLU) over the mixing of church and state in using a Christian facility for a public school ceremony. It was not clear at the time I started writing this chapter whether the ACLU would actually bring suit over the matter. A compromise has since been reached. The graduation was held in the Auditorium, but the cross was not illuminated, and religious signs inside the Auditorium were temporarily covered over.

How should we look at this issue? As a secularist and member of the ACLU, I might simply endorse the complaint and insist that the graduation ceremony be held elsewhere or, as was actually decided, that all signs of Christianity be temporarily removed or covered over. But think of it from a Deweyan/Whitmanesque perspective. We have an opportunity to encourage communication and cooperation across secular-religious lines. There is no intention on the part of either group to convert, repress, or discriminate. In arranging the graduation ceremony, representatives of the public (state) and church groups (neighbors) work together to provide a lovely and satisfying experience for the graduates and their families. The occasion also provides an opportunity for students and teachers to discuss issues related to church-state separation. The very essence of democracy is captured in such an occasion for cooperative activity.

The Deweyan argument can be augmented by a brief evaluation through the lens of care ethics. The situation involves groups who have direct contact in a local community. The high school has an expressed need for a large attractive facility in which to hold its graduation exercises. The Camp Meeting Association is not only willing to meet the need; it also wants to enhance its own image in the larger community. There is no need to introduce or refer to a *principle* that governs the assignment of legal authority in church-state affairs. Indeed, principles invoked unnecessarily can impede rather than enhance democratic relations. Unless there is a directly applicable principle forbidding friendly negotiations, groups would do well to address themselves to direct communication and cooperation.

To help in filling out Dewey's (1927) notion of democracy as a mode of associated living, we might turn to Walt Whitman, "the seer of democracy" (p. 184). Recognizing democracy as an ongoing, controversy-laden project, Whitman (1982) called for a new literature that would portray the wonders of the natural world and the new spirit of human fellowship and equality. He wanted the arts, especially literature and music, to deepen and broaden the expression of democracy. He sang of an end to authoritarianism, of religiosity without churches, the equality of women, the renewal of moral character, love and respect (poetic adoration) for nature, and a genuine appreciation for ordinary working men and women—the People! He sought neither a blueprint created in the past nor a mythical ideal of the future, but a continuous struggle to communicate, to share, to celebrate ordinary life in its best, most honest forms.

Stranger, if you passing meet me and desire to speak to me, why should you not speak to me? And why should I not speak to you? (Whitman, 1982, p. 175)

Such thoughts are also found in the work of Ralph Waldo Emerson. Emerson celebrated ordinary life and made it glow. Dewey clearly admired Emerson's understanding of the vital connection between creative individuality and cooperative social relations. In *Individualism, Old and New*, Dewey (1929–30/1988) cited Emerson's views on the dynamic, interconnected nature of individuality and democracy. Acknowledging with Emerson that the network of relations (society) can undermine individuality, he points out (again in agreement with Emerson) that recognition of the possibilities inherent in continuous change can have a positive effect on both individual and society:

> But "the connection of events," and "the society of your contemporaries" as formed of moving and multiple associations, are the only means by which the possibilities of individuality can be realized. (p. 122)

The views expressed by Whitman and Emerson might be labeled romantic, but they do not express impossible ideals, and they are not intended as recipes, bodies of law, or constitutional clauses. They express a spirit of care, fellow-feeling, friendship, sympathy, regard, and the like. Combining their views with that of Dewey's method of intelligence and with care ethics (which also puts great emphasis on dialogue and continuous practice), perhaps we can develop an approach that is stronger than any one view so far expressed. In making this attempt, I will also consider the views of social reproduction and critical theorists. They are right to point out that schools are controlled by powers in the society that work largely to maintain the social/economic status quo (Apple, 1996; Spring, 1997). We must be alert to how easy it is to support this power inadvertently. The current movement to force academic studies on everyone—proposed ostensibly to promote equality—may, paradoxically, help to maintain the status quo and even reduce opportunities for upward mobility. We should remember also that Dewey had socialist leanings that strongly influenced his views on democracy.

Throughout this book, I will urge readers to consider a host of ideas, theories, and concepts that have been introduced into education with enthusiasm and discarded when it was discovered that they did not yield panaceas. We should avoid buying views and methods "hook, line, and sinker," but we should also avoid simply discarding them. Instead, we should ask how some of the ideas can be used, for what purposes, at what time, and with which students.

DEMOCRACY IN SCHOOLS

Following Dewey, Emerson, and Whitman, I think of democracy as first of all participatory, and with Gutmann, I see an important role for teachers in both promoting the participation of students and in guiding them toward deliberative thinking and communication. With Dewey, I believe that communication (dialogue) precedes the establishment of common values, and guided participation in conversation and dialogue is a means of learning to deliberate. Teaching for deliberative participation is not easy in even supportive situations; in our schools today, with so many forces opposing such teaching, it is very difficult. The prevailing idea is that we already know what constitutes the educated person and the democracy we cherish, that all we need to do is teach this material in didactic form—from specific learning objectives to easily measured items on a test—to produce a new generation of intelligent, dedicated citizens. My claim is that this will *not* produce deliberative thinkers. Further, many teachers are not themselves deliberative thinkers.

Those teachers who are deliberative thinkers, encouraged by supervisors, should set an example by asking relevant questions about every school policy. For example: Given financial shortages across the country, many schools have decided to cut back on extracurricular activities and concentrate greater effort on academic basics such as math and reading. Is this a wise choice? What purposes are served by extracurricular activities in our high schools? Student government groups, clubs, and performance groups provide opportunities for students to work together, elect officers, and establish goals and plans for their achievement. In the comprehensive high school, these activities bring together students from different programs and, thus, increase points of contact across the student population. It is not an exaggeration to claim that healthy extracurricular activities act as a cradle of democracy, an important center of practice for young citizens. If the choice is to double the time in formal language arts and drop extracurricular activities or to maintain the typical one period in the former and promote the latter, there is good reason to choose the second option. Moreover, communication directed at their own democratically chosen projects may do more to increase facility in language than would more formal language instruction.

Consider another example of the sort of thinking to be encouraged. Suppose a city or large district is considering the establishment of a magnet school in, say, the arts. There is something enormously attractive about organizing a school around the expressed interests of the student body. But is a separate school the best way to do this? When we think again about Dewey's criterion of communication across groups with very different interests, we might prefer to find a way to satisfy students' special interests without placing them in separate schools. We want to develop citizens who can do more than use the formal procedures of a democracy; we want citizens who respect their interdependence and can work cooperatively across groups with whom they share some values but have different central interests. This is not to say that magnet schools should be rejected. Rather, it is to warn that careful deliberation should be used in making the decision. When magnet schools and vocational schools (to be discussed in Chapter 8) are established, thought should be given to interschool activities designed to enhance mutual respect and cooperation.

Another example: Should a democratic society permit private schools? Gutmann (1987) discusses this question at some length, but she uses language somewhat different from the Dewey/Whitman pattern I've been exploring. In a fine example of deliberation, she acknowledges that a strong argument can be made for the prohibition of private schools in a democracy, but she suggests:

> A better alternative to prohibiting private schools would be to devise a system of primary schooling that accommodates private religious schools on the condition that they, like public schools, teach the common set of democratic values. (p. 117)

But if we agree with Dewey that democracy is primarily a mode of associated living, we might have strong reservations about this alternative. Can we teach democratic values without living them? It is one thing to use democratic procedures within a closed group; it is quite another to work across groups in a genuine pattern of democracy. Consider the ancient Greeks. Supposedly, we learned something about democratic *procedures* from their example, but Athens was by no stretch of the imagination a democracy. We might conclude that it would have been better for our democracy if private schools had never been allowed to exist. At the same time, we might acknowledge that trying to eliminate them now would be counterproductive in the campaign to strengthen our democracy. Such a move would surely be regarded as anti-democratic. Instead, we might now work to increase the points of contact across schools and discourage further increases in privatization.

Choice is another matter that arises regularly in discussions of democracy. One argument against the elimination of private schools centers on the right of parents to choose their children's schools. In a democracy, it is argued, parents should be allowed to send their children to religious schools, and this right is especially important when the public schools are forbidden to promote the religion advocated by parents. This is a right long accepted in the United States, but there are strong counterarguments. One counterargument concerns the rights of children to an education that

is culturally broad and scientifically sound. Pointing to Gutmann's democratic aim of rational deliberation, one might object strongly to the sort
of education offered in Fundamentalist Christian schools, as well as that
presented in radical Muslim or Jewish schools (Peshkin, 1986). Generally,
however, the rights of parents are upheld, and the decisions are guided by
First Amendment guarantees to freedom of religion. We should remember,
however, that even some of the Founding Fathers believed that children be-
longed more to the state than to their parents (Wood, 2011a). When the
rights of the state are not threatened, the rights of parents have generally
been upheld. In the 1972 *Yoder* case, the Supreme Court went so far as to allow Amish parents to remove their children from school after the 8th grade.
(See the discussion in Gutmann, 1987; also in Greenawalt, 2005.) Justice
William O. Douglas filed a partial dissent arguing that the children might
be deprived of an education to which they were entitled, but he nevertheless
voted with a unanimous court. It seems clear, in reviewing *Yoder* and other
cases, that, if the Amish had been politically active and interested in making a widely applicable case, the Court would probably have denied their
request (Greenawalt, 2005).

STUDENT CHOICE

I asked earlier whether it is enough to insist that students be "taught" democratic values or whether schools must be organized to provide opportunities
for students to practice democracy as a mode of associated living. Now I
want to ask questions about the kind of choices that should be offered to
students. Should we sharply limit students' choices while ostensibly educating them to make intelligent choices as adults, or should we carefully guide
them through the provision of age-appropriate choices at every level?

The lack of student choices in today's schools should be deeply disturbing to those who embrace the central ideas promoted by Dewey, Emerson,
and Gutmann. From kindergarten through elementary and middle school,
student choices have been curtailed. Kindergartners have less time for free
play and are expected to master certain academic tasks before entering 1st
grade. Many elementary school children have been deprived of recess—a
time during which they could choose what games to play and with whom
to talk. Recently, a middle school principal told me proudly that his school
had achieved silent halls; his students were forbidden to talk to one another
as they passed between classes. I was shocked to hear that he hoped next to
achieve silent cafeterias! Kids are told what to read, when to do homework,
where to play and with whom, where to sit in every class, and exactly what
they must do to receive the A's they are taught to covet.

Teachers too are deprived of choice. Increasingly, they are expected to follow a curriculum that is tightly aligned with the achievement tests by which they will be evaluated. Many teachers do not feel free to depart from the text or script, even when they think it might profit their students to do so. One result of this rigidity is that teachers have little incentive to stretch themselves intellectually. Some have told me that they do little planning for the lessons they will teach because it is all laid out for them. What a pity. Planning can be—should be—at the heart of what a teacher does, and it is certainly essential to the teacher's continued intellectual growth. In planning, teachers prepare not only a lesson; more important, they prepare themselves for an array of questions that they hope will arise. Being thoroughly prepared for a host of challenging possibilities allows teachers to meet their students with both confidence and enthusiasm, and it gives teachers what might be called authoritative confidence—the confidence that permits them to encourage appropriate student choices (D. Hawkins, 1973; F. Hawkins, 1997).

Parents and teachers are often afraid that students will make bad choices and thereby harm their progress in school and even their life chances. This fear led Mortimer Adler (1982) to recommend that students should have no choice in the subjects they study through high school. He wrote:

> To give the same quality of schooling to all requires a program of study that is both liberal and general, and that is, in several, crucial, overarching respects, one and the same for every child. All sidetracks, specialized courses, or elective choices must be eliminated. Allowing them will always lead a certain number of students to voluntarily downgrade their own education. (p. 21)

But, I will argue, it should not be possible for students to downgrade their own education by choosing anything the school offers. Every course should be rich in intellectual possibilities and relevant to the lives of students. A primary purpose of schooling in a democratic society is to produce thoughtful citizens who can deliberate and make wise choices. There should indeed be features of schooling that are "in several, crucial, overarching respects, one and the same for every child," but how do we identify, describe, and implement these features? That is a central task undertaken in this book. To provide the "same quality" of schooling to all does not mean to force everyone through exactly the same, prespecified curriculum. Equality does not mean sameness. But how shall we describe *equality*? We turn to that topic next.

3

Equality

Equality is a core concept in democracy, but there has been a long struggle to honor it in practice as well as words. Today, although we are much closer to achieving equality before the law than we were a century ago, Americans are still divided over whether equality should apply to economic as well as political entitlements. All adult citizens are equal in the sense that all have a right to vote and all are entitled to equal treatment in courts of law. But is everyone entitled to decent housing, food, medical care, and a poverty-free retirement? Probably few would argue that there should be an absolute or even nearly equal distribution of wealth among individuals and families, but should there be economic equality in the sense that no one should live in dire need of the basic necessities just mentioned? Those who lean toward democratic socialism answer this question affirmatively; those favoring a more individualistic political position respond that everyone should have a fair chance at achieving these goods, but it is *opportunity* that should be equal, not outcomes. And then there are those who claim that if opportunities are truly equal, equal outcomes will follow.

These views and several variants of them lie at the heart of today's educational debates. For example, there are those who argue that democratic equality requires that all children have exactly the same curriculum from kindergarten through high school. Sometimes they (and others) argue that a uniform curriculum will contribute to the achievement of greater equality in the larger society. Some, while not insisting on the sort of traditional curriculum espoused by Hutchins and Adler, argue for a general academic curriculum that will prepare all students for college; their argument is primarily economic—that preparation for college will give all students an equal opportunity for economic success. There are still others (there is some overlap here) who believe that all children should have an opportunity to develop intellectually regardless of economic factors and that the schools should not be distracted from the task of intellectual development by other aims and interests such as preparation for a satisfying personal life.

All of these arguments are to some degree unconvincing. In the last section of this chapter, on equal opportunity, I will argue that a reasonable approach to equal opportunity requires the recognition of differences in student talents and interests. Indeed, I will argue that, from the perspective of democracy in the 21st century, there is nothing quite so *unequal* as sameness in curriculum and pedagogy.

EQUALITY THROUGH A COMMON CURRICULUM

A popular slogan over the past several decades has been, "All children can learn!" Mortimer Adler (1982) wrote, "There are no unteachable children. There are only schools and teachers and parents who fail to teach them" (p. 8). But, although such statements are appealing, they are virtually meaningless until we specify what it is that *all* children can learn and why they should learn it. In Chapter 1, I described a course in second-year algebra that allowed all students to make decent scores on a standardized test. These were students who had *chosen* a college preparatory program; those within it who chose the minimum option were bright but not mathematically inclined. I still believe they would have been better served by an entirely different course in mathematics or, still better, being allowed to pursue non-mathematical studies.

Hutchins and Adler simply assumed that the curriculum traditionally presented to the "best" was the curriculum all children deserve. E. D. Hirsch (1987, 1996) has gone so far as to list exactly what children should learn in every grade before high school. When children have great difficulty with the material presented in, say, 5th grade, Hirsch says it is because they were not adequately taught in 4th grade, and so on. I am not going to brush this criticism aside, although I believe it is too simplistic. I have, after all, already described the course in second-year algebra that required students to pass a chapter test on one unit before moving on to the next. There is such a malady as cumulative ignorance that makes learning more and more difficult over time. Hirsch's claim is not easily dismissed, but we should consider carefully why we are forcing the material on all students.

In the algebra course discussed earlier, we teachers had to decide which material in Chapter 1 had to be mastered in order to get started on Chapter 2, and so on. Persistence on the part of both teachers and students paid off in results showing few students in the bottom quartile of a standardized test and none in the lowest decile. However, the difference between the top students and those who completed the minimum course was substantial. No honest observer would claim that all of the students had the same course. Responsible educators should take the problem of cumulative ignorance seriously.

But to move on with a real chance of success, what must students know? It is much more difficult to answer the question, What must children learn in 4th grade in order to succeed in 5th? than it is to answer, What must a student know about factoring in order to add algebraic fractions? Given a small, well-defined set of skills, we can persevere until the student has acquired sufficient skill to move on to the next topic. Even so, the end result is a dramatic difference in achievement across students, not equality. The only sense in which our math students were equal is that all of them had "Algebra 2" listed on their transcripts. I'll say more about this in a section on the value of degrees and certificates.

After doing the hard thinking required to answer the question of what students need to know in order to move on with some chance of success, we are still faced with the highly challenging question: How do we do it? This is a question tackled by Ted Sizer (1984) in his thoughtful study of American high schools. In that study, Sizer considered smaller classes and the closer relationships that can be achieved by having teachers spend more time with a group of students. He suggested as one possibility that a teacher might teach two subjects (say, English and social studies) to one group of students rather than one subject to two different classes of students. The closer relationship between teacher and students thus developed should enhance achievement. I, too, have considered what might be gained through patterns of continuity such as having teachers work with the same students for 3 years rather than the typical 1 year (Noddings, 2005). Valuable as this work is, it cannot reduce the inequality in summative achievement on standardized tests, although it can make a substantial difference, as our algebra course did, in reducing abject failure. At the same time, it illustrates vividly how unequal students are in aptitude and interest. To capture a range of achievement in topics and projects related to the central subject, we need to look beyond standardized tests.

I have not yet tried to answer the question that opened the above paragraph. What must all students know and why? I will defer most of that discussion to Chapter 4 on aims and standards. Here, I want to point out that much of the material taught and learned in schools is forgotten when the courses and tests are over. Again and again, we are reminded by various polls, interviews, and questionnaires that Americans know (remember) little about their history and form of government. Each time one of these stories comes out, there is a clamor for the schools to teach this material. But the schools *do* teach it! We forget it, and we forget the math we were taught, too. Try this: Develop the equation for converting the Centigrade measure of temperature to Fahrenheit. I know you learned how to do this in 9th-grade algebra. You may (or may not) remember the formula, but can you *develop* it?

Or, for a chuckle, consider the material specified for grade 6 in a curriculum much admired by Hirsch:

> [Students are to] identify the Hwang, Yangtze, and Hsi rivers; the Himalaya Mountains, the Tlin Ling Mountains, the Central Mountains of Japan, and

Mount Fuji; the Gobi Desert, the East China Plains, and the Manchurian Plain; Hong Kong, Taiwan, and Yokohama; the Pacific Ocean, the Sea of Japan, and the Yellow Sea. (cited in Hirsch, 1996, p. 31)

One can argue that learning these facts induces powerful habits of mind, and that may be so (let's stay open to the possibility), but we are still left with the question: Why learn this particular set of facts? Might some students develop desirable habits of mind by memorizing a list of the most popular rock stars, baseball hitters, or Academy Award winners?

Hirsch (1996) does not use the "habits of mind" argument but, rather, claims that the material he has listed (in *Cultural Literacy*) is essential to the cultural literacy of all Americans, and he suggests two ways in which such common knowledge should improve American life for everyone. First:

Improving the effectiveness and fairness of education through enhancing both its content and its commonality has a more than educational significance. The improvement would, as everyone knows, diminish the economic inequities within our nation. (p. 238)

Would it? That is not obvious to many of us. Although college graduates typically have higher lifetime earnings than those without degrees, there are many exceptions, and shocking inequities that have nothing to do with degrees exist across occupations. The typical bachelor's degree holder working in home health care or child care earns about half that of someone working in the tech industry with just an associate's degree (Sparks, 2011). Indeed, many of the people working with children—college graduates—earn so little that were it not for two-income families, they and their families would live in poverty. And women still earn about 80% of what men receive for the same work. Schooling can do little to diminish these inequities. Further, as the information world grows, so does the service world, and a just, democratic society would not allow its service workers (those who provide caregiving services) to live close to the poverty line despite their full-time work.

A second contribution of common cultural literacy, Hirsch (1996) claims, would be a renewal in civility and communitarian spirit.

Bringing our children closer to universal competence is important. But an equally important contribution of the truly common school would be the strengthening of universal communicability and a sense of community within the public sphere. In the long run, that could be the common school's most important contribution to preserving the fragile fabric of our democracy. (p. 238)

On one level, this is a lovely ideal. America today certainly needs more civility and a more generous spirit of community. But Hirsch may have things backwards. With Dewey, I believe that working together, communicating on a variety of tasks and interests, generates community and common values. Common values are an achievement, not a starting point. Moreover, the concept of community is not without its problems. Common education and a strong sense of oneness, of community, are core features of fascism (Noddings, 1996). Giovanni Gentile, described by Hirsch as an admirer of the progressive ideas coming out of Teachers College, Columbia, served as minister of education under Mussolini. He thought of himself and became widely known as the philosopher of fascism, and he wrote passionately about community spirit and the oneness of that spirit. Perhaps it makes a significant difference how we approach the ideal of community. If we assume that it is already somehow *there*—constituted by God or by a specific ideology or by a specified body of knowledge—we may suppose that the task of teachers is one of almost pure transmission. However, if we agree with Dewey that democratic community is a work under continuous construction, the task is one of inviting communication, of building upon and extending common interests, and encouraging reflection and deliberation. It isn't that we need a common body of knowledge in order to communicate; it is that we need to communicate in order to build a common body of knowledge.

So far, we have noted two facets of the argument for a common curriculum. One is that such a curriculum is required in a democracy; it is demanded in the name of equality. The second is that a common curriculum will produce or enhance equality in the existing democracy. Both of these claims are questionable, and neither of them necessitates a particular form for the common curriculum. Why should the common curriculum be constructed and enacted as it was described by Hutchins or by Hirsch? We will have to probe more deeply into this question.

None of this discussion should be taken to mean that there is no value in common learning. But the question remains: What must all children know and be able to do? And a second question arises in connection with Hirsch's work: How are the facts specified by Hirsch best learned? Without a big idea or central concept to which facts are tied, it is unlikely that they will be remembered, and if the big idea or concept is well developed, the facts can usually be found or recovered. There is no need to put them at the center of the curriculum. Many well-informed people were never required to memorize these facts; they picked them up through conversation and reading. Clearly, however, not everything can be "picked up" informally. What material should everyone know and how is it to be learned? The questions remain.

To this point in the discussion of equality in schools, two things stand out. Children are not equal in their capacity for academic learning, and a universal, academic curriculum may well aggravate academic differences. A richer, more varied curriculum might help students find out what they are suited to do and also to respect the wonderful differences in talent that they should be encouraged to see in their classmates. Even within a particular course, there should be a balance between common learning and individualized units and topics that provide students with opportunities to exercise their special talents and interests on related work. Again, this is a topic on which much more will be said.

EQUALITY THROUGH DEGREES AND DIPLOMAS

In the discussion of Hirsch's work, I acknowledged that holders of a college degree could expect higher lifetime earnings than those without a degree. This has been true in the past, and will no doubt continue to be true into at least the near future. However, as I pointed out above, the picture is complicated when we consider the field chosen by graduates, and it is further complicated by the current financial condition of young graduates—enormous debts accumulated to pay their tuition.

In addition to the personal problems of choosing a field and repaying loans, young people may become caught in a structural problem. It is possible that, if college education for all becomes an active government policy, America may produce too many college graduates. China is already struggling with that problem, and many young Chinese graduates are working at jobs that do not require a college education. To some degree, given the troubled labor market today, this is true for young Americans as well. Consider what would happen if everyone were to achieve a bachelor's degree. Many such graduates would of necessity be employed in occupations usually associated with the working class. Would they be better paid for this work because they have degrees? Some argue that they would be, but the evidence is not clear.

It is true that the BA now has economic value, but in large part the economic advantage is a result of its use as a marker. Charles Murray (2008) remarks:

> Employers do not even interview applicants who do not hold a BA. Even more brutal, the advantage conferred by the BA often has nothing to do with the content of the education. Employers do not value what the student learned, just that the student has a degree. Employers value the BA because it is a no-cost (for them) screening device for academic ability and perseverance. (p. 92)

This claim is not universally true. At the present time, for example, there is a large, unmet need for computer experts who can work in cyber-security, and doubtless there are other labor shortages that require specialized training. But Murray's point holds up fairly well over the whole field of college graduates. This may change as the number of college graduates seeking employment increases and complaints about the quality of college education and its graduates grows. (See Hacker & Dreifus, 2010; also Arum & Roksa, 2011.) For the foreseeable future, however, degrees and diplomas count whether their holders are adequately educated or not.

We now encounter a dilemma. If we agree with those who want to raise standards in our high schools—so that a high school diploma "means something"—we may in effect deprive many students of the credential required for a job or continued training. Of course, those who are determined to raise standards usually argue along the lines we have already discussed. They insist that "all children can learn," that all children should have a rigorous secondary school program, and that teachers and schools are at fault if students do not succeed. In opposition, I have argued that not all children are academically inclined and that a detailed universal curriculum will magnify differences and aggravate inequality. Instead of worrying about preparing more students for college, we should be working to get our kids through high school and prepared for work they might find satisfying.

What should a high school diploma mean? It should mean what it has always meant—that a graduate has satisfied the school's requirements in courses and grades. There should be no exit test. If there are deficiencies in the school's courses and/or programs, they should be analyzed and corrected. As I said earlier in a discussion of Adler's fear that student choices would lead some students to "downgrade" their own education, this should not be possible. Every course offered by an accredited high school should be intellectually rich, practically relevant, and continually evaluated. That is the goal toward which we should put our educational efforts. Addressing legitimate, well-understood aims for the 21st century, we should ask of *every* course: In what ways does this course contribute to these aims?

In the meantime, as we work on this challenging task, we should get rid of useless and frightening exit tests, keep our children in school, and pull out all the stops to help them graduate. Much as I deplore intellectual shoddiness, I'd rather have students graduate knowing too little than not graduating at all. Recall that the Algebra 2 course our team created was designed to allow students to meet the university requirement for 3 years of academic math. Our test results proved that our students had learned some math, but they had a credential, not a full course in algebra. Perhaps it shouldn't be that way, but Murray is right that a credential at the high school or college level often means more than what a graduate actually knows. We have to start our thinking from where we are.

EQUALITY AND ANTI-INTELLECTUALISM

Some advocates of a common, traditional curriculum put less emphasis on the equality demanded by democracy or the equality that might be achieved through the common curriculum. Instead, they contend that schools, by definition, are designed primarily to promote intellectual development. Other admittedly important goals for child development should be the province of homes, religious institutions, communities, and other organizations. We might note that this attitude is characteristic of the bureaucratic thinking of the 20th century—assignment of every task and problem to the properly designated institution or agency. The basic idea of bureaucracy, the hope, was to make society's tasks manageable.

Since its inception in the early 20th century, the American high school has come under attack periodically for anti-intellectualism. It was attacked vigorously in the 1950s, and not without reason. A movement called Life Adjustment had become popular with the National Association of Secondary-School Principals. In one of their bulletins, it was written:

> When we come to the realization that not every child has to read, figure, write, and spell . . . that many of them either cannot or will not master these chores . . . then we shall be on the road to improving the junior high curriculum. (quoted in Kliebard, 1995, p. 223)

A statement like this should make us cautious about claiming—as I do now—that not all students need to (or can) master academic mathematics. I could be wrong, and we should move carefully. Surely, life adjustment advocates were wrong, and probably no one today would argue that not all students need to read, figure, write, and spell. But the underlying questions of how well they must do these things and of what else they must learn remains. These are not easy questions, and we must remain open to opposing answers.

Arthur Bestor Jr. (1953) was one of the strongest critics of the life adjustment movement, and a careful review of his criticisms is worthwhile even today. His criticisms were pointed and impassioned, but he was careful not to blame progressivism or John Dewey for the anti-intellectualism he saw as rampant in the schools. His target was the life adjustment movement and statements such as the one quoted above. However, he and several other strong critics seemed to believe that the movement was much more influential than it was in actuality.

Bestor was among those who have claimed that the school has a special task—that of intellectual development—and he challenged the life adjustment movement as anti-intellectual and anti-democratic. In a series of powerfully worded essays, he insisted that it is wrong, anti-democratic, to suppose that the majority of children are incapable of intellectual work. We can agree with him tentatively on this, but press the question of what is meant by the word *intellectual*. If we restrict the designation *intellectual* to mean the content usually associated with traditional academic work, it does not seem at all anti-democratic to believe that many children are not cut out to do intellectual work. Indeed, Charles W. Eliot (1908) argued earlier in the century that *not* recognizing this truth about human beings actually puts our democracy at risk:

> If democracy means to try to make all children equal or all men equal, it means to fight nature, and in that fight democracy is sure to be defeated. There is no such thing among men as equality of nature, of capacity for training, or of intellectual power. (p. 13)

Forcing all students into a common curriculum at the high school level might indeed put our democracy at risk. With this arrangement, it is easy to rank students from top to bottom, ignoring their special talents and interests, and it is likely—in a "rigorous" academic curriculum—that the same students in class after class, year after year, will rank at the bottom. In a 21st-century democracy, one of our most important goals is to recognize and appreciate interdependence. John W. Gardner (1984), who also believed that the school's primary task is intellectual development, nevertheless spoke out strongly for the recognition of a full range of excellence:

> We must learn to honor excellence in every socially accepted human activity, however humble the activity, and to scorn shoddiness, however exalted the activity. An excellent plumber is infinitely more valuable than an incompetent philosopher. The society that scorns excellence in plumbing because plumbing is a humble activity and tolerates shoddiness in philosophy because it is an exalted activity will have neither good plumbing nor good philosophy. Neither its pipes nor its theories will hold water. (p. 102)

Gardner was somewhat constrained in his first edition of *Excellence* (1961/1984) by his belief that the primary purpose of schooling is and must be intellectual development in the form of academic studies. In the revised edition (1984), he expressed greater appreciation for post-secondary education other than traditional college work, and he spoke of shared purposes as well as the pursuit of intellectual excellence.

We might argue against Adler, Bestor, Hirsch, and the early Gardner that the school must recognize and pursue many aims, not simply that of intellectual development. But even more important, we might reconsider the definition of *intellectual* as the pursuit of traditional academic studies.

CONFUSION OVER THE MEANING OF *INTELLECTUAL*

John Dewey (1916) made it clear repeatedly that no subject is inherently more intellectual than another, and I have also made that argument in several places (Noddings, 2003, 2007). If we identify the intellectual with the exercise of intelligence, the algebra taught in schools is not inherently more intellectual than cooking or motorcycle repair. Calvin Woodward made the argument even before Dewey, referring to young workers in a forging shop as "young Vulcans, bare-armed, leather-aproned with many a drop of an honest sweat. . . . They are using their brains and hands" (quoted in Kliebard, 1999, p. 1).

Today, Mike Rose (1995, 2005) has reminded us that thinking and doing are mutually supportive, tightly connected activities. No useful activity or preparation for an occupation involving hands-on work need be simply manual labor; such work can be taught and learned intelligently, and classroom discussion can move beyond specific "doings" to matters of citizenship, mutual respect, and prospects for a satisfying personal life. Rose connects his discussion to the meaning of democracy and the centrality of respect in a growing, evolving democracy. In such a democracy—we might call it "Whitmanesque"—honest workers are worthy of respect. One should not need a college degree to earn this respect.

I should note, however, that Rose has recently expressed concern that his appreciative appraisal of the "mind at work" might be used to launch a renewed effort to direct minority and low-SES students away from college preparatory courses and into dead-end vocational programs. I share that concern, but I will argue in Chapter 8 that vocational programs can be, and should be, intellectually rich. They need not consist of mere training.

I have an even greater concern, however, and that centers on the high school dropout rate. We may comfort ourselves by bragging that we now prepare *all* students for college, but we lose a huge number before high school graduation. My enthusiasm for vocational education rests on two essential premises: first, that we will get to work seriously in creating rich and relevant vocational programs and, second, that we will provide extensive counseling and mentoring services so that students can make intelligent choices of program.

In many of the most prosperous European countries, high-quality vocational education and training (VET) is deemed essential:

> Countries with strong VET systems have a different conception about learning for jobs. They make a distinction between a calling or occupation and learning the specific skills needed to weld or solve banking problems or manage the IT system in a corporation . . . work is related to active citizenship and thus education and training needed for work are seen as the joint responsibility of the government and what are called nicely the "social partners" (employers and labor unions). (Hoffman, 2010, p. 1)

In Chapter 8, we will discuss vocational education and its connection to both democracy and individual thriving.

Before turning to a discussion of equal opportunity, we should say a bit more about the meaning of *intellectual*. When we speak of persons as intellectuals, we usually mean that these people deal with ideas at a general and abstract level; they are concerned with ideas and topics for their own sake, not for practical purposes. One might think here of the mathematician G. H. Hardy, who claimed that he had never done anything useful (Newman, 1956, p. 2026). The work of intellectuals (including Hardy) often turns out to be useful, but that is not why they engage in it. They may be captivated by it, drawn to it by its beauty or by the challenges it presents.

Some of our high school students are budding intellectuals in this sense, and they should be encouraged. They are often cheated in today's schools. Just as we should make adequate educational provision for young musicians and artists, mechanics, and those with outstanding social skills, so should we also encourage young intellectuals. There should be opportunities for such students to pursue topics in far greater depth than their classmates would enjoy. By pretending that everyone will now participate in the same intellectual program, we are pushing young intellectuals to distinguish themselves only in terms of the highest possible GPA, not the richest level of understanding and creativity. The young intellectual should not be regarded as an example for all students to follow, nor is the life of an intellectual necessarily better than other ways of life. In our faulty attempts at intellectual equality through a common curriculum, we may be depriving everyone— even young intellectuals—of real opportunities to develop intellectually.

EQUALITY OF OPPORTUNITY

So far, I have argued that a highly specified common curriculum is not required by democratic principles, nor is equality likely to be increased by such a curriculum. There are those, however, who contend that a common curriculum through high school—one preparing everyone for college—provides equal opportunity for all. In opposition, I have pointed out that ignoring the talents and interests of many students can hardly be described as providing equal opportunity. (For an interesting and comprehensive analysis of the concept of equal opportunity, see Kenneth Howe, 1997.)

Talk of equality pervades the discussion of schooling today. Advocates of vouchers, for example, claim that with vouchers poor parents could choose a school for their children just as wealthier parents have been able to do. This claim borders on deceit. The best private schools in this country charge more than $30,000 a year in tuition (many closer to $50,000), and many wealthy parents pay that much and more for additional tutoring.

Further, independent schools with costs in the typical voucher range live a tenuous existence, often unable to manage on their meager funds. They often simply fold up.

Paradoxically, voucher advocates often support a free-market system of schooling, claiming that a vigorous market will force failing schools (usually public schools) out of business. But schools are not like corner gas stations or convenience stores. Schools are like second homes to children, and continuity matters. What does a family do when the school it has chosen closes? And what has happened to their children in the year or years just prior to closing? It is starkly clear that the expensive, prestigious schools available to the wealthy are not in jeopardy of being forced out of the market. Many of them are justly proud of their long histories and assured futures. The only reasonable answer to failing public schools is to improve them.

How do we accomplish that improvement? I am not at all sure, but I think the task must be undertaken by teachers, parents, and administrators *on site*. There are no panaceas for today's problems of schooling, and the current mania for "scaling up" is a product of delusion. The problems require the cooperative work of an energetic committee (or set of committees) that will begin work in an analytic frame of mind, not one that attempts to fix blame and throw everyone into a panic of guilty accountability. That committee should involve families and the community in appropriate ways, but it should not turn the whole project over to them. That sort of meddling at every level helped to doom earlier efforts at local control. The lines of communication must be kept open, and the project should be under continuous construction (see Meier, 1995; Meier & Wood, 2004). Helpful suggestions of the sort I offer in this book should be considered, but there are no recipes.

To provide equal opportunities for all children, the public schools must be preserved and strengthened. Every time a child leaves a "failing" school, that school becomes weaker and the children left behind suffer further. Responsible experimentation can be guided by project committees as suggested above. There is no need to complicate matters with charter schools or vouchers. Money and effort should be concentrated on existing public schools.

Financial equality for individual wage earners is often claimed as a benefit of a prescribed, common academic curriculum, and I have acknowledged that a college degree (as a credential) makes it possible for many graduates to earn more than they would have without it. Indeed, the most frequently heard argument for a single, traditional academic track today does not emphasize intellectual content but, rather, the economic benefits of a college degree. However, the benefits are not as clear and certain as we are led to believe. Unless students and their families make judicious choices, they are likely to incur costs that will take a long time to repay.

The present emphasis on preparing everyone for college may itself be perversely motivated by monetary considerations; it may not be driven entirely by a mistaken democratic commitment to social justice. Good vocational education is far more expensive than the usual college preparatory course of study. It often requires more space, expensive equipment, smaller classes, a specially trained faculty, and a commitment to add new equipment regularly. It is far less expensive to place all students in regular academic courses, whether or not such placement suits them. Even if we provide extra help to assist students in passing academic courses for which they are not suited, we still save money while ignoring the present and long-term interests of students. We feel justified in claiming that we have provided equal opportunity when in fact we have hurt many students doubly: We have forced them into studies at which they do not do well, and we have deprived them of courses at which they might succeed. As a result, many do not graduate from high school, and even those who do may wind up in jobs by default instead of by choice. They may well believe that they are doing this work because they are not good enough for anything else.

In Chapter 8, I will return to the topic of vocational education and the possibilities for genuine intellectual engagement in vocational courses. We must also admit, however, that some jobs—jobs someone must do—are essentially mindless and even demeaning. Digging ditches, cleaning toilets, scrubbing pots, and picking beans all day, every day are not jobs likely to engage the intellect. Utopian writers have long recognized the difficulty of reconciling economic justice and respect with the dirty, boring nature of some necessary work. Writers as different as Edward Bellamy (1897/1960) and B. F. Skinner (1948/1962) have explored the idea of utopian societies in which such work is shared by everyone so that no one person need spend his or her full work week in hard, dirty, mindless labor. So far, we have not succeeded in the utopian quest.

Schools can do little by themselves to change these conditions. Substantial change will require the cooperation of several agencies. Schools can, however, promote that spirit of cooperation, and they can work conscientiously to develop appreciation for social/economic interdependence. Perhaps most important, they can take seriously the task of preparing the young for full and satisfying lives beyond the economic realm—in the personal, occupational, and civic domains. All three of these aims must figure prominently in 21st-century education.

We can also take fuller account of the variety of talents and interests among our students. Howard Gardner (1983) gave us a rich start on this with his theory of multiple intelligences. My approach differs in emphasis. First, it does not depend so heavily on psychological theory; it is more "everyday" in its identification of interests. Second, whereas Gardner gives plentiful advice on how to use the intelligences in teaching the regular curriculum, I would like to build these interests into the curriculum and thus transform it.

Before moving on to a fuller discussion of the aims of education, a bit more should be said about equal opportunity. The first phase of equal opportunity is experienced by children in their homes. Many knowledgeable thinkers have insisted that the first 5 years of a child's life at home are crucially important in preparing the child to take advantage of opportunities that will arise later, especially in school. Given that this fact is widely known, it is almost inexplicable that the schools still do not teach anything about homemaking and parenting. Looking at the history of education, we can see that the omission of this material is in large part due to the development of education by men for men in public life. How might the school curriculum have developed if women had been actively involved in it from the start? I said in Chapter 1 that the entire discussion of this book would be based on the assumption that the ages-old, disciplinary structure of the curriculum would not change radically. Our task, then, is to explore how this vital material—homemaking, parenting, caregiving—can be incorporated into the existing immovable structure. That will be a major topic in Chapter 6.

Before leaving this chapter for a discussion of aims, I want to add just a warning note on equality and race. We have come a long way from the days in which we automatically and cruelly shoved our minority students into dead-end programs. A main point in this book is that there should be no dead-end programs in our schools. Everything we offer should be rich and relevant. But as we reject the old forms of discrimination, we introduce students to the new, universal inequality. Their legitimate differences of talent and interest may be ignored.

4

Aims, Goals, and Objectives

Regular, continuous discussion of aims is essential to both democracy and education (Noddings, 2003). As Dewey (1916) advised, good aims are an outgrowth of an analysis of existing conditions. We point to aims when we are asked, or ask ourselves, why we are engaged in certain activities and why we are committed to certain beliefs and practices. When dramatic social or political changes occur, we may modify our aims, create new ones, or reorder our emphases. As I suggested in Chapter 1, the realities of global life in the 21st century have led many of us to believe that cooperation should be valued more highly than competition. Peace and prosperity are primary aims not only for the nation but for the global community, and collaboration is a value, instrumental technique, and practice that supports both of these.

In education, aims-talk is addressed to large questions seldom asked today. Most *why* questions, if they are asked at all, arise in connection with objectives and goals—ends at a lower, more specific level. I am suggesting here, for conceptual clarity, a hierarchy of ends: aims, goals, objectives. We may ask, for example, why a teacher or textbook has included as an objective a particular skill or concept in a given lesson. We expect an answer that connects the lesson material to what comes next in the course or to the larger goals of the course. Generally, we identify objectives with lessons and goals with larger units or courses of study. A social studies teacher may, for example, pursue a series of objectives on longitude and latitude, so that students will be able to achieve the larger goal of reading maps. A geometry teacher may begin the year with lessons on logic so that students will grasp the idea of proof in mathematics.

We might pause here to remark that there is today a scarcity of *why* questions even at the level of goals and objectives. Unfortunately, some teachers do not know how the material they are teaching on a given day connects to the larger goal of their subject. The lesson material is simply there to be "delivered" by the teacher and "received" or learned by the students. The students sign for the delivery by passing a test of some sort. This is a topic of huge importance to be considered in methods courses. Good teachers must be able to engage in task analysis; that is, they must know what students need to know before tackling a new task. They must know how every concept and skill they teach fits in with other concepts and skills and how they all connect to the larger subject. The Algebra 2 course described earlier could not have been designed without this knowledge.

But fitting objectives to goals is not the whole story. Large, overarching aims suggest that we engage in discussions, raise questions, and debate issues as needs arise.

AIMS

Education is an enterprise with multiple aims. I suggested in Chapter 1 that these might be organized within and across three great life domains: home and personal, occupational, and civic. In the 21st century, if we are to make progress under the guidance of the aims and values outlined in Chapter 1, it will be important for teachers to know not only the connections among topics in their special subject but also how their subject is linked to many others. Aims thoughtfully written and reflected upon regularly guide us to seek topics and skills across the disciplines that complement one another and together enrich the guiding aims.

Dewey (1916) did not use the hierarchical category of aims just suggested—possibly because he did not say much about the high school curriculum—but we would do well to follow him on the basic meaning of aims (ends), and that meaning should extend to all three categories. Dewey distinguished between *ends* and *results* (ch. 8). All sorts of natural events bring results, for example, but these results are not ends; they are not the intended products of planning and directed effort. Moreover, aims construed as ends-in-view provide continuity to the educational process. Each activity exhibits some connection to the activities that precede and succeed it, and they are all demonstrably connected to the large, overriding aims.

Looking at the list of learning objectives admired by Hirsch for its specificity, we are led to wonder what overriding aim or goal guides the selection of learning objectives: to identify three rivers, four mountain ranges, Hong Kong, Taiwan, and Yokohama. Hirsch would no doubt say, "cultural literacy," but—without denying the value of cultural literacy—we must probe more deeply into how such an aim directs our choice of content and method. Unless the individual objects of learning are connected to a basic concept and to ends-in-view of which students are conscious, the objects are likely to be quickly forgotten. Alfred North Whitehead (1929/1967) wrote forcefully on this problem. He suggested "Life in all its manifestations" as the connecting aim of education. As educators, we have to think how our lesson objectives are connected not only to one another and to larger course goals but to the big, central aims of life. But instead of connecting our objectives to life, Whitehead complained:

> We offer children—Algebra, from which nothing follows; Geometry, from which nothing follows; a Couple of Languages, never mastered; and lastly, most dreary of all, Literature, represented by the plays of Shakespeare, with philological notes and short analyses of plot and character to be in substance committed to memory. (p. 7)

Whitehead criticized the conventional lists of things to be learned as "inert ideas," and his warning is highly relevant today:

> In training a child to activity of thought, above all things we must beware of what I will call "inert ideas"—that is to say, ideas that are merely received into the mind without being utilized, or tested, or thrown into fresh combinations. (p. 1)

It is not just philosophers writing in the early 20th century who see the danger in inert ideas. E. O. Wilson (2006), the great biologist, has made an elegant plea for the thinking that should characterize 21st-century education:

> There is, in my opinion, an inevitability to the unity of knowledge. It reflects real life. The trajectory of world events suggests that educated people should be far better able than before to address the great issues courageously and analytically by undertaking a traverse of the disciplines. We are into the age of synthesis, with a real bite to it. (p. 137)

Wilson argues that specialists today need to know far more than their main discipline and that, as teachers, they must be able to move laterally into other subjects related to the special topic under discussion. I'll say more about this work in a discussion of stretching the disciplines from within (Chapter 5). To achieve the continuity sought by Dewey and avoid the inert ideas abhorred by Whitehead, Wilson (2006) recommends that we "teach each subject from the general to the specific" (p. 131). This approach provides students with motivation, reasons for learning the details to follow. It also suggests that education should become "less discipline-oriented and more problem-oriented" (p. 136).

Wilson's suggestions conform to our description of 21st-century thinking. With available technology, we can always find facts and details; we need not memorize long lists of them. But we must have a reason—a problem, concept, issue—that impels us to seek details.

Concern about the thoughtless pursuit of prescribed learning objectives is deepened when we see that questions about objectives and goals are actively discouraged. All over the country, we hear accounts of teachers who have been reprimanded for ignoring the posted lesson objective on a day when student interests or events strongly suggest a different topic—one that may be beautifully aligned with major aims but is not listed formally on the day's prescribed plan. Good teachers eagerly seize and capitalize on such teachable moments, but today they are too often actively discouraged from doing so.

If *why* questions are discouraged at the level of objectives and goals, consider how difficult it will be to raise questions guided by large, abstract aims: Why must all children learn geometry? Why do we persist in organizing history courses around wars? Why is Shakespeare more important for high school students than a serious study of fairy tales and other children's literature? Why is a course in academic chemistry more important than one on nutrition? Why do we suspend students for skipping classes? Why, if we accept an emphasis on collaboration, do we insist on maintaining GPAs and class rankings? Why have we allowed the liberal arts to degenerate into a set of narrow, seemingly unrelated, specialties? As possibilities, the questions abound. In reality, almost every education question today is raised and answered in economic terms. We educate our children so that they may qualify for better-paying jobs and to increase our nation's ability to compete economically. By narrowing the discussion so drastically, we are putting the future of our children, our nation, and our world at risk.

Looking at the aims mentioned in Chapter 1, we see that they support one another and the continued development of democracy. For example, collaboration, communication, and appreciation of interdependence should promote the aim of achieving peace and prosperity. Similarly, critical thinking, self-understanding, creativity, and living a full and satisfying life should promote both intellectual development and community spirit. But each of the aims needs elaboration.

Consider the aim of education for a full personal life. This is an aim that has appeared in every educational philosophy since such thought began. Periodically, since universal education was established, schools have been criticized for neglecting components of this aim. Paradoxically, they have also been criticized when attempts have been made to restore it. In 1918, the Cardinal Principles Report argued that universal secondary education required attention to aims beyond the traditional academic aims that had earlier defined intellectual development. The report advocated seven aims: "1. Health. 2. Command of the fundamental processes. 3. Worthy home membership. 4. Vocation. 5. Citizenship. 6. Worthy use of leisure time. 7. Ethical character" (quoted in Kliebard, 1995, p. 98).

Although the report was widely praised, it was also criticized for asking the schools to do too much. Whereas the earlier report of the Committee of Ten, chaired by Charles Eliot, was thought to be too intellectual (academic) for general education (Eliot himself came to believe this), the Cardinal Principles were criticized as anti-intellectual. Even today, that report is charged with starting a lasting trend toward "hostility to academic subject matter" (Hirsch, 1996, p. 49). Hirsch (1996) admits that the report could be viewed as recommending a balanced approach to the nation's needs—a concern for the whole student rather than just his or her intellectual side, and a desire to democratize public education by accommodating teaching to children's "individual differences in capacities and aptitudes." (p. 48)

But although he has concern about the "whole child," he believes that the major responsibility of the school is to promote intellectual development. From the perspective advocated as 21st-century thinking, Hirsch is mistaken in separating the intellectual from the whole child, and he is mistaken also in assuming that 20th-century schools rejected standard academic work. It is clear that, with a few exceptions, most elementary schools went right on with the usual academic work. The big difference occurred at the secondary school level, where several tracks were offered. The standard academic studies in elementary schools were used to sort students into tracks, only one of which represented the traditional college preparatory curriculum. I have already acknowledged that the sorting process was often morally and socially deplorable, but this does not mean that the idea of a variety of tracks is itself wrong. Indeed, despite the questionable methods of tracking employed, the enormous increase in high school attendance and graduation over the first half of the 20th century was a remarkable achievement that almost certainly could not have been attained under the plan offered by the Committee of Ten.

The basic idea of the Cardinal Principles actually offers a good starting point for aims-talk in the 21st century. Thinking seriously about education for a full life, which of these aims would you abandon? And why should we suppose that addressing them is necessarily anti-intellectual? All of them can be richly intellectual; that is, they can all actively engage the mind.

The fear that such broad aims will be too much for schools was voiced early and repeatedly throughout the 20th century. As we saw, even such a generous thinker as John W. Gardner worried whether schools could handle so great a task. In part, this worry is a product of 20th-century bureaucratic thinking. We continue to suppose that every agency and institution has an assigned responsibility that may be sacrificed or confused by additional responsibilities. Today, we should think about both interagency collaboration and broader aims within institutions.

In Chapter 1, I suggested a shift in thinking about intellectual development away from narrowly defined academic disciplines and toward critical thinking, self-understanding, creativity, and effective and responsible use of technology. This is not to say that every student will achieve critical thinking as logicians and philosophers might define it, nor do I claim that all students will become creative. Aims, properly defined, guide our thinking. We should not try to translate them directly into goals and objectives that can be measured numerically. Rather, we examine everything we do in schools in the light of the stated aims. What critical issues are involved in the subject matter at hand? How will we encourage thinking and discussion of these issues? Are there opportunities for creativity in this unit of work? Without insisting that all students will be creative (and prove it on some numerical scale), we think about the opportunities to be offered. For example, instead of rushing from one math problem to the next when the first has been satisfactorily resolved, we might pause and ask students to consider other ways of solving the problem. Teachers should know when the possibilities are especially rich.

We might consider educating for self-understanding as part of critical thinking. It is so important, however, and so neglected that I would list it as a separate aim, one to be discussed in Chapter 9. At the deepest level, educating for self-understanding is a way of involving students in all of the other aims. It is also an aim that connects the list of democratic aims with the list of aims for education. Students should achieve a critical and appreciative understanding of their nation as well as an understanding of themselves as individuals. There is much to be proud of, to celebrate and maintain, but there should also be opportunities for students to examine the less admirable acts in their nation's history, betrayal of our stated principles, and questionable positions taken on the world scene. They should also consider how traditional patriotism has functioned to close minds and ranks and whether it is time to reject notions of world domination in all forms.

In the chapters that follow, I will not offer a detailed list of aims, but I will make suggestions for how we might think about aims in the personal domain (Chapter 6), the civic domain (Chapter 7), and the occupational domain (Chapter 8). In each of these exploratory discussions, I will draw attention to the 21st-century aims of cooperation, critical thinking and problem-solving, and creativity.

FROM AIMS TO GOALS

Aims are general statements of concern to which we turn when asked (or asking ourselves) why we are doing certain things. When we mention health, happiness, citizenship, and a host of other important topics as *aims*, we draw attention to an overall, significant concern with these matters. We do not specify beforehand exactly what we will accomplish or what provisions we will make for individual differences.

In contrast, when we set goals in accordance with the aims, we must consider particular subject matters, local resources, and the individual needs of students. In the Algebra 2 example used earlier, we set different goals for students with different aptitudes and interests. Consider, in contrast, national statements such as Goals 2000 and No Child Left Behind (NCLB). In Goals 2000, for example, it was stated that by 2000, America's students would be first in the world in mathematics. Why? What great aim or ideal prompted this goal? Almost every educator in America knew that this goal was ridiculous, and many of us questioned the wisdom of even aiming at such an end. *Goals should be attainable.* For a variety of plausible reasons, we may fail to achieve a goal, but the goal should be, in principle, realistically attainable. Deluded policymakers must have thought the goals were attainable, because they blithely proceeded to apply penalties for not achieving them. Making America's students first in the world in mathematics by 2000 was not an attainable goal. Similarly, a goal established by NCLB—that all students would be proficient in mathematics by 2014—was obviously impossible, and yet federal, state, and local governments treated it as a genuine goal and instituted penalties for those schools that failed to make adequate progress toward it. Think of the time, money, and effort wasted in trying to achieve the impossible, and the corruption induced by the fear of incurring penalties for failing to do so. Not only were the mandated goals impossible, but they actually harmed our system of education by encouraging corruption and widespread demoralization (Nichols & Berliner, 2007). The goals posited actually worked against the broad great aims under discussion here.

Moreover, in the wake of corruption, officials have reacted by trying to ferret out the cheaters and hold them accountable. This would be reasonable and ethically appropriate if the cheating had been ethically unmotivated and the structural causes less obvious. I am not defending cheating. As educators, we should deplore it. But consider what has happened in its wake. Instead of changing the rules to motivate responsible conduct, officials have employed stronger methods of detection. Intelligent people now spend hours identifying and counting the number of erasures on standardized tests, counting those erasures from wrong to right answers. Then an average number per student is calculated for each class, school, and district. When the number of erasures (from wrong to right) is above average, further investigation is required. A recommendation has also been made that teachers should not be involved in marking the tests of their own students. A further suggestion has been made that teachers should not even be involved in monitoring the tests. Thus, more expense will be incurred to support a system that should be radically changed.

A few years ago, a graduate student in one of my classes actually defended the practice of cheating by teachers who, without telling students the right answer, would keep pointing to or tapping on incorrect answers until the right blocks were filled in. He said the practice was morally justified; it was, he said, civil disobedience. At that point, I stopped the class and spent some time on a discussion of the meaning and history of civil disobedience. Civil disobedience involves not only breaking the law but, more important, *accepting the consequences.* Thoreau and King broke the law and went to jail; they did not sneak about and cheat. A courageous, concerted effort at genuine civil disobedience—refusing to administer the tests, for example—might have effectively put an end to high-stakes testing. In contrast, cheating invites stricter rules, heavier surveillance, harsher penalties, and greater separation of teachers from control of their own teaching.

Goals should be attainable, and they should be established cooperatively in the light of aims to which we are committed. Whereas aims are stated at a general and ideal level—"thorough and efficient education" for all students—goals depend on a careful analysis of the subject to be taught, the interests and talents of students, available resources, and the social and economic needs of the larger community.

In the approach taken today, several bad mistakes are being made. First, we have confused aims and goals. Because we are committed to an education for each child that will promote a full personal life, satisfying occupational life, and responsible citizenship, we suppose that the *goals* must be the same for all. The budding mathematician, machinist, hotel manager, police officer, writer, musician, and health-care worker must all have the same mathematics courses in high school. This is both harmful and ridiculous. But at what point should differentiation begin and on what basis? Accommodation of individual differences should characterize our educational efforts from the start, but serious planning for differences should start at about the middle school. I will suggest (Chapter 8) that the middle school years should be used to discover the talents and interests on which differentiated plans will be provided for the high school years. I will not recommend a sorting process based solely on test scores or one that ignores the interests and talents of individual students.

Another mistake made today is to let subject-matter goals dominate all other possibilities. This is perhaps understandable given the current emphasis on higher academic standards and the traditional division of the curriculum into separate, narrowly defined subjects. But we should resist it, and this can be done in at least two ways. First, when a significant social problem arises, we should rethink our goals. For example, too many children in the United States are obese. A few days ago, an article in the *New York Times* told about a fine organization that has started a project to teach parents and children about nutrition. No matter how hard it works, however, it will reach relatively few children. Why, I thought, are we not teaching this material in our schools? Where better to reach all of our children? Science classes might put aside lessons on levers, batteries, and genetic formulas or integrate those materials into a substantial unit on nutrition. Education should interact usefully with the world around us. It should be, as Whitehead advised, aimed at life itself.

A second way to resist the domination of formal subject-matter goals is to stretch the disciplines from within and to increase interdisciplinary work. That will be an important topic in the next chapter.

Construction of realistic and respectable goals requires collaboration among high school faculties, subject-matter experts, employers, community college faculties, and unions in addition to the usual college/university connections. What jobs will be available in the next decade? How are people best prepared for the relevant post-secondary training?

In addition to questions about occupational preparation, we need to ask how we can include goals that contribute to the large aims of citizenship and full personal life. Such goals have been increasingly neglected in an atmosphere heavy with inert academic learning. The great aims long associated with liberal education have too often been sacrificed to what some call "cultural literacy"—volumes of disjointed facts and skills detached from real-world uses and from each other. I'll address these issues also in the next chapter.

In both past and present, we have ignored the construction of rich goals for the non-college-bound. Too many of us have supposed that such goals are necessarily embedded only in the academic curriculum; this result was, in part, caused by confusion over the meaning of *intellectual*, as discussed in the last chapter. Guided by that false supposition, policymakers have concluded that the only way to provide a culturally rich education for all students is to insist that they all participate in the same standard academic curriculum. This is woefully impoverished thinking. A vocational curriculum can be exciting and rich in goals inspired by universal aims, but we have to treat this curriculum and its students with respect and creative effort.

It should be possible to open some courses to students from both academic and vocational programs—art, music, drama, and literature, for example. Some years ago, when Discipline Based Art Education became popular, some of us warned that such courses would appeal more to academically oriented students than to those with real artistic talent, and that turned out to be true. Courses established for those with particular talents should be maintained and extended. Doing this well might require changes in teacher licensing rules that would allow hiring artists, musicians, writers, and actors to teach in these programs. This practice should not be confined to magnet schools.

The growth of excellent vocational education will almost certainly require changes in teacher certification. This argument has been made by, among others, Frederick Hess (2010), who argues more broadly that teacher licensing should be rethought in light of 21st-century needs. One need not agree with Hess's argument in its entirety to consider the ways in which such rethinking may be valuable. Indeed, he argues—as I will throughout this book—that we should reject the "hook, line, and sinker" approach involving a wholesale adoption of methods that will later be rejected entirely when they prove not to be panaceas. His cautionary message is well taken:

When a fresh idea does happen to come along, it is all too often oversold as a miracle cure rather than a useful tool. Advocates demand that favored measures be adopted everywhere, as rapidly as possible—until a sensible idea is turned into an ill-conceived fad that eventually loses favor, to be replaced by another. (Hess, 2010, p. 11)

A more rational approach would review and evaluate both old and new ideas. Can we use some of this? How can we use it? With whom? In the Algebra 2 course described earlier, we drew heavily on Benjamin Bloom's (1981) discussion of mastery learning. We did not agree with Bloom and his colleagues that mastery learning and teaching could bring as many as 90% of students to mastery. And how should we define mastery? We did believe, however, that most students in the population with which we were working could be brought to minimal mastery if we defined the goals reasonably and insisted that students show competence on one unit before proceeding to the next. Results showed us to be right on this. If we had been faced with a more general population at the level of, say, Algebra 1, we might well have had to establish goals that would define a course in pre-algebra. When that happens—when many students cannot cope with algebra—the challenge should be accepted creatively. Perhaps it would be better to drop the thought of algebra. What sort of mathematics can we teach with a reasonable chance of success? How can our universal aims guide the construction of goals? What we must *not* do is to present our students with a fake algebra course masquerading as the real thing.

I cannot lay out a full plan for vocational education. This must be done locally in cooperation with employers, unions, and post-secondary educators. Some forms of vocational education are very expensive, and all forms require continual updating. The single most important thing we can do as educators is to encourage respect for all forms of work and talent. Today's politically correct insistence that all children can succeed at academic work is hurting, not helping, many students. Lots of adequately intelligent, morally decent, creative people are not good at math. Our job as educators is to help students find out what they *are* good at and assure them that, in an interdependent society, they are appreciated. I'll say more about the educative possibilities of vocational education in Chapter 8.

LESSON OBJECTIVES

The educational ends most familiar to today's teachers are learning objectives. In many schools, teachers are expected to have a stated learning objective for every lesson, every day. In some schools, the objective is stated for them; there is nothing for them to decide. Sometimes even the means of reaching the objective—the pedagogical method—is prescribed. What these particular students need, the methods that evoke their interest, the strategies at which the teacher is expert, what is currently happening in the school community—all of these are taken to be irrelevant.

Those of us who have been in education for a long time can remember the heyday of behavioral objectives and how some schools rewrote their entire curriculum in terms of such objectives. Teachers (and lesson writers) were told to state exactly what students would do as a result of instruction (for example, add fractions with different denominators up to 12), to what level of proficiency (say, 80%), and under what conditions (for example, a paper and pencil quiz of ten questions). (See Cronbach, 1977, for a full and fair discussion of the use and construction of such objectives.)

Behavioral objectives are enormously helpful when a teacher sets out to teach a particular skill or application of a concept. As a high school mathematics teacher, I often used behavioral objectives to guide my instruction (although I didn't call them that), and if most of my students did not achieve the 80% or better on the quiz that followed, I discarded the quiz and retaught the material. But not every class session was guided by a behavioral objective, and some that were so defined were interrupted when something socially vital or intellectually exciting came up. Not every lesson was teacher-centered, and sometimes the objective was simply awareness, not learning as strictly defined. Some valuable class sessions were aimed at reflection, some at social/political issues, some aimed at inspiration, some at discovery, some at practice, some at self-understanding and time management, and some at the connections of mathematics to other subjects.

The discussion of behavioral objectives illustrates the educational penchant for going whole-hog on promising ideas. The critical thinking we tout as an educational aim is too seldom used by teachers and their supervisors. Good teachers think critically, analytically, about when to use teacher-centered methods and when to use student-centered methods; they do not settle permanently for one or the other. Over the years, we have lost or disparaged some wonderful ideas by stretching them too far: discovery learning, cooperative small groups, role playing, Socratic questioning, intuition, structure of the disciplines, repetitive practice, whole language, overt thinking. . . . Even something as simple as "drill" is too often overused or discarded entirely. I have never addressed an audience that didn't know the words popularly used to follow "drill": "and kill." But drill can be employed reasonably. It can even be restful to simply practice a well-defined skill and stop thinking for a while. Instead of analyzing, evaluating, and employing these ideas and techniques reasonably, we set up ideological oppositions such as whole word versus phonics, teacher-centered versus constructivism, drill versus discovery, and so on. The fruitless demand for school plans to "scale up" extends to a continuing search for the best methods to teach everyone particular subjects and skills. The hopelessness of this form of inquiry was noted more than 40 years ago by Lee Cronbach (1966):

> I have no faith in any generalization upholding one teaching technique against another. . . . A particular educational tactic is part of an instrumental system; a proper educational design calls upon that tactic at a certain point in the sequence, for a certain period of time, following and preceding certain other tactics. No conclusion can be drawn about the tactic considered by itself. (p. 77)

Cronbach also warned that we must look at outcomes other than the successful learning of some skill. For example, if, using some method, kids learn to compute but also come to hate mathematics, the method cannot be deemed advisable. Everything we do as educators must be evaluated in light of our aims and goals as well as lesson objectives.

In the discussion so far, I've suggested choosing judiciously among various pedagogies and using both teacher-centered and student-centered methods. But even that dichotomy is too simplistic. What about methods that are neither teacher-centered nor student-centered but are, rather, whole-class-centered? My favorite lessons were of this sort. When getting ready for a new topic, I liked to pose a problem instead of launching into a formal introduction of the topic. For example, when the coming topic was exponential equations, I might write on the board: $2^x = 8$. The kids were quick to see that x = 3. But then I would write: $2^x = 10$, and we would spend some time coming up with approximate answers; x was certainly not an integer, and (if there was an answer) it had to be between 3 and 4. Then I would ask whether we had any method of solving an equation such as this: $y = 2^x$. This gave us an opportunity to explore all of the methods we had so far learned to solve equations. The *students* decided the equation did not fit any earlier pattern. What to do? They decided on graphing and discovered several important facts about the equation and about our assumptions in addressing it.

Rueben Hersh (1997) uses this method in introducing readers to various topics in mathematics. Since his readers are not physically with him, he says things such as, "As you saw . . ." and "If you guessed . . ." or he makes up realistic skits similar to the real-life account I gave above. The effect is to be immersed in a problem instead of being, without motivation, introduced formally to a topic. I suppose we could call such lessons *guided discovery*, but a label is not necessary. What is necessary is to analyze a unit of work and decide when the method is applicable.

A fascinating follow-up to the introductory lesson on $y = a^x$ is to ask: Why must "a" be a positive integer? This can motivate a terrific lesson. Well, this is perhaps enough math for one day. For present purposes, it is important to emphasize that such lessons are motivated by large aims: encouraging creative and critical thinking, cooperating, and communicating clearly.

Guided by well-considered aims and goals, we must look at intellectual inputs as well as a variety of outcomes. This is another area in which we have gone too far in one direction. It may be true that attention was for a while too closely focused on inputs such as money, facilities, and various resources; perhaps not enough attention was given to outcomes. But look at where we are now. Almost all attention is now focused on outcomes in the form of test scores. This is doubly foolish. It ignores valuable outcomes such as intellectual curiosity, moral concern for classmates and the larger community, and even academic honesty. All over the country, too many students are slaving for high grades with little concern for an appreciative learning of the subjects they study (Labaree, 1997; Pope, 2001). Our concentration on specific learning outcomes also ignores valuable intellectual inputs aimed at providing *opportunities* for individual student pursuit.

One of the most important and enjoyable teaching tasks is to present ideas from which some students will construct their own learning objectives. There is no specific learning objective per se in such lessons. The idea is to present a stimulating array of ideas from which students may choose topics or problems for further study. Dewey (1938/1963) wrote on this:

> There is . . . no point in the philosophy of progressive education which is sounder than its emphasis upon the importance of the participation of the learner in the formation of the purposes which direct his activities in the learning process, just as there is no defect in traditional education greater than its failure to secure the active co-operation of the pupil in construction of the purposes involved in his studying. (p. 67)

This does *not* mean that students must *always* construct their own learning objectives and the activities through which they will pursue them. Teachers are well-educated adults who know many things that students must learn—like it or not. Good teachers make these necessary learnings as palatable as possible, but there will be many teacher-centered instructional sessions. When I taught geometry, about 3 weeks before introducing the Pythagorean theorem, I explained to the students that they would work more easily with that theorem if they acquired some facility with the simplification of radicals, square roots, and the number line. I even had them memorize the squares of the integers from 1 to 25 and approximations for the square roots of 3 and 2. One of my proudest teaching moments came when one boy expressed what seemed to be the class's opinion: "Okay, if you say so." . . . Which brings us to another point about aims and objectives. Time spent developing relations of care and trust is not time wasted. Everything goes better as a result. Telling stories, listening to complaints, deliberating on social problems all have a place in good teaching.

As planning goes forward from aims to goals and objectives, and evaluation continues to circle back from objectives to goals and aims, consideration must be given to the use of technology in instruction. Over the past few decades, there has been some debate about the use of technology—some declaring it a panacea, others arguing that its efficiency has not been proved and that it dehumanizes the process of teaching and learning. Remember the debates over audiovisual aids back in the 1960s and 1970s? This is another example of sacrificing powerful methods by going too far and failing to integrate various tactics into a well-planned instructional system.

The great promise of a computerized curriculum—and I endorse it heartily—is that it can take over the routine instruction in skills. A well-designed computer course can move students along at their own pace, monitor their success, and keep track of their progress. Done well, this would mean no more worksheets, no more teacher time wasted correcting boring homework exercises. Highly effective programs can relieve teachers of the almost impossible task of differentiating instruction for students widely dispersed across the achievement spectrum. They can also free teachers to conduct discussion, inspire creative work, and encourage the deliberation so necessary in a democratic society. Freedom from the tedium of routine skill instruction should make it possible for teachers to do the important work described by E. O. Wilson—moving discussion of their own specialized subjects laterally into other disciplines and areas of human interest such as ethics, religion, and social problems. A word of caution should be added. Teachers should regularly review their students' computerized progress and occasionally ask them to think aloud about exercises involving important skills. No one method will accomplish all of our objectives and help us to meet all of our goals.

In the next chapter, we will see that working toward significant aims and goals for the 21st century will require changes in both teacher education and the K–12 curriculum.

5

The Liberal Arts in Schools

The liberal arts—literature, history, philosophy, mathematics, science, and arts (with emphasis on their development, not technical expertise, in the last three)—have long been the backbone of higher education. That emphasis has influenced the curriculum of precollege schooling, and everywhere we see the high school curriculum defined in terms of English, mathematics, social studies, science, and a foreign language. But for a hundred years or so, scholars have expressed fear that the tradition of liberal arts education is being lost (De Nicola, 2011). How concerned should we be about this possibility?

In this chapter, we'll look first at the tradition and its purported aims. Then we'll review its decline and how that decline is manifested in the high school curriculum. Finally, we'll consider whether the tradition should be renewed and, if so, how that renewal might be approached.

THE TRADITION

Although I listed above the subjects usually identified with the liberal arts, the tradition is better defined in terms of its aims and values than by its curricular subjects. First, above all, the tradition values learning for its own sake. Hutchins (1936/1999) was careful to tell readers that he did not denigrate *usefulness*, but he wanted to distinguish a long-term, life-guiding usefulness from everyday, practical usefulness. He wrote:

> The trouble with the popular notion of utility is that it confuses immediate and final ends. Material prosperity and adjustment to the environment are good more or less, but they are not good in themselves and there are goods beyond them. The intellectual virtues, however, are good in themselves. (p. 62)

In liberal arts education, then, the paramount aim is to cultivate the intellect. Hutchins (1936/1999) quotes Cardinal Newman to support his view:

> If then the intellect is so excellent a portion of us, and its cultivation so excellent, it is not only beautiful, perfect, admirable, and noble in itself, but in a true

and high sense it must be useful to the possessor and to all around him; not useful in any low, mechanical, mercantile sense, but as diffusing good, or as a blessing, or a gift, or power, or treasure, first to the owner, then through him to the world. (pp. 63–64)

From one perspective, this is a beautiful message; from another, it is a haughty example of privileged knowledge praising itself. But in either case we must wonder as we explore it further whether liberal education has had the effects attributed to it by Hutchins and Newman. If so, why is it being lost? Wayne Booth (1988; through his fictional speaker, Professor Zukunft) remarks sadly:

The simple value of cultivation of the powers of thought, for the sake of the value of thought itself and not for some ulterior practical use, has disappeared; the massage of the media has finally produced a gloriously comfortable and permanent mental torpor. (p. 159)

The elevation—almost worship—of pure thought and contemplation is a legacy from classical Greece, and it carries with it the seeds of its own destruction. For Plato and Aristotle, the life of thought represented the highest form of human life, and those incapable of it were expected to serve those who could do so. Today, many of us who have strong sympathy for the intellectual way of life nevertheless feel more than a twinge of discomfort when that life is placed at the top of a hierarchy of human talents. Am I— working thoughtfully at my library table, supported by Beethoven in the background—superior to the man who is now working physically to repair a leak in our porch roof? Even if we insist that it is not the person who is superior but the type of work, we can still ask: In what does this superiority consist? Can we find a way of life that retains and extends the appreciation of truth, intellectual beauty, and learning for its own sake without elevating this way of life above all others?

Looking at the world as it is, I can find little evidence that learning for its own sake has done much to improve the human condition. Indeed, one might be discouraged by the divisions it has aggravated. We need only to read J. G. Farrell, E. M. Forster, Edith Wharton, Noel Coward, even Conan Doyle to be reminded of the snobbery that has so often accompanied this learning. Remember Hardy's *Jude the Obscure* (1894/1961)? How Jude suffered, longing to be accepted in the circle of learned men. *Jude the Obscure* is fiction, of course, but it hit home in its devastating criticism of Oxford. Hardy's hard-hitting observations of Oxford and of England's hypocritical sexual mores were met with outraged critiques of the book. Hardy never wrote another novel. (Ah, but then such poetry emerged, and he made some of the same points poetically.)

But the ideal of pure thought, untainted by practical purposes, remains seductive. Must we elevate it above the obviously directly useful? There is another troubling feature of "learning for its own sake." Can one be *required* to study something for its own sake, or does such study acquire of necessity a subversive purpose? Surely, someone may suggest to another that Plato's *Republic* is worth reading for its own sake, but if that someone forces me to read it, if I can't pass a course without reading it, what has happened to the idealized purpose? Must there not be personal choice involved if I am to be truly engaged in learning for its own sake? And is the essence of that learning lost if I am motivated by practicality?

The dilemma appears in every discipline at the high school level. In a recent op-ed piece in the *New York Times*, the writer suggested that the high school mathematics curriculum should be revised to make it more practical. Of what use is algebra to people who will never use it? And why, the writer asked, are we not teaching people the basics of finance, budgeting, and household mechanics? I agree heartily with the writer, but published responses to the article were *all* critical to some degree. One letter, from Jonathan David Farley, sounded like the mathematician Hardy reborn: "You do not study mathematics because it helps you build a bridge. You study mathematics because it is the poetry of the universe. Its beauty transcends mere *things*" (*New York Times*, September 2, 2011, Letters). When I read statements like this, I want to ask: For everyone? Is this why everyone should study mathematics? I want to keep open the possibility that some students will see mathematics as the poetry of the universe, but I know from experience that few will do so.

The questions I would like readers to consider are these: Can we, in a democratic society, find a way to admire and encourage intellectual life (defined as by Hutchins and followers) without labeling it as "better" than every other form of life? To the degree that it *is* better, can we find a way to include liberal thought in all of our courses, including those in vocational education? Are the practical and the beautiful necessarily separate and distinct? Should we concentrate on helping students find subjects of study that they can willingly engage in for the sake of learning instead of prescribing and requiring those subjects?

Besides extolling learning for its own sake, advocates of the liberal arts have claimed that immersion in the history of thought and great literature encourages the development of intellectual virtues and thus of character. This does not imply endorsement of what we today call character education. Hutchins, for one, rejected attempts to teach the virtues directly. Probably his view was influenced by Socrates's carefully argued claim that the virtues cannot be taught directly. Despite the almost certain failure of direct instruction, Socrates advised that teaching must have *something* to do with the development of virtue. Hutchins and other advocates of the liberal arts agree; they believe that learning from good teachers in the liberal arts encourages the development of wisdom and virtue.

Much as we may be moved by the rhetoric of Hutchins, Newman, and Booth, we also suspect that there is no certainty in this approach. If there were, surely the world would be a much more sane and compassionate place. When we read David Halberstam's *The Best and the Brightest* (1992), for example, we may swing in the opposite direction and suffer a real fear of "eggheads" devising national policy. For thoughtful educators, the conflict continues to nag at us.

We should not, however, refuse to engage in the "immortal conversation" invited by the liberal arts. The great existential questions demand our attention: What is the meaning of life? What is truth and how can it be found? What is beauty? What is good? (For a new take on these questions, see Howard Gardner, 2011.) Is there a God? What is love? How should I live? What do I owe to others? Today, in a time of environmental turmoil, we must also ask: What must we do to preserve the Earth? Should we seriously consider a political move toward One World? Notice that these questions are relevant in all three domains of human life. The great gift of the liberal arts has been to keep this conversation alive. It is in this sense that it is better than other forms of education.

In the last section of this chapter, I'll explore some possibilities for renewing and extending it to include all students. I do not think, however, that it is either wise or feasible to maintain the liberal arts as a study of the great books or, in high schools, as a set of narrowly defined special disciplines. Although the literature of the great books contains much wonderful material, the world has changed and continues to change. This obvious fact was emphasized by Dewey but very nearly denied by Hutchins (1936/1999), who said:

> Education implies teaching. Teaching implies knowledge. Knowledge is truth. The truth is everywhere the same. . . . Hence education should be everywhere the same—the heart of any course of study designed for the whole people will be . . . the same at any time, in any place, under any political, social, or economic conditions. (p. 66)

The suggestions made in the last section of this chapter will challenge every sentence in this passage.

My focus throughout this book is, however, on American secondary schools, and my main challenge will be directed at the present organization of the curriculum into specialized subjects that rarely make connections across disciplines and almost totally ignore the great existential questions.

DECLINE

The liberal arts tradition has been declining for more than a hundred years. I do not mean that the quality of liberal arts courses at colleges and universities has declined. I have no knowledge of that. I mean that their place in the overall curriculum has been usurped by courses in business, technology, applied political and social sciences, and professional studies. The changes are welcomed by some who believe that the liberal arts are simply not that useful in either the short run (with which advocates of liberal education proudly agree) or in the long run. Where is the evidence, critics ask, that a liberal education produces wisdom, good character, or serenity of soul?

Quite the opposite, the most vocal critics might say. Liberal education has produced snobbery, a Sneetch-like society in which those who have heard of Matthew Arnold and Friedrich Nietzsche look down upon those who have not. We have only to read the novels of E. M. Forster and J. G. Farrell to get a taste of the class divisions aggravated by liberal educa- tion. One of Forster's (1908/1995) characters briefly describes life in that society thus:

> Life, so far as she troubled to conceive it, was a circle of rich, pleasant people, with identical interests and identical foes. In this circle, one thought, married, and died. Outside it were poverty and vulgarity for ever [sic] trying to enter, just as the London fog tries to enter the pine-woods. . . . (p. 89)

The "identical interests" alluded to above included cultural literacy defined by the liberal arts.

Advocates and opponents of liberal education both recognize the perni- cious social barriers described in Western literature. But today's advocates suggest an answer: Educate everyone in the liberal arts. This is the solution recommended by Hirsch. I agree with him on one point—that all children should learn and should use standard oral English. This accomplishment will not remove all social barriers and lead to perfect democracy, but it will block the immediate judgments we are so quick to make on the basis of spo- ken language. So we have identified one subject/skill that all children should master. Even this is controversial, and I will have to say more about it in the chapter on vocational education. At this point, I will just say that one way to promote this skill is to have all children engage regularly and at length in conversation with people who have already mastered the skill. It is not learned effectively through disconnected drills or the sort of exercises once associated with "punish lessons." Remember the little boy who wrote on the blackboard, "I have gone," 100 times and finished by saying, "I wrote it 100 times, and I have went home"?

What might be gained from actual study of the liberal arts? Here, we are tempted to break our exploration down into individual subjects, and that is, of course, the way our high school curriculum is organized. Specialization has contributed to the decline of the liberal arts in universities (Booth, 1988), and it has virtually eliminated the tradition at the high school level. The sharp separation of subjects, narrowly defined, makes it almost impossible to uphold the tradition of the immortal conversation.

Consider some examples. In biology, most schools now teach evolution, but very few spend time on the fascinating history of debate over the topic. Some brush that topic aside, claiming that it belongs in a "history of science" course, not in "real" science. But high schools do not typically offer a course in history of science, so the debate is neglected. Discussion of that debate might lead into one on the exclusion of women from scientific activities and the collusion of religion with science in maintaining that exclusion (Noble, 1992). I'll say more about this in the last section of this chapter when we consider how the spirit of liberal education might be renewed in our high schools.

In mathematics, the curriculum is so tightly controlled that students rarely get a glimpse of connections to other disciplines, much less a sense of mathematics as the "poetry of the universe." They may never hear of the conflict between followers of Leibniz and those of Newton over who should be credited with the invention of calculus. Many geometry students remain unaware that there are non-Euclidean geometries; they do not hear how mathematicians tried for centuries to prove Euclid's parallel postulate. And how many hear anything about the religious beliefs of the Pythagoreans?

In English class, the teaching of literature emphasizes reading great authors, not reading and contemplating great themes. It would be easy and so much more powerful to start with themes and then select fine writers who have written on them. Students should hear Aristotle's comments on friendship—that friends point each other upward; good friends help their friends to become better people. In *The Challenge to Care in Schools*, I suggested several other books that might be read and discussed on the theme of friendship: *Huckleberry Finn* (Huck and the slave Jim), *The Color Purple* (Miss Celie and Shug), *Of Mice and Men* (Lennie and George), *The Diaries of Jane Somers* (Jane and Maudie).

If we selected "caring for self" as a theme, for example, we might have students read Butler's *The Way of All Flesh* to see a long struggle for selfhood. We could choose biographies that might help students with their own everyday problems of time management, working style, abhorrence of homework, and the like.

Before turning to a closer look at how we might renew the spirit of liberal education, we should note that current advocates often make matters worse by suggesting that everyone should read a prescribed set of books. In a recent *Newsweek* column, for example, Niall Ferguson (2011) listed

11 books from Columbia University's core curriculum, including Virgil's *Aeneid*, Ovid's *Metamorphoses*, Saint Augustine's *Confessions*, Goethe's *Faust*, and Woolf's *To The Lighthouse*. The predictable reaction to such a list is to ask what use such reading might satisfy. Indeed, when a young person entering college announces that she might major in English literature, her parents might fear for her future. What will you do with that? they may ask. And if you decide to read *Faust*, you had better learn to pronounce "Goethe" or you will join the small legion of those "trying to enter" the circle of the cultured like the London fog into the pine-woods.

HOPE FOR RENEWAL

If we are to renew the spirit of the liberal arts, we may have to reject the emphasis on their content as cultural literacy. E. M. Forster (1910/1993) captures the problem in the thoughts of another of his characters, one who would like to set a young man right in his pursuit of learning through great books:

> No disrespect to these great names. The fault is ours, not theirs. They mean us to use them for sign-posts, and they are not to blame if, in our weakness, we mistake the sign-post for the destination. (p. 101)

And that is exactly what I fear we are doing when we reduce the liberal arts to a list of books, words, and facts. The essential idea is to get students thinking deeply and broadly. There are many fine books and many valuable individual interests—too many to squeeze into a prescribed list. Good teachers offer excellent possibilities from which students with different interests may choose, and then encourage discussion among students who make the same choice. When common reading is required, good teachers spend time on the ways in which that work connects to the immortal conversation. They take students on excursions into the depths of the subject at hand and laterally into a host of connections to other subjects.

Consider, for example, the topic of large numbers. Students should, of course, understand place value: ones, tens, hundreds, thousands, millions, billions, and—these days—trillions. Douglas Hofstadter (1985) wants students to consider what can be bought with a billion dollars, but even more he wants to overcome number numbness, to think in cosmic terms. Mulling over the possibilities, he comments:

> I wonder what percentage of our population, if shown the numerals "314,159,265,358,979" and "271,828,182,845," would recognize that the former magnitude is about 1,000 times greater than the latter. (p. 130)

I wonder, too. But I also wonder whether mathematics students would recognize these numbers if we placed a decimal point after the 3 in the first and after the 2 in the second. What remarkable numbers are these? What are they used for? And how are they computed? Perhaps students would like to see pi computed to 100,000 decimal places. (If so, see Posamentier & Lehmann, 2004, pp. 246–273.) This could be, in itself, a lesson in cosmic wonder, and it could be supplemented with biographical stories, historical accounts, and geographical explorations. None of this should be followed by a test. Those who are intrigued will know what "learning for its own sake" can mean. Those who are not will understand that this teacher—this *teacher*—will someday offer another glimpse of cosmic wonder in which they *will* be intrigued.

As we explore possibilities in each of the subjects we teach, we should keep in mind our 21st-century aims, especially collaboration, creativity, preserving Earth, and critical thinking. Hofstadter closes his discussion of large numbers and cosmic wonder with a quotation from *Cosmic View: The Universe in Forty Jumps* by Kees Boeke, a Dutch teacher:

> When we thus think in cosmic terms, we realize that man, if he is to become really human, must combine in his being the greatest humility with the most careful and considerate use of the cosmic powers that are at his disposal. . . . It is therefore an urgent need that we all, children and grown-ups alike, be educated in this spirit and toward this goal. Learning to live together in mutual respect and with the definite aim to further the happiness of all . . . is a clear duty for mankind. (quoted in Hofstadter, 1985, p. 131)

Because I taught high school mathematics for about 12 years, my cross-discipline thinking starts with math and moves out laterally. There is clearly a role for specialization, but math teachers need preparation that is quite different from that of other specialists in mathematics. One of the great mistakes of teacher educators has been acceptance of arguments in favor of educating teacher specialists in exactly the same way as others who specialize in the subject. On this argument, people planning to teach high school mathematics should have the same college program as all other math majors, and their promotion should depend on similar graduate courses. This is wrong. Teachers need a breadth of knowledge not necessary for other math majors, and they do not need technical expertise in complex analysis or topology or graph theory. They should know something about how these fields are defined and how they have grown, but they do not need the intense technical preparation required by those who expect to work in one of the many mathematical specialties. In an important way, the education of math *teachers* should be richer and broader. Educators bought into the "same courses" idea as a matter of status. The idea was to show that math teachers are as good as other math majors. As a result, math teachers are often not as good as they might be as teachers.

The practice in higher education has been to require a variety of courses in different disciplines in order to achieve breadth. For example, many engineering schools require their students to take two or three courses in the humanities. Unless they are lucky enough to get a teacher like Wayne Booth, they will not emerge enriched by the experience. Instead of connecting students to the great existential questions and everyday human dilemmas, these courses will simply introduce them to one or two other specialties.

A better answer, certainly at the high school level, is to stretch the disciplines from within. Wherever possible we should start our units of study with big ideas as suggested by E. O. Wilson—not with unmotivated details—and then move down the line to details as they are needed and laterally to the consequences or relations in other disciplines. Lateral excursions can be fairly lengthy if the topic is highly significant and students are interested or, in other cases, very brief, mere mentions. A history teacher in a unit on the Napoleonic era might pause to mention that Beethoven had planned to dedicate his third symphony to Napoleon but, disgusted with Napoleon's betrayal of the democratic cause, scratched out that dedication and called it the "Eroica." Casual but relevant mentions of this sort also contribute to what psychologists call "spaced repetition," but the repetitions need not be planned and deliberate. It is true that, if we hear things several times over a considerable period of time, we are more likely to remember them, and sometimes this repetition *should* be planned and carefully embedded in the curriculum. The powerful idea behind the spiral curriculum (Bruner, 1960) is to revisit concepts over time at ever deeper levels. Too often, crammed curricula encourage students to learn things for the test and then forget them. Ideas, facts, anecdotes, names that arise again and again are less likely to be forgotten. The informal repetition suggested here is not designed to aid memorization for tests; it contributes to genuine, connected education as well as the support of memory. When teachers of English, mathematics, history, science, and music all mention Beethoven, Gauss, Goethe, and Napoleon, students get a sense of the world and its wonders at a given time.

Stretching the disciplines from within supplies the connections that Whitehead saw so lacking in schooling. The practice also provides opportunities to discuss highly controversial topics without indoctrination. Recall how George Counts wanted to teach social justice by "imposition." In that discussion, I said that I agreed with Dewey that we should reject imposition and indoctrination. Instead, we can provide students with the arguments made by others, using their own words where possible. This approach is a great strength of the liberal arts tradition. The readings provide well-expressed arguments on all sides of every issue. On economics and politics, students read Marx, Hayek, and Keynes. On religion, they read Saint Augustine, Cardinal Newman, and Nietzsche.

At the high school level, biology teachers can broaden the discussion of evolution by quoting Darwin on Christianity and noting that some evolutionists have embraced atheism whereas others have retained a religious faith. Noteworthy here is the ongoing friendship of evolutionists Richard Dawkins (atheist) and Simon Conway Morris (Anglican). Both are scientists, but one believes that evolution is God's plan, and the other believes that evolution is one sign that there is no God.

To present such material in schools requires pedagogical neutrality—a willingness to consider all reasonable points of view without endorsing one as the absolute truth. This is hard. One has to decide first what constitutes a reasonable point of view. Teachers should not be expected to accept Hitler's Nazism as reasonable; it violates the most basic moral commitments. Nor should they, out of respect for religion, acknowledge creation science. When a concept or theory is scientifically supported by a mountain of evidence, it should be presented as fact. Pedagogical neutrality is out of place in the case of evolution just as it is when someone wants to question 2 + 3 = 5. Simon Conway Morris (2003), Anglican evolutionary biologist, warns his readers:

> . . . if you happen to be a "creation scientist" (or something of that kind) and read this far, may I politely suggest that you put this book back on the shelf. It will do you no good. Evolution is true, it happens, it is the way the world is, and we too are one of its products. (p. xv)

Pedagogical neutrality is required, however, in discussing the debate among evolutionists over whether evolutionary activity is entirely random or progressive. The arguments are fascinating, and there are recognized experts on both sides.

Pedagogical neutrality is an ethically and strategically effective way to introduce students to controversial issues. It is a great strength of the traditional liberal arts that they draw so effectively on rational, opposing views. Teachers need not claim that there is a God or that there is not a God. They can let the Karamazov brothers carry both sides of the argument. Students can read the *Iliad* and celebrate war and warriors. They can read the poet Wilfred Owen and turn from war with disgust, then listen to William Butler Yeats criticize Owen for cowardice and lack of patriotism, and experience renewed confusion.

At the high school level, a good strategy is to encourage critical thinking by introducing exciting arguments that are no longer highly controversial. The story of the long-lasting feud between Thomas Hobbes, political philosopher, and John Wallis, mathematician, is valuable for several reasons (Hellman, 1998). First, it shows vividly how uncivil—even nasty—two renowned intellectuals can be in their opposition. Second, it contains fascinating mathematical problems such as "squaring the circle"—a problem some amateurs in mathematics still tackle, even though the proof of its impossibility has long been established. Third, it can be used to inform students about the origin of two familiar mathematical symbols invented by Wallis ($\leq$ and ∞). Fourth, and perhaps most valuable from the perspective of critical thinking, it demonstrates that a person's thinking in one field may be admirably creative and unmarred by logical errors, yet surprisingly off the mark in another field. Hobbes, a great political philosopher and writer, was no match for Wallis in mathematics. Students may also be interested to learn that Wallis appears prominently as a character in *An Instance of the Fingerpost*, a fascinating historical novel by Iain Pears (1998). Finally, reading about this feud, we can vow to be more generous in our own debates.

Past debates should arouse student interest in critical thinking and consideration of the great existential questions. This is one reason I have suggested repeatedly that science teachers spend time on the Huxley-Wilberforce debate over evolution. Students usually enjoy the excitement and humor in this story. But they should also be asked to assess the arguments. To whom or what do we turn in trying to do this?

Pedagogical neutrality does not imply personal neutrality. When teachers feel strongly about an issue, they should feel free to say so and why, but they should also remind their students that there are other views. Like Counts, they may believe strongly in social justice, but as Dewey advised, they should avoid indoctrination.

Possibly the most difficult problem for today's thoughtful teachers is finding a way even to include controversial issues and existential questions in a curriculum stuffed with trivia. The problems of effectively handling controversy and finding a way to introduce it are large and, unfortunately, largely neglected. At the college level, the best liberal arts programs still manage, but even they are under some attack from those who accuse them of "liberalizing" their students. Do the critics understand what it means to "liberalize"?

At the high school level, there has always been a tendency to construe the liberal arts as a set of discrete subjects, not as the setting for deep thinking on eternal questions. That tendency is aggravated today by the proliferation of Advanced Placement courses for which curricula prescribed in detail press teachers and students to "master" skills, factual detail, and prespecified applications that leave little time for the exploration, wonderment, and creative thought once considered to be at the heart of the liberal arts.

Still, the case is not hopeless. Good teachers can stretch their disciplines from within, and they can talk to one another across disciplines. When teachers of science, history, literature, and mathematics all mention the Hobbes-Wallis feud, students get a glimpse of a larger intellectual world. But teachers need to be intellectually prepared to do this work, and they must be freed to do it. That means that we simply must reduce the emphasis on test scores, GPAs, and rankings. Our aim is not only to increase cooperation as a way of working and relating but also to encourage creativity and get students to think for themselves. In urging an increase of interdisciplinary study and lateral excursions into ethics, religion, and politics, E. O. Wilson (2006) concludes with sound advice: "Therefore, *Sapere aude*. Dare to think on your own" (p. 137). And Richard Dawkins also believes we should work toward that end. If he were to start a school, he says, "It would be a 'think for Yourself Academy'" (quoted in Powell, 2011, p. D4). If they are right, and I think they are, we are making a very bad mistake by prescribing our curricula in more and more standardized detail.

We should initiate and extend an invigorating discussion of educational inputs. For the last 2 or 3 decades, we have construed *inputs* in economic terms and, in opposition to this emphasis, have insisted that we should concentrate on *outputs* or *outcomes*. Why are we so attracted to narrow dichotomies? Surely, there are inputs besides money to consider, and there are important outcomes besides higher test scores to be sought. There should be reawakened interest in *intellectual* inputs. What is offered? Who accepts our various offers and with what results? How do good teachers broaden the outlook of their students with stories, allusions, questions, and quotations—none of which appear on tests except as students may refer to them in constructing their own answers to various challenges? It would be interesting to study how often and in what ways students draw on these "free gifts" bestowed on them by intellectually alive teachers.

So far, I have been looking at the liberal arts tradition with some admiration and some misgivings. The admiration is for its devotion to existential questions and the immortal conversation. The misgivings are directed at the certainty and snobbery that sometimes accompany it. Both admiration and misgivings are aroused by its emphasis on learning for its own sake, and I'll say more about that in a bit.

Hutchins's declaration that "knowledge is truth" generates misgiving in me and should be worrisome for all educators. The claim is characteristic of the Platonic idea that truth exists in some eternal and certain world of forms; *knowledge*, then, is that bit of truth we manage to snag off in our efforts to learn and discover. On this view, knowledge is discovered, not created. This view has long been popular among many mathematicians, but it has not obstructed what others might call the continuous creation of mathematics. But in the philosophy of life (political philosophy, ethics, philosophy of education), it can be troubling. It leads to the supposition that if x is an accepted piece of knowledge, then x is true. This, then, leads us to hang on stubbornly to schemes thought to be true or to discard them entirely as untrue. Throughout this book, I've been cautioning against this all-or-nothing approach.

Dewey and the pragmatists offered a different approach. In the pragmatic view, knowledge is bigger than truth. It is that material that, often unproven, effectively guides our action for at least a time. With sufficient experimentation and confirmation, we may say—as Conway Morris says of evolution—"it is true." Or we may find that a bit of knowledge works only sometimes, in some conditions, with some people, in some places. Knowledge is not everywhere and for all time the same. Dewey reminds us, too, that our actions affect the objects of knowledge, and he argues against all theories that insist on a sharp demarcation between object and observer, essence and existence, sense and reason.

A full discussion of this philosophical problem is not possible here (but see Dewey's *The Quest for Certainty*, 1929), and an attempt would take us too far afield. The important point for present purposes is that, although the liberal arts illustrate vividly the enormous variation in human attitudes, values, and activities, they have somehow inherited the longing for universality and certainty in answers, not just in questions. Hence, we hear recommendations for one best curriculum for all, for methods that will always work, for values that are unassailable.

Consider the great emphasis put by liberal arts advocates on "learning for its own sake." I confess to being afflicted by it. Mention *The Quest for Certainty*, and I find myself reading parts of it again. In discussing the Hobbes-Wallis feud, I was reminded of the novel casting Wallis as one of the characters and so took *An Instance of the Fingerpost* from the shelf and reread parts of the relevant chapters. Those of us who share this affliction could spend hours telling stories of our absorption in learning for its own sake. Some—those who share the particular interest pursued—might be fascinated; a conversation would ensue. Those not interested in the topic that fascinates me would be truly and thoroughly bored. Learning for its own sake should be encouraged by teachers, but we cannot specify exactly *what* should be learned for its own sake. That depends on the interests, aptitudes, and dreams of the learner. We are reminded, too, that choice is a basic concept in democracy. That is why it is so important that teachers offer a large set of "inputs" from which students may choose for further study.

I'll close this chapter by affirming the belief that the main purposes of education are to help students find out what they are good at, what they would like to do with their lives, and how to live responsible and fulfilling lives. To satisfy these purposes, we need to include serious discussion of personal life—parenting and homemaking—in our curriculum. We turn to that topic next.

6

Educating for Home Life

The general outline of today's curriculum has been with us for centuries. It was designed by men for the public life of men. When practical subjects have been added—at, for example, the university level—they have been held in lower esteem, sometimes very nearly in contempt. That has changed dramatically in the last few decades, and many critics lament the declining prestige of the liberal arts. Similarly, until the 20th century, the secondary school curriculum was designed to prepare privileged boys for college. With the creation of the comprehensive high school and its variety of programs (or "tracks"), the United States soon led the world in the percentage of its population enrolled in secondary education. But the difference in perceived status remained, and today—instead of trying to build upon and improve what our visionary predecessors created—the "reform" movement recommends that everyone receive the traditional privileged curriculum and be prepared for traditional college studies.

Throughout this process, the experience of women has been largely ignored. Even when girls were formally educated, their education usually consisted of a watered-down version of that offered to men; rich girls, educated to be culturally literate, were prepared to be socially acceptable and interesting as companions to the men who controlled public life. Poor girls sometimes got a smattering of reading, sometimes nothing at all. With the advent of women's colleges (1821) and the admission of women to some state universities in the last half of the 19th century, some women received the sort of education previously reserved for men. There was, of course, vigorous debate over the wisdom of educating women. What would they do with this education? Might they give up on motherhood? Might their reproductive organs be damaged by too much mental work? Might they forsake marriage? Linda Kerber (1997), in her work on women's intellectual history, titles one of her chapters "Why Should Girls Be Learn'd and Wise" after a verse written at the end of the 18th century:

> Why should girls be learn'd and wise?
> Books only serve to spoil their eyes.
> The studious eye but faintly twinkles
> And reading paves the way to wrinkles.
> (quoted in Kerber, 1997, p. 232)

A few early schools designed for the education of women paid some attention to the duties of women as homemakers and mothers, but such schools never acquired the status of schools that allowed women to participate in the curriculum designed for men. Any course or topic specifically made for women automatically had low status. Even at the high school level, courses in home economics and home nursing were not considered respectable on a transcript for college admission. A respectable education for women became the exact image of one for privileged men.

Through a lengthy struggle for equality in education, something of crucial importance has been lost—careful attention to the work that women have done for centuries. Are homemaking and parenting less worthy of attention than geometry and English literature? It has long been supposed that these activities—women's work—are taught at home, and the long, strongly endorsed, separation between public and private life supported this view. To the degree that personal life has been considered part of education, it has been confined to the construction of character and cultural literacy espoused and developed by the liberal arts. There was apparently no need to teach homemaking and parenting because these were taught at home by people of good character, well versed in their culture and history. When educators tried to introduce "worthy home membership" (in the Cardinal Principles Report), critics decried the attempt as anti-intellectual.

Even today, we find resistance to teaching these matters in our schools. Often, since our public schools are state-operated, proposals to teach homemaking and parenting are rejected as invasions by the state into private lives. Critics insist that such material be taught at home, even though they know that it is often not done. Educators and policymakers write article after article making suggestions for what the schools should do to assist children whose early years do not prepare them for school. Why are they not prepared? Clearly, many biological parents are not prepared to do the work of parenting, and this includes some economically comfortable parents as well as those living in poverty. The deficiencies of the poor are, however, often more noticeable in that facet of parenting that prepares children for school. This is not a moral failure on the part of parents but, rather, a product of a way of life influenced by both poverty and various lacks passed from one generation to another. Educators have been, understandably, reluctant to consider so-called deficit or deficiency models because their acceptance suggests that there is something wrong with the people exhibiting the deficiency; it seems to be blaming the victims. But there are deficiencies, and they are largely deficiencies of education. If we are to make progress in helping all children to succeed, I think we must accept as a fact that many parents, although they may love their children, do not have the knowledge and parenting skills needed to guide their children's education. And, of course, there are parents at every socioeconomic level who do not have the parenting skills to guide their children more generally toward satisfying lives.

We insist that all children must now study academic mathematics, although few will ever use it. However, all adults must make a home even if it is just for themselves, and most become parents. Why, when a task is so vitally important, do we not teach parenting in our schools? In a recent *New York Times* column, a Yale study was cited in which one middle-aged graduate bemoaned the fact that Yale does not require all students to study parenting. He had, apparently, experienced some difficulties in his role as a parent.

If we accept as a guiding aim that education should prepare students for full and satisfying lives, then clearly homemaking and parenting should be part of formal education. How might schools include these topics? We obviously cannot simply add a course or two. The school day is already too full, and reduced resources make it difficult to maintain the present courses. Even if we were able to add courses in homemaking and parenting, the courses would likely be treated as second- or third-class material unworthy of college preparation. The best solution is to plan along the lines suggested in the last two chapters; that is, we should stretch the disciplines from within to include material central to the topics of homemaking and parenting. Given two such huge topics, what material should we try to include? In what follows, I do not intend to recommend a specific curriculum. Rather, I want to show how, through exploration and reflection, we might go about doing this.

HOME AND HOMEMAKING

What is a home? There are several meanings to consider. First, a home is a dwelling place, a place of shelter. It need not house a family; a home for the aged or for orphans is a home in this sense. Second, a home as we usually think of it is a domicile chosen and organized by a family or family-like unit. Third, a geographical region or community may be thought of as a home. For many people, a region such as Appalachia is home; the United States, Peru, or Russia is thought of as a *homeland*. Fourth, we sometimes speak of having "found a home" when we've settled into an occupation or become part of a stable group devoted to some favored activity. All of these meanings are important, but the second and third will be of primary interest here. In this chapter, our concern is with what occurs in family homes, and in the next, with how people relate to their regional and national homes.

Let's consider the family home. What does it mean to make a home? We usually associate home with safety, physical comfort, and renewal. Privacy is also high on the list for many of us; when we enter our home and close the door, the world is shut out for a while. Most of us would like a place within the house where we can retreat even from family members. How do people achieve privacy in crowded households? This is an important question to explore with young teenagers. Some kids have to leave the house to get away from their families. Where do they go?

There was a day when kids just "went out." Sometimes they played with other kids, sometimes they walked in the woods or just sat under a tree in the yard. Some built tree houses; others pitched tents in their backyards (Smith, 1957). Today, children in education-conscious homes have little time to wander, and many parents would feel negligent if their children were allowed such unsupervised time. In the past, some could find a quiet place on the porch or in a corner of the attic. These quiet places—sometimes within the house itself—provided a shelter for thinking and daydreaming.

Gaston Bachelard (1964) has given us a beautiful description of the role played by a house or dwelling in our lives:

> [The] house shelters daydreaming, the house protects the dreamer, the house allows one to dream in peace. . . . It is the human being's first world . . . man is laid in the cradle of the house. . . . Life begins well, it begins enclosed, protected, all warm in the bosom of the house. . . . (pp. 6, 7)

Bachelard wrote about a physical place, the house, not about the people who live in it and make it a home, and his description of the human experience does not fit that of everyone. But this may be an important place to begin. As homemakers, we will want to explore how we shape our living places. But our houses—dwelling places—also shape us, and Bachelard helps us to think about this. Not only do our houses shape us, but so do the geographical locations in which we live and work. Philosophical thinkers from Socrates to Heidegger, Woolf, and Sartre have talked about the interactive effects of human consciousness and place.

Some discussion of dwelling places can be provided in units on history and geography. Far too little attention is given in the history taught in our schools to sanitation, the development of the structures we call homes (Rybczynski, 1986), and the fairly recent (17th-century) interest in the privacy and comfort we cherish today. In art classes, too, some attention can be given to the settings depicted as well as the artistic techniques. Witold Rybczynski (1986) uses Albrecht Durer's painting *St. Jerome in His Study* to remind us that the room in the painting is typical of 16th-century architecture, not that of the time in which Jerome actually lived (5th century). In the painting, Jerome is swathed in robes from shoulders to feet. Was there a source of heat? Of light? And why is there a lion lying peacefully beside a small dog in the room? Wait. Is the little creature a dog? Look more closely. Is it a lamb? Is there a biblical prophecy illustrated here?

Let's return to Bachelard's poetic description of the house as a shelter for our deepest thoughts and dreams. If we admire this description, how can we as homemakers shape our living spaces to provide the setting in which all family members can thrive? The Victorians believed that rooms should be designed to encourage proper behavior and that proper use of these rooms should be enforced (Ford, 2000). No shouting or horseplay in the library, no lounging about half-dressed in the drawing room. Today in popular cartoons we see the man of the house in his undershirt, unshaven, shoeless, beer in hand, watching TV in the living room. Most of us probably prefer the informality depicted in the cartoon to the stodginess of Victorian times. But is there something positive to be said about assigning special functions to certain places? Should everyone have at least a corner designated as his or her own? Should there be a place for reading and study with no TV or loud talk? Should there be a public space, always clean and ready for guests? In talking about family living spaces, the historical account is largely uncontroversial, but if discussion moves on—as we hope it will—to how we live today, uncomfortably large differences may emerge. How will kids feel if their homes have no public spaces and/or no private places? I think we have to remind them that we are talking largely about the future, about how we might plan our future homes, just as we talk about future college attendance and a future occupation. We do not tell them dogmatically what they *should* want, but we help them to think about, imagine, and plan for it.

There is help for us in the current small home movement. Students may enjoy collecting pictures and plans of small houses for which it clearly is important to think of the functions each area will serve. What activities will go on regularly in this dwelling place? How does the dwelling-place—house, studio, small apartment—fit into its geographical place? For city dwellers, the current movement for rooftop and community gardens should be interesting. What might we grow, and what shall we do with our produce? Some city schools now maintain their own gardens and introduce students early to the tasks and joys of growing things.

For the connection between space and function, Bill Bryson's (2010) *At Home* is rich in information as well as stories and humorous anecdotes. Here are the titles of some chapters: The Hall, The Kitchen, The Dining Room, The Cellar, The Study, The Bedroom, The Bathroom, The Nursery, The Attic, The Stairs. On this last, Bryson remarks, "In terms of the history of stairs, not a great deal can be said" (p. 369). Indeed, Bryson says little about any of these rooms; he uses them, rather, as meeting places to talk about all sorts of things. However, math teachers might have students measure risers and treads (called "goings" in England) on their school stairways and see if their measurements conform to formulas proposed by a mathematician (Bryson, 2010, p. 369):

$$R = 9 - \sqrt{1/7}(G - 8)\ (G - 2)$$

and

$$G = 5 + \sqrt{7}(9 - R)\ 2 + 9$$

Can this formula help explain why some stairways are uncomfortable, even dangerous?

Math teachers can find another promising example to discuss in Michael Pollan's (1997) *A Place of My Own*. In learning to build his own studio, Pollan and his contractor (and teacher) decided that the length and width of his study should be determined by the Golden Section, a proportion in which the length is calculated by multiplying the width by 1.618. The Golden Section (or Golden Ratio), Φ (phi), appears in architecture, nature, aesthetics, fractals, geometry, and many other fields (Livio, 2002). Math teachers can create any number of lessons involving phi—especially relevant in studying quadratic equations—and students might enjoy measuring various rooms in their homes and school. Are those with measurements close to the Golden Ratio more pleasing aesthetically than others? It is not my purpose here to provide lesson plans, but I hope teachers will have fun creating them.

Let's return briefly to Bachelard's writing on the house. He examines every room poetically and psychologically. The cellar holds special psychological meaning, enclosing the fears harbored in our unconscious. Dark, damp, and cold, the cellar is a place most people prefer to avoid. Indeed, many people today are glad to live in houses that have no cellar. Teachers of literature can surely find many stories and poems to illustrate cellar-fears. Remember Robert Frost's "Two Witches" in which a skeleton "carried itself like a pile of dishes" from the cellar (where it belongs) to the attic? Bachelard (1964) remarks on the exaggerated fears inspired by the cellar:

> The cellar then becomes buried madness, walled-in tragedy. Stories of criminal cellars leave indelible marks on our memory, marks we prefer not to deepen; who would like to re-read Poe's "The Cask of Amontillado"? (p. 20)

Teachers, without getting morbid, can help students recognize common fears and also the curative powers of sunlight. They can also help students make choices in recreational reading. There are some very good, well-written mystery stories, for example; many involve cellars, attics, narrow stairways, and locked rooms. During this writing, for example, I started to read *The Vault* by Ruth Rendell—a dark hole, corpses, a blocked stairway . . . brr.

I am not suggesting that we should develop detailed sub-curricula on houses and homemaking for each of the traditional subjects. That might well defeat our purpose. Teachers would revolt against one more demand on their time. Students would regard the material with the resigned dread of coming tests, after which most of it could safely be forgotten. There are some things that all children *should* learn about houses and homemaking, and I'll say more about that material a bit later. Here, I'm concentrating on the lateral moves that teachers can make to stretch their specialties into other disciplines and actual life.

Every teacher should be on the watch for material that can be used to make lateral moves into the topic of houses and homemaking. Consider what creative teachers might do with eating and hospitality as subjects. Some work with well-chosen cookbooks might be more effective in teaching geography than the unconnected details prescribed by Hirsch. Where might we encounter 300 varieties of potato? Why did such a proliferation of varieties occur there? And what does this history tell us about the dangers of monoculture?

There are several ways in which such discussion might get started. Conventionally, the curriculum might require a study of the Andean region, and a creative teacher might move from basic map and climate details to the exploration of potatoes, recipes, and the perils of monoculture. She might even mention the Irish potato famine as a calamity of monoculture (Pollan, 2001). Or the discussion might start in a biology class with monoculture and move from there to the Andes and potatoes. Or a creative English teacher might conduct a unit based on cookbooks—the sort of books that include cultural accounts, not just recipes—and the discussion would move laterally into geography, cultural habits, and agriculture. For English teachers, a main aim is to get students reading. If the reading permits some choice (which cookbook or mystery story from an approved list) and if it contributes to building a satisfying personal life, it passes an important test, guided by a significant aim.

To teach in the way suggested here requires some changes in teacher education. Instead of concentrating on the development of narrow expertise in a subject, teacher education must help teachers to acquire the breadth that will enable them to stretch their disciplines from within.

So far in this discussion of houses and home life, I have concentrated on how our dwelling places shape us. How do we shape our houses and living spaces? This topic is in several ways more difficult to treat in our schools. Notice that in the references I have included, all of the writers have been men, and it was relatively easy to move from the existing curriculum to lateral topics on the subject. When the question is how we shape our homes, however, we face a problem of long standing. The task of shaping home life has largely fallen to women, and there is almost nothing in our school curriculum on women's work in the home. There is no shortage of fine writing on this topic, but it has rarely been translated into material for K–12 education. In a popular American history textbook, there are more than 30 entries under "women" in the index, but not one has anything to do with women's work in the home. Women only appear in the story when they contribute something to the projects dominated by males or gain attention in trying to do so.

I said earlier that I do not believe that the general outline of the American secondary school curriculum will change in the next few decades and that we have to work across disciplines and stretch each of the disciplines from within. But there is no course called "history of homes" or "women's work" or "housework" to start with or link to. When there were courses in home economics in our high schools, they were taken by girls who did not expect to do anything in the public world, and the courses were not held in high regard.

Perhaps, then, an addition to the formal curriculum is required. Since history courses other than U.S. history are usually elective, why not offer one on the history of homes or women's history? One discouraging answer is that only girls would take such a course, and a second is that the course would have to be high-powered enough to qualify for Advanced Placement status. With the fine material produced in the last 40 or so years, it would not be difficult to do this. However, it would not address the problem to be discussed later in this chapter—the basic problem of parenting. There are some matters on which we should educate all children, and an AP course taken by a few good students would not accomplish this.

Women have shaped the lives of their families in homes. This has always been true, but starting in about the middle of the 19th century, women began to professionalize homemaking and to make important suggestions for the design of homes. Catherine Beecher (sister of Harriet Beecher Stowe), for example, was concerned with the organization of housework and with the comfort of its inhabitants. She and her sister (Beecher & Stowe, 1869) recommended smaller, more efficient homes in which the kitchen was carefully designed to save steps, and provision was made for heat, ventilation, and water. Rybczynski (1986) draws attention to the ingenuity of the Beecher sisters in designing a house of about 1,200 square feet for eight persons:

> This appreciation for smallness was something that had disappeared from the domestic scene since the snug Dutch home. Its reappearance marked an important moment in the evolution of domestic comfort. In this, as in so many things, Beecher was ahead of her time, for the nineteenth century still associated comfort with spaciousness. (p. 162)

Today, the rage for McMansions seems to have given way to a renewed interest in small houses.

Beecher argued for the importance of women's role in shaping the house and family; she did not argue for women's equality in public life (Martin, 1985). As the women's suffrage movement grew, followed by waves of feminism, it became hard to defend the notion that there should be a "women's sphere," distinct and separate from the public sphere. Whereas Beecher had extolled the professional expertise of the female homemaker, later writers such as Barbara Welter, Aileen Kraditor, Betty Friedan, and Gerda Lerner criticized the notion of a women's sphere, referring to it as a cult or mystique of "true womanhood" (Kerber, 1997). The image captured in the separate spheres position is that of an "angel in the house"—an intensely sympathetic, unselfish, self-sacrificing prisoner in the house of which she was supposedly in charge. Virginia Woolf (1966) described this paragon of Victorian female virtue and rejected it. Referring to the purported "angel," she wrote: "It was she who used to come between me and my paper when I was writing reviews. It was she who bothered me and wasted my time and so tormented me that at last I killed her" (1966, 285).

Students may be interested in women who managed successfully in both spheres. The story of Lillian Gilbreth in *Cheaper by the Dozen* (Gilbreth & Gilbreth, 1966) is quite fascinating. Gilbreth managed a distinguished career as an industrial engineer and also raised 12 children. Her example illustrates the importance of order and efficiency in household management, and it also shows that efficiency and creativity are not necessarily at odds.

I have spent a bit of time here on the idea of a women's sphere and important objections to it, because I want to suggest that, although I too reject the notion firmly, I worry that we too often overlook, even dismiss, the significant contributions of homemakers. There is, after all, a sphere of homemaking. When I refer to the "homemaker," I do not mean the model described by Beecher. The homemaker to whom I refer may well be professionally employed in the public world; "she" may even be a man. The possibility that men may engage in maternal thinking, for example, has been beautifully described by Sara Ruddick (1989), and I'll say more about that in the next section on parenting.

Can we learn something important from women's experience as described by Beecher and others who saw homemaking as a challenging task requiring expertise? The physical tasks of homemaking have often been emphasized in home economics courses: cleaning, washing and ironing, cooking, preserving food, sewing, caring for young children, tending the ill. But when we think of home—the sort of house described by Bachelard—as a shelter for the dreamer, as a place of security in which people *grow* and learn not only to cope with the outside world but to contribute to shaping that world, we see that the influence of the homemaker stretches far beyond the physical tasks so easily identified. And these tasks have changed over time. There is little ironing done today, and few people darn socks or even know what "to darn" means.

A homemaker is responsible for the physical well-being of those in the household. She plans healthy meals and rarely relies on fast foods. She makes sure that there are fresh fruits available for snacks. Smoking is not allowed in the house. In this age of growing worries over obesity, the homemaker's responsibility to plan a good family diet is more important than ever.

The competent homemaker somehow establishes an atmosphere of psychological comfort in which family members and guests feel welcome, "at home." Conversations are invited. Everyone is expected to participate in household tasks, but the work is distributed democratically where possible; kids get to choose the tasks for which they will be responsible. The homemaker provides a supportive structure—for example, regular mealtimes at which everyone will be present—and she encourages other family members to establish and communicate their own schedules of activity. She invites discussion on these matters.

The homemaker sets the tone for language use in the home. I do not mean to conjure up the vision of Victorian hostesses skillfully guiding dinner table conversations. I mean simply that she does not permit the use of objectionable language—"We do not use that word in this house." She tries to include everyone in family conversations. She gently corrects grammatical errors in the young. And she listens.

She conveys a sense of what is precious, to be valued and cared for. Houseplants are not allowed to die of neglect. Pets are not abused but treated with love. Furniture is rarely broken or marred by anger or carelessness (it does happen occasionally), and spills are cleaned up without undue fuss. Perhaps, above all, the competent homemaker establishes a sense of balance among structure and freedom, choice and responsibility, rest and activity, pleasure and toil, social interaction and privacy. She provides a democratic environment.

I have no desire to resuscitate the glorified doormat known as the angel in the house, but I do not want our aversion to her to lead us to neglect the attitudes, knowledge, and skills required for good homemaking. These days, both parents and children must share in the work of homemaking. Where do people learn these things? If they do not learn them at home, they may never learn them. In schools, we try to compensate for poverty by providing early childhood education. We know that the home environment is the single most important factor in a child's education. And yet, while stuffing algebra into everyone, we stubbornly refuse to teach homemaking and parenting in our schools.

PARENTING

Some people object strongly to the teaching of parenting in schools on the grounds that such teaching is an invasion of family privacy. This objection is a product of a long-standing belief that the public and private should be sharply separated—two different life spheres. In the last several decades, feminists have challenged this separation in a campaign, in part, to eliminate the abuse of women and children in their homes. Social reproduction theorists might object to this separation because it plays such a strong part in supporting the current class structure, and they would be right to do so.

But educators should be sensitive to the need for privacy in family matters and should also recognize that parenting takes different forms in different cultures and families. I have already rejected Counts's recommendation that we should *impose* a defensible view of social justice, and I think we must also reject teaching an authoritarian, dogmatic pattern of parenting. There is a risk, too, that open, critical discussion of parenting may invite personal disclosures that students will later regret. As in the earlier discussion of homemaking, public disclosure and analysis of present conditions can be avoided by focusing attention on the future. We freely ask students to talk about their future college attendance and anticipated occupation; similarly, we can encourage them to think about what sort of home they want and what they hope to be like as parents.

Educators and policymakers should consider the strong possibility that our failure to teach parenting supports class differences that impede social justice. Today, large amounts of money are spent on early childhood education, and this is defended as a compensatory measure, a way of giving children experiences of which poverty has deprived them. But poverty is only part of the problem. Very poor parents have sometimes provided their children with excellent preparation for learning and participating in school. Our national history is rich with such examples.

I am not arguing against programs designed to alleviate poverty or to provide early education for poor children; they are clearly important, and deserve our strong support. But when we turn our attention to what schools can do, we should recognize that the school and home are interdependent. If we can do something to strengthen the home life of future children—particularly its educational climate—we should do it. Otherwise, we risk having our efforts in school countermanded by what goes on in homes. This is not "blaming the victim" or making harsh, unsubstantiated judgments about some parents. It is not a matter of blame at all. It is a matter of facing facts well known to veteran teachers; some children come from homes that do not facilitate education. Shirley Brice Heath (1983) has provided a powerful ethnographic study that illustrates some of the problems caused by cultural ways of using language that work against the ways we use language in schools. When, for example, parents read and children listen—a tightly scripted performance—there may be no discussion, no exploration of how what is read might be extended to other situations. At the opposite extreme, there is no reading at all in some families. Further, we may not be able to do much about the ineffectiveness of people who are already parents. However, we may be able to reduce the number of people who will be ineffective parents in the future.

Where might we begin? As I admitted earlier, we have to work with the structure of curriculum in place. If we were free to design and implement a full course on parenting—one that would be required of everyone, I would start with the three great demands on maternal thinking identified by Sara Ruddick (1989): preservation of life, fostering growth, and guiding the young toward moral and social acceptability. Since it isn't likely that such a course will soon be offered in our high schools, we must ask how we can use the subjects already in place to get some of these ideas across. In what follows, I'll concentrate on the first two demands; a later chapter will be devoted to the third, moral acceptability.

Consider what might be done in the English program. Surely, one semester of high school English could be devoted to the literature of childhood. As we explore some possibilities, we will run into problems introduced in earlier chapters—the demand for detailed learning objectives, overdependence on specialization, and helplessness in devising forms of evaluation that do not depend on tests.

The first question is which childhood literature to include. We have to keep in mind that the primary purpose in teaching the literature of childhood is to prepare our teenage students for one of the most delightful parental activities—reading to and with our children. A familiar cartoon (appearing repeatedly over the years) shows a parent sitting, book in hand, by the bedside of a young child, presumably reading a "bedtime story." The cartoon inadvertently suggests that the purpose of bedtime reading is to put the child to sleep. If that is what the parent intends, it would be far better to sing lullabies. The picture we should invite is that of parent and child sitting close together sharing a book—both with a hand on it, both looking at it, both talking about it.

Suppose the child is quite young—prekindergarten—and the book selected is a "picture book." With our teenage students, we can look at a variety of these books, and students can learn to check on the recommended ages for which a book has been designed. They should also learn about the Newbery and Caldecott medals and what they signify. Now let's say we have a good age-appropriate book in hand. What do we, as parents, do? Obviously, we read. But we also talk, listen, and spend time looking carefully at the illustrations. (Again, see Heath's (1983) comments on the sort of scripted reading that does little to prepare children for critical thinking in later school life.) A book I looked at recently pictures a variety of wild animals in the woods. A parent might ask, "What do you see?" If the child says, "Bears," the parent might say, "How many bears?" This is a wonderful opportunity to find out whether the child has mastered the basic idea of one-to-one correspondence—she puts a finger on one bear and says, "one," then the finger on another says, "two," and so on. This is vitally important in learning arithmetic. Too many parents suppose their children can *count* when they simply recite, "one, two, three . . ." as they would a jingle. When the child does not yet have the concept of one-to-one counting, the parent does not make a fuss about it, but shows how to do it when opportunities arise. The picture I am looking at shows three owls and three raccoons as well as three bears, so the parent can take the child's finger and point-count at each of the owls and each of the raccoons. And what is an owl? What is a raccoon? And what is that bristly creature clinging to a tree limb? See how it is almost hidden by leaves. The parent extends the reading into names, shapes, nature, fears, fun. And the child is encouraged to comment and question.

At this point, we may encounter a familiar problem. The English teacher may protest that she is an *English teacher*, not an early childhood teacher, certainly not a math teacher, not a biology teacher. She is supposed to be teaching British literature, American poetry, and/or how to write a clear five-paragraph essay. We are face-to-face with the problem of specialization. Recall E. O. Wilson's advice that future scientists should know a lot beyond their own specialty, and I have offered the same advice in education. But we have not been able to convince teachers that they must do this despite the powerful reminders of thinkers like Whitehead that what we teach should have something to do with actual life.

It is somewhat more realistic to expect an English teacher to identify and review great children's classics with her students, and these works should surely be included in the course. In addition to the readings selected, there should be some discussion of how these books have been evaluated by psychologists and other experts on child care. *Grimm's Fairy Tales*, for example, have been the object of some debate, because their content has sometimes been disturbing to sensitive children. Dr. Spock (2001) noted the ambivalence of experts on the wisdom of reading fairy tales that involve cruelty and violence, and Bruno Bettelheim (1976) advised parents not to read stories to their children in which the mother is a witch or the father an ogre. If we accept this caveat, is it otherwise acceptable to include violence and cruelty? The teacher need not endorse one side or the other on this debate, but she should make her students aware of it.

Before turning to other subjects in which we might find ways to teach something about parenting, we should recognize another impediment to this work. The demand for a detailed, prespecified curriculum has already been mentioned; another is the straitjacket of specialization in which we are confined. A third is the sort of evaluation that might be demanded if the course is to be accepted on transcripts for college admission. It might be counterproductive if the course were constructed to satisfy a test typical of today's evaluations: "Name three books written by A. A. Milne." Or "Which of the following was featured in *The Wind in the Willows*: Whitehouse, Windsor Castle, Toad Hall, Liberty Hall?" In contrast, a course envisioned here might look quite different from year to year, and a more sophisticated method of evaluation would be required.

What might be done in science classes? With our insistence today on preparing everyone for college, we have perhaps gone too far in designing high school science courses as preparation for college science courses. "Popular science" is looked down upon as non-rigorous. But consider the real world in which we live. Highly educated nonscientists depend on "popular science" for information on health, the environment, the latest experiments on relativity, nuclear energy, and advances in chemistry. Further, in some cities, there is a near-epidemic among teenagers of obesity, asthma, and diabetes. Surely, high schools should find a way to incorporate these topics in regular science classes. And why not offer a year of psychology in which parenting, learning, and mental health are discussed?

A course in psychology might also be the right place to study drugs and the history of human addiction or, perhaps, this could be done in a chemistry class. Instead of addressing the topic as a problem to be treated in highly moralistic special sessions, it should be incorporated into courses "that count." Theodore Zeldin (1994) provides us with a fascinating historical account of worldwide drug use over the ages in the context of a larger story of how people have tried to escape from their troubles. Zeldin, a historian, tells the true story of the human desire to live more fully and to escape troubles of all sorts. So, on reflection, much of this material could be built into a history course. Notice that the strategy mentioned earlier of approaching familiar teenage problems by focusing on their future as parents reduces the likelihood that students will be turned off by what they might see as a heavy dose of moralizing. Focusing on the future, we ask: What would you tell your children about drugs and addiction? How would you best protect them from such problems?

In the last few paragraphs, I have nearly ignored the practical problems that arise again and again when we try to add important topics to the curriculum. If we were seriously to propose a psychology course, which department would sponsor it? Science or social studies? And what would it displace? We might easily find ourselves in a battle very like the never-ending one over history versus social studies. It is reasonable to affirm the recommendations I have made repeatedly throughout this book. The disciplines must be stretched from within. Teachers in every discipline must be asked what their subject can contribute to the knowledge essential to everyday life and to the connections among subjects that make each of them more relevant and interesting. And everything we do—selection of readings, pedagogical strategies, methods of evaluation—should be guided by our aims of cooperation, critical thinking, and creativity.

Let's look briefly now at what more could be done in history. In addition to the history of homes and homemaking, the history of childhood and of child-rearing should be considered. As recently as the 1960s, it was thought that childhood was not recognized as a distinct period of life in the Middle Ages. Philippe Aries's popular book, *Centuries of Childhood* (1962), depicted a time in which children were treated as small adults. More recent research has revealed a genuine culture of childhood in medieval and early modern times (Orme, 2001). Today's history students might enjoy looking at and discussing the painting *Children's Games* by the Flemish painter Pieter Bruegel. This painting (1560) appears as the jacket cover of Nicholas Orme's (2001) book *Medieval Children*, and it "depicts more than two hundred children and adolescents, playing with toys or taking part in games" (p. 166). More than 70 activities are shown. Can our students figure out what the children are doing? There is an opportunity here also for art teachers to get involved. Indeed, historians may have been misled by early paintings that pictured children—even babies—with bodily proportions like adults.

Although medieval children were expected to do some work and life was hard, there was time for them to play. We are not surprised to hear that medieval children had to work. It is harder for most of us to understand why children were so exploited in Victorian times. In the new industrial age, children as young as 7 and 8 in England often worked 10 or more hours a day, and even in 20th-century America, children were employed at an early age and for long hours. Scott Nearing (2000), who worked with others to introduce laws governing child labor, gives us a powerful quote from Sally Cleghorn: "The golf links lie so near the mill that almost any day the working children can look out and see the men at play" (p. 39). And, of course, the children were very poorly paid. It is believed that Nearing lost his faculty position at the Wharton School (University of Pennsylvania) because of his social activism, although that could not be proved. Later, he lost his position at Toledo University for his opposition to World War I. These are important lessons in the consequences of social activism. Students should be encouraged to look carefully at the period from about 1905 to 1938 when child labor was legally eliminated. The aim is for teachers to help students make connections among the phenomena of industrial growth, labor movements, child labor, socialism, home life, and parenting.

Before child labor was outlawed, it was children of the working class who suffered; children from better-off families often had the sort of childhood depicted in stories and poems. By the 1980s, however, experts again expressed concern about the "adultification" of children; this time, however, worry centered not on their exploitation as labor but on the increasing influence of television and other social forces outside the family. There seemed to be an alarming tendency for kids to dress like adults, engage in adult social activities, use adult language, and demand adult independence. For more than a century, there has been debate about what constitutes the best parenting for life in a democratic society, and there has even been discussion of democratic parenting (Hulbert, 2003). Discussion of these matters in a historical perspective might provide useful information for both current students and their future children.

In this chapter, I have tried to show how some traditional disciplines might be stretched to include material on homemaking and parenting. The idea was not to prescribe a set of topics (I have barely scratched the surface), but simply to show through a process of exploration and reflection what might be done. By choosing to neglect this material, we contribute to a long-standing form of social injustice and weaken our democracy. Compensatory measures in early childhood education are commendable, but they probably can never make up for the lack of informal education that should be supplied by parents.

This is not an expensive recommendation; it makes use of existing courses in our high schools. It will, however, require substantial changes in teacher education. In particular, we should reject the status-conscious notion that high school teachers should be prepared in their major subjects through exactly the same courses required of others majoring in the subject. On the contrary, teachers need a much richer, broader education.

We turn next to how we might think about preparation for civic life in the 21st-century global environment.

7

Toward Ecological Cosmopolitanism

We think of our country as both our homeland or home-place and our nation, but throughout the 20th century the emphasis was on the concept of nation—that is, a group of people with a distinctive form of government. The prevailing attitude in America was one of enormous pride in a democratic nation that had become the world's greatest national power. We need not give up pride in our national heritage, but in the 21st century, we might adopt a more humble and critical attitude toward the nation and a more appreciative one for the home-place on which the nation has been built. The shift signifies deeper concern for natural resources—land, air, water, and the interdependence of all living things. The same shift of emphasis is required at the international level. Of course, we should continue to be concerned about international (world) affairs, but we should be especially concerned about how these interactions affect the health of Earth, our universal world home. It is a shift toward ecological cosmopolitanism.

In the last chapter, we noted that our dwellings shape us, and we shape them into homes. Similarly, our natural environment shapes us, and we shape it. As we build cities and villages, this new environment shapes us, and we continue to modify it. The first European settlers in America encountered an incredible bounty of land, woods, water, wildlife, and mineral resources. It is not surprising that the generosity of the natural environment led to profligacy in the growing population of new Americans. Everything, it seemed, could be had by working hard to capture it or, often, by simply grabbing it. Today, Americans lead the world in consumption, using an inordinately large part of the world's resources. The habit is so strong that, even in an economic recession, we are urged to buy things; the economy needs consumers to continue consuming. We assume that people are not buying because they have less money, but what if people have come to believe that they just don't need all the things offered in malls and catalogs? Apparently, only a few of us think this way, and most of us who do are already richer than we need to be.

Like homemaking and parenting, conservative consuming does not appear prominently in our school curricula. There may be some discussion of living within one's means in a unit on economics, but there is far more talk of raising one's income by investing in higher education and not just any education—the more prestigious, the better. Further, the media flood us with temptations to buy, and the dominant political answer to economic woes is *growth*. Yet careful thinkers urge us to think in terms of sustainability (Martenson, 2011). It is simply not possible to continue growth as we have come to think of it.

In this chapter, we will look first at our local environments and how schools might introduce some significant ideas on ecology. We'll look at examples of ecological problems such as pollution, overconsumption, and mountains of garbage, and then we'll consider how the study of history and geography might be transformed by the new emphasis on ecological cosmopolitanism. Finally, we'll explore how to connect some of this thinking to world peace. Throughout the chapter, we will emphasize the aims of 21st-century education: collaboration and critical thinking, with special attention to individual growth and world citizenship.

LIVING IN PLACE

Whereas our ancestors lived in an age dominated by place, we humans today live in an age dominated by time. Edward Casey (1997) begins his study of place with these remarks:

> Whatever is true for space and time, this much is true for place: we are immersed in it and could not do without it. To be at all—to exist in any way—is to be somewhere, and to be somewhere is to be in some kind of place. (p. ix)

So thoroughly governed by time, however, we pay little attention to place until something dramatic happens to draw our attention to it. Sitting in an airport, at the gate that displays my intended destination, I sometimes have to think about where I am, but I quickly realize that it doesn't matter. I will board a plane that will take me to a planned destination, and—unless that place is *home*—it, too, may not matter. What matters is my schedule and what I will do when I get there. John B. Jackson (1994) also notes the dominance of time over place:

> What brings us together with people is not that we live near each other, but that we share the same timetable: the same work hours, the same religious observances, the same habits and customs. . . . It is our sense of time, our sense of ritual, which in the long run creates our sense of place. (p. 160)

But this is not true for all of us. A personal story—not unique, I'm sure—may help here. During my 30 or so years at Stanford, my family lived in a pleasant, nearby community. In all those years, we knew almost none of our neighbors. Our "community" was organized, just as Jackson has described it, around our workplaces, hours, and rituals. But for periods each summer, we lived in a village on the Jersey shore. We came to realize that we knew more people by face and name in that village where we spent relatively little time than we did in our California town where we lived all year for more than 20 years. When I took formal retirement, we moved permanently to that village. Here, we know the names of our neighbors and even those of their pets.

There is another difference that I treasure. Although I keep a very busy professional schedule and love my professional community, I am now much more attuned to natural time. Clock-time still governs my professional life but, living on the ocean front, I am deeply aware of sunrise, seasonal changes, tides, winds, and rain. I keep a garden log and rotate my vegetable plantings. Place shapes much of my life.

Living here, I am affected by what the Greeks called *philochoria*, love of place. Sometimes, in some places, people are moved by what seem to be the spirits of a sacred place. Socrates, apparently resisting the feeling, nevertheless confessed to divine inspiration as he and Phaedrus rested by the River Ilissus (Walter, 1988). Some of us experience philochoria in the mountains, some at the seaside, and some in human-made wonders such as cathedrals.

Jackson (1994) notes an important difference in beliefs about our sense of place:

> It is my own belief that a sense of place is something that we ourselves create in the course of time. It is the result of habit or custom. But others . . . believe that a sense of place comes from our response to features which are *already* there—either a beautiful natural setting or well-designed architecture. (p. 150)

I think both beliefs capture something of our human experience. Local place shapes us, and we shape our places—just as we shape and are shaped by our houses. As we talk about these things in our schools, we should discuss how our school-place affects us and how we affect it. Rena Upitis (2010) has asked an important question: Why are school buildings over much of the world so much alike? They should differ, one would think, at least by physical location. In designing schools, Upitis identifies several important factors: "the need to pay attention to natural settings, the need to provide facilities that encourage learning through play, through conversation, and through the body . . ." (p. x). She recognizes that we shape our schools and, then, the schools shape us: "Schools ought to shape the ideas of the people who dwell in them in ever-changing ways, leading students to unpredictable and creative encounters with ideas, with one another, and with the natural world." (p. 180) Schools should open minds to a wider world, but they should also induce reflection and appreciation for the particular place in which we live.

Our love for particular places has led to movements to preserve those places, sometimes with little thought to the urban centers in which many people spend their lives. As population grew and moved westward in America, a movement grew to preserve the wilderness (Steinberg, 2002). Within the movement to save the wilderness, two major forces contended. One advocated wise, conservative use of the wilderness and natural resources to serve human needs. This movement opened wild areas as national parks to allow people to enjoy the wilderness. It promoted the construction of great dams to supply water to the arid west, and it largely ignored warnings that the naturally arid west would become even more drought-stricken if artificial attempts at supplying water to it continued (Reisner, 1993). The second conservation movement, forerunner of the current ecological move-ment, advised closer study of particular regions and their living populations. This movement concentrated on natural environments in cities as well as wilderness and the interdependence of all their life forms. The history of the ecology movement is important, and we'll say more about it as this chapter progresses. It vividly captures the spirit of cooperation and connection so important in 21st-century education.

Schoolchildren are often taught to admire the wilderness/conservation movement, and certainly we should be grateful for the establishment of our great network of national parks. But we should also be aware of the short-sighted and bureaucratic nature of much that went on in the name of conservation. When fruit trees were threatened by insects, for example, the response was to use powerful insecticides to destroy the predators and preserve the trees. But what happened to other living creatures and the en-vironment that sustained them? The wilderness movement tacitly accepted a sharp separation between cities and wilderness. It gave little attention to the urban ecology. The move away from wilderness and other piecemeal approaches to the environment was given a big boost in 1962 by the pub-lication of Rachel Carson's *Silent Spring*. In the tradition of John Muir and John Wesley Powell, Carson argued for a move away from human-centered conservation to ecology:

> Although she used the word sparingly in her book, Carson helped to transform *ecology* into the rallying cry of the environmental movement. Unlike *wilder-ness*, conceived as a world apart, the word *ecology* suggested, in a sense, the reverse—that all life was bound up in an intricate, interconnected web. Human beings, she believed, were thus part of the balance of nature, not divorced from it in the way that some wilderness advocates implied. (Steinberg, 2002, p. 247)

This way of looking at the life-world has led to a renewal of interest in particular places and how they might be studied and preserved. Instead of looking at one type of insect, tree, or mammal, ecologists look at a holistic life domain to study patterns of interdependence. Sara Stein (1993) captures the ecological approach:

> But let's look at something smaller than the Colorado. Let's look at seeps, rivulets, sumps, hollows, bogs, ditches, frog ponds. Let's examine the face of the continent through a magnifying glass, noticing less the large protuberances and declivities than the fine texture of its skin, its pores and little wrinkles. Let's get down to the minutiae of puddles. Let's look at our own back yards and ask where butterflies can drink. (pp. 175–176)

Science teachers should read parts of Stein's book to their students. It would take a hard-hearted child not to be moved by the plight of frogs, toads, turtles, and butterflies whose habitats are so often destroyed by drainage, buildings, and lawns. Students might also enjoy planning an ecologically healthy garden along the lines suggested by Stein. The study of ecology is a continuing search for balance and harmony:

> Balance is what happens when nature is in harmony with itself. By harmony, I do not mean peace—there is no peace in nature. . . . What you perceive to be an immutable scene is a constant unseen struggle, progressing second by second, minute by minute, hour by hour, and not just between plants and soil, plants and light, plants and water, but between plants and insects, plants and deer, plants and rabbits. Add to this the untold millions of interactions between insect and insect, insect and bird, insect and bat, and you have created a palette of intricate interdependencies. . . . (Grissell, 2001, p. 211)

How do lawns fit into this "palette of intricate interdependencies?" Among projects students might find interesting is the study of lawns. Why are they so popular and extensive in the United States? There are about 30 million acres of lawn under cultivation in the United States (Steinberg, 2002). (Incidental math problem: How many square miles are we talking about?) Lawns require an enormous amount of water and fertilizer (Stein, 1993), and mowing them contributes substantially to air pollution. Steinberg (2002) estimates, "One hour spent mowing grass [by power mower] is the equivalent in terms of emissions produced to driving a car 350 miles" (p. 222). The end result is a beautiful green carpet:

> an ever more impenetrable mat until it is what its owner has worked so hard or paid so much to have: the perfect lawn, the perfect sealant through which nothing else can grow—and the perfect antithesis of an ecological system. (Stein, 1993, p. 138)

Michael Pollan (1991) tells an amusing story about one man's resistance to maintaining a lawn:

> [A] Thoreau scholar . . . has spent the last several years in court defending his right to grow a wildflower meadow in his front yard. After neighbors took it upon themselves to mow down the offending meadow, he erected a sign that said: "This yard is not an example of sloth. It is a natural yard, growing the way God intended." (p. 67)

When Pollan last heard, the Thoreau scholar's "act of suburban civil disobedience had cost him more than $25,000 in fines" (p. 68).

There is an opportunity here to encourage practical critical dialogue. What can be said in favor of well-tended, fresh green lawns? Surely, suburban streets edged by acre after acre of beautiful lawns are lovely. Lawn and garden companies urged Americans to accept lawn care as a patriotic duty: "Your lawn is the symbol of peace at home and its proper maintenance a vital factor in keeping up morale" (quoted in Steinberg, 2002, p. 222). But, if the upkeep of lawns costs too much in water and air pollution, if lawns really are the "antithesis of an ecological system," should we continue to maintain them?

It is important for students to consider both sides of the issue if—for no other reason—we wish to avoid confrontation at home. If students go home to denounce lawn-keeping and criticize their parents for ecological insensitivity, teachers can expect angry responses from those parents. When anything new—anything unfamiliar to parents or at odds with their customary behavior—appears in the curriculum, an attempt must be made to inform parents about the purpose and content of the new material. I remember vividly an incident that arose when I was teaching the "new math" to high school students. I had assigned homework that involved simple arithmetic problems in base 12. One father was incensed when he saw his bright son writing 6 x 3 = 16 and, forbidding him to complete the assignment, he wrote me an angry letter. I had to reassure him that 6 times 3 was still 18 and that 16 (base 12) was another way of writing 18 (base 10).

When we introduce new or controversial material in the classroom, we should spend time discussing how students might share the new ideas with parents and other classmates. Why might these others be shocked, even offended? What arguments do they offer against the ideas under consideration? Such explorations lie at the very foundation of critical thinking. If our intention is to turn out citizens capable of critical thinking, we must encourage students to listen and to present their arguments both logically and considerately. We should not want to send home wild-eyed revolutionaries but thoughtful, effective change agents.

Even though it is today more important than ever to focus attention on our local ecology, it has become difficult because many children are not allowed to roam freely outdoors. Since fewer children get to build tree houses or shacks out of branches and twigs, a form of alienation very like homelessness afflicts many of our children. E. O. Wilson (2002) notes that children seem to have an instinct for biophilia (love of nature and life forms) and that, with the opportunity to explore, this love develops steadily (see also Kahn, 1999; Nabhan & Trimble, 1994). If opportunities for this development do not occur at home, perhaps schools can offer them. Wendell Berry (1995) remarks:

> I believe that for many reasons—political, ecological, and economic—the best intelligence and talent should be at work and at home everywhere in the country. And therefore, my wishes for our schools are opposite to those of the present-day political parties and the present-day politics of education and culture. Wes Jackson has argued that our schools—to balance or replace their present single major in upward mobility—should offer a major in homecoming. I agree. (p. xi)

Science teachers might encourage students to undertake projects in their own backyards and neighborhoods. They might, for example, observe and record activity in a spider web, the variety of insects in one tree, the copycat-like appearance of weeds that pop up in flower beds, the behavior of ground wasps, the songs of mockingbirds. Such projects should require real, time-consuming observation. Recommending "learning in depth," Kieran Egan (2010) suggests having students undertake projects that will last through all the years of elementary and middle school. I do not agree with his advice to assign students particular topics, nor would I insist that students follow a topic for years, but I agree enthusiastically with Egan when he recommends that we find a way to help children learn in depth about the natural world:

> I just want to add the observation about our catastrophic ignorance of the natural world, and its cognitive consequences, as another reason to consider the educational value of LiD [learning in depth]. Especially if we choose our topics from the natural world, we can enable every student to build up both a quantity and a richly meaningful intensity of knowledge, which might go some way toward saving us from our current inability to think well about the natural world and our place within it. (pp. 17–18)

At least, encouraging such projects might reduce the nonsense that is often portrayed as "observation" in our science classes. Some years ago, I was asked to comment on a high school biology lesson that was supposed to teach students about observation. Here is the teacher's explanation of what she was doing:

> I planned what I thought was an exciting practical lesson which focused on ob-
> serving characteristics of eight different types of living things. Each specimen was
> located in a "station," and students, working in groups of four, rotated between
> the stations every five minutes. At each station, the students were required to note
> their observations on a record sheet. (Wallace & Louden, 2002, p. 100)

This is a parody of observation. It might be useful for small children to
look briefly at two or three different insects and note differences, but it is a
highly misleading exercise for high school students who should learn something about the time and care required for scientific observation. Further, if
our aim is to encourage thoughtful care for our local ecology, such faulty
methods are morally, as well as scientifically, questionable.

There is another facet of the observation story worth discussing. One of
the creatures to be observed was a cockroach, and a group of rowdy boys
killed it. This event distracted both the teacher and commentators from a
discussion of science to one of discipline and classroom management. In my
comments I acknowledged that it "was just a cockroach," a creature we
regularly try to exterminate. But there was a larger, potential lesson lost. I
noted that cockroaches have survived for centuries despite human efforts to
eliminate them:

> What did the students learn about these hardy creatures? . . . How long does
> an individual cockroach live? How many familiar types are there? How do they
> reproduce? Why are they so hard to eliminate? . . . Do they bite? Are they dirty?
> People do associate cockroaches with dirt and, in fact, cockroaches are said to
> create an objectionable odor. But this may occur as a result of their cleaning
> themselves and leaving behind a smelly residue. Could students think of a way
> to test this conjecture? (Noddings, in Wallace & Louden, 2002, p. 104)

I also wondered (and still do) whether the students learned anything at
all about the work of naturalists. Would the names Tinbergen, Wilson,
Andrews, Muir, Audubon, or Fabre mean anything to them?

There were lost opportunities here to discuss the work of naturalists,
the history and biology of cockroaches, insect communities, and even evolution. Surely, when creatures show a remarkable ability to survive and re-
produce, humans studying them might feel a surge of wonder. Carl Safina
(2011) describes the plight of horseshoe crabs threatened with extermina-
tion by people who collect and destroy them for bait. He describes one
beautiful moonlit night on which he had been watching the yearly mating
and egg laying of the crabs:

> Their rite is beyond reassuring: it's sacred. Nothing is more venerable than the
> act of creating new generations of living beings—or more vulnerable. And that

puts my heart on alert. Something in the pit of my stomach tells me that, after 450 million years, the only way to go from this feeling is down. (pp. 132–133)

Sure enough, on that moonlit night, the collectors arrived and began flinging the living crabs into a truck bed like so much garbage. Should not 450 million years of survival trigger astonishment and, as Safina suggests, a sense of the sacred? This is part of what Egan is getting at when he recommends forms of learning in depth that may reconnect us to the natural world.

Readers will recognize, of course, that recommendations of the sort made here require substantial changes in our school curriculum. Contact with animals and plants should not be limited to the elementary school years. An entire secondary school science curriculum can be organized around the study of our home-places and ecology. Further, every subject in the curriculum should be asked to contribute to this universal curriculum. Such a curriculum should be acceptable for college admission and would provide a rich alternative for college-bound students who do not need the traditional courses in science. A strong curriculum in natural history also offers opportunities for community service, involvement in the preservation of rivers and ponds, wildlife, and plants. And the courses can be offered at various levels of technicality and with a variety of topical foci.

Notice that these suggestions do not require the addition of courses outside the established curriculum. They require changes within the disciplines. In the previous chapter, I recommended that a year of high school science be devoted to nutrition and matters of health. Here, I have suggested another year of science concentrating on local ecology. Both concentrations would connect science to real life.

EARTH: MORE THAN A COLLECTION OF NATIONS

I have already suggested that we need a broad new curriculum in natural history, and I want to carry that further as we consider a de-emphasis on national history and a greater emphasis on the lives of human beings in natural environments. Again, I do not intend to present an actual curriculum. That is beyond my expertise, a collaborative project for representatives from all of the disciplines. Rather, I suggest a way of thinking about ecology and the curriculum. Further, there is no intention here to eliminate political and military history; that would be counterproductive. Instead, I suggest that the traditional material be somewhat reduced and that the remaining material be convincingly connected to the new material on ecology. An effective 21st-century curriculum emphasizes connections, connections among the subjects taught and connections between school subjects and real life.

We might build on our earlier discussion of lawns and their problematic ecological effects. The amount of water they require is itself problematic, but the runoff loaded with chemical contaminants from fertilizers is another problem. Where lawns thrive, lakes and streams are likely to be polluted. Whereas industrial sources of water pollution have been somewhat reduced, the problem of contaminated runoff from residential development is still unsolved (Anderson, 1999).

Students might become interested in both the problems and the history of attempts to solve them. Ted Steinberg (2002) tells the story of how reformers insisted on the removal of pigs from our cities in the mid-1800s. Clearly, the presence of pigs on city streets was unsanitary. One can imagine how disgusting it was to walk on a street littered with pig excrement, piles of discarded vegetables on which the pigs fed, and the pigs themselves. It was the practice then for workers to come in at night and collect both the pig offal and human waste from homes ("night soil") and deliver it to the nearby countryside to enrich the soil for agriculture. Although this practice was unsanitary, it was—in a basic way—ecologically sound. Discarded vegetables fed the pigs, the pigs were an important food source for the urban poor, and their waste was returned to the earth to enrich it for the production of vegetables and fruits.

The system had to change, and human health improved when pigs were removed from cities. But concentrated deposits of animal and human waste brought about by intensive animal farming and sewers led to an increased contamination of waterways. Steinberg refers to the banishment of food animals from cities as the "death of the organic city," a dramatic change that has since characterized the difference between city and rural life in America. It is worth noting that ecological thinking is now working to restore natural connections between urban and rural areas and trying also to restore both organic and social life in our cities (Ford, 2000; Walker, 2007).

Human life generates piles of refuse—not only the "night soil" now carried away by flush toilets and sewers, but all the material we call "garbage," "rubbish," "trash," or "junk." Paper products alone accounted for 35 million tons of trash in 1967 (Steinberg, 2002, p. 226), and the use of paper has not been reduced by the widespread use of computers. We are deluged with electronic messages, and the temptation is to print them out. Recycling can handle only part of this growing mountain.

For some time, small cities and towns tossed their refuse indiscriminately into "dumps." Because something had to be done to reduce the mass and odor, cities began to use incinerators, but incinerators damaged air quality, and the odor they emitted was not a great improvement over the open dump. Moreover, some things do not burn easily, if at all. After World War II, cities began to depend on landfills to dump their garbage. The idea was to pile refuse into low-lying wetlands and cover the fresh load with soil daily, thus reducing the smell of rotting organic matter and, eventually, providing a dry foundation for new building. But urban landfills began to literally fill up about 30 years ago, and so garbage had to be transported over many miles. The trend, of course, has been to truck it from fairly wealthy areas to poorer ones. There are stories—tragically funny—of truckloads of refuse leaving the city only to be turned away at their proposed destination, returning, and passing other trucks hurrying along on the same frustrating mission.

Another problem with the use of landfills illustrates the lack of ecological thinking employed in trying to solve the garbage problem. Not only were some of these sites permanently contaminated, making building on them hazardous, but it turns out that the loss of wetlands is itself a problem. The wetlands (or swamps) that were used for landfills actually serve an important ecological function, filtering and purifying the water that runs through them. They also provide homes for birds and other wildlife. "There was little understanding in the 1940s of what we now call an ecosystem," Diane Ward writes. The damage done by ignorance was enormous. Ward (2002) tells the story of the Florida Everglades in some detail, and it is both a sad and hopeful one. Development in the form of agriculture and housing caused the loss of bird and marine life, increased saltiness in bay waters and inlets, and a decrease in rain. How might dredging and draining affect rainfall? We now know much more about the harm caused by trying to solve problems one by one without regard to the whole community of life. All students should learn something about the near-catastrophe in the Everglades, and then they should begin to explore their own local environment for ecological problems. (For a deeply moving account of the near-destruction of the Everglades, see Douglas, 1997.)

One of the great contributors to environmental pollution continues to be careless consumption. The history of consumption from the perspective of consumers' habits and consumer protection is a fascinating tale (Cohen, 2003). For educators, it is especially interesting to know that John Dewey was involved in the creation of the League for Independent Political Action (LIPA), an organization founded to advance the interests of consumers who were at that time (1929) badly exploited by producers and the business community. Politically, the LIPA was a disaster. The common concern for the welfare of consumers was not strong enough to overcome political differences within the group (Westbrook, 1991). Our main concern here, however, is not the protection of consumers but rather the protection of the environment from overconsumption.

Dramatic improvements in transportation by the early 1990s made it possible to ship foods over long distances. We have already noted the "death of the organic city," part of the growing separation in space of production and consumption. Because foods once inaccessible to most of the

population were now available, demand grew. But the increasing separation of production and consumption promoted the need for personal/family
transportation, and the market for cars and small trucks also grew. People
had to travel to and from work. Steinberg (2002) points out that suburban-
ization and increased consumption have taken a toll on the environment.

Earlier, we noted that increased consumption has led to an incredible
increase in waste. So much to buy! Steinberg (2002) notes:

> Montgomery Ward and Company established the first mail order company in
> the 1870s. In 1874, it put out a 72-page catalogue. In the 1880s, the catalogue
> grew to over 500 pages and, by the turn of the century, had ballooned to 1,200
> pages. (p. 228)

And such catalogs had to be revised and reissued every year. As we know,
the United States today is the world's largest consumer of energy and the
largest producer of refuse.

A rapidly growing business in advertising supported the growth in consumption. In an earlier discussion, I mentioned the highly successful advertising campaign that promoted the cultivation of lawns as a moral duty.
There are other stories of impressive success in advertising, slogans such as
"breakfast of champions," "melt in your mouth, not in your hands," and
the currently popular, "You deserve it!" Probably the most successful gam-
bit in advertising has been the segmenting of groups to be targeted: by age,
gender, race, economic class, and entertainment preferences. Segmenting
then spread into political advertising, where it plays an increasingly heavy
role.

Not only have the schools failed to inform students about the ways
in which they are manipulated by advertisers, but they have even allowed
commercial companies to provide televisions, ostensibly for educational
purposes, complete with the usual ads for which students serve as a captive
audience (Molnar, 1996). Instead, schools should promote critical thinking
on the topic of advertising (Noddings, 2006).

Educators, parents, and policymakers must look carefully at educational aims for our 21st-century democracy. One of the worst betrayals
of those aims appears in the single-minded obsession with future incomes.
Everywhere students are urged to prepare for college so that they will *earn
higher incomes.* Policymakers and educators use as an excuse for forcing
everyone into an outdated college preparatory curriculum that such preparation is necessary in the name of equality, for upward mobility. At the same
time, the dream of upward mobility is becoming more and more just that—a
dream. Education, instead of guiding thoughtful consumers in both education and the wider world, has joined big business. Too often, we are engaged
in false advertising, promoting the pursuit of useless degrees, and distracting

the young from thinking critically and reflecting about what they would like to do in life and what kind of persons they will become. In the next chapter, we'll consider an approach to vocational education that is more honest and perhaps more fruitful as well.

If happiness is embraced as an aim of education—and it should be—students should have opportunities to engage in dialogue on the topic. They should learn that research has shown convincingly that, beyond what is necessary for a reasonable level of economic security, there is little correlation between increased wealth and happiness (Lane, 2000). What does make people happy? It is not our task as educators to *tell* students what will make them happy, nor is it our job to *make* them happy. Rather, it is our job to introduce them to how people have thought about happiness—how they have pursued it, failed at it, or achieved it—and to open doors for them to explore their own paths to happiness (Noddings, 2003).

Intelligent dialogue on happiness should contribute to the personal development aims of education. It is also essential for the development of commitment to the preservation of our loved places and Earth itself. Students should at least consider the advice offered by Carl Safina (2011):

> The revolution is as simple as this: Don't buy the products by which they drain you and feed themselves. . . . Do the unadvertised and the unauthorized. . . . Plant seeds. . . . Go to formal dinners in great-looking thrift-store clothing and brag about how much you paid. React badly to every ad and every exhortation about what you need, as though they are lying. . . . (p. 310).

Now, notice that I said that students should *consider* the advice offered by Safina. Who is the "you" to whom Safina speaks? Who are the "they" who exploit the "you"? Are there words of caution to be added to Safina's advice? What would happen if we all stopped buying "stuff" we really do not need? The dialogue should be extended. How should we live in order to preserve Earth? What should we do locally? And what do we need to learn?

GEOGRAPHY WITH A PURPOSE

We talked earlier about water pollution as an essential topic in ecological studies. A unit of study concentrating on water pollution is obviously interdisciplinary. What substances pollute our waterways? Both chemistry and biology are involved. Can these substances be removed? How do we approach the problems politically? What are the economic implications? How bad are the problems? Noting that Earth's increasing population has led to a tripling of water use since the middle of the 20th century, Diane Raines Ward (2002) comments:

We now face the need to feed unheard-of numbers of people on the earth while at the same time accommodating the toll exacted by growing so much food—increases in fertilizers, pesticides, salination, deforestation, erosion, and over-grazing. More than half the world's major rivers are either polluted or going dry. (p. 3)

We face two large, related ecological problems, each of which contains within it many interrelated subproblems. The first is population growth and the second is the increasingly rapid loss of species. We'll look at the population problem in the last section of this chapter, where we'll see that it is not simply a matter of too many people. Paradoxically, the greater problem seems to be that smaller, more wealthy populations consume far too much of the Earth's resources. For example, in "1988, the United States used more energy per capita than any other nation in the world . . . with just five percent of the earth's population, consumed 25 percent of all the world's oil and released roughly a quarter of all the world's atmospheric carbon" (Steinberg, 2002, p. 234). The United States, so fond of being number one, also "leads the industrialized world in waste generation, producing twice the amount of trash per capita as such countries as France, Britain, and Japan" (Steinberg, 2002, p. 234).

In this section, however, I would like to consider school studies in connection with environmental destruction and species loss. We have an opportunity to teach geography that matters. Instead of asking students to memorize the names of rivers, mountains, and deserts—as suggested by E. D. Hirsch—we might start with ecological problems and/or promising solutions.

E. O. Wilson (2002) tells the story of forest conservation in Suriname. Suriname, situated next to Guyana in South America, with its southern border on the mountains with Brazil, has "the highest percent rainforest cover of any country on Earth" (p. 175). In the mid-1990s, the country was threatened with an enormous logging operation but, by working closely with several conservation groups, environmentalists created the Suriname Conservation Foundation, which was successful in securing "the establishment of large natural corridors that connect existing parks and reserves" (Wilson, 2002, p. 178). These natural corridors provide protection for the reserves that otherwise often are overwhelmed at the edges by tourists and other commercial endeavors. Wilson suggests that such corridors should be created in North America from the Yukon to Yellowstone National Park, from upland New Mexico and Arizona to northern Mexico, and from western Pennsylvania to eastern Kentucky. Here is a nice geography lesson for 5th- or 6th-graders.

Wilson (2002) also draws attention to parts of the world called "hotspots"—the Earth's land areas where species extinction is most active. Twenty-five hotspots "take up only 1.4 percent of the world's land surface. Yet, astonishingly, they are the exclusive homes of 44 percent of the world's plant species and more than a third of all species of birds, mammals, reptiles, and amphibians" (p. 61). Can students locate some of these hotspots: tropical Andes, Greater Antilles, Madagascar, Indo-Burma, New Caledonia?

As teachers teach from the "top down," starting with ecological problems, they might move from the hotspots on land to problem spots in our oceans. Why is the Mesoamerican reef having problems? How does a coral reef form? How does a baby coral grow? And where is the Mesoamerican reef? Why is seaweed bad for corals?

Obviously, there is a lot of biology to be learned—or at least to be astonished by—in reading about coral reefs. But in addition to the biology, there is geography. In contrast to the deterioration of the Caribbean reefs, those in the Pacific near the islands of Palau seem to be recovering (Safina, 2011). (Note: Although the reefs seem to be recovering, many of the islands will likely disappear under a rising sea—another reason to study global warming.) Where is Palau? Students should be encouraged to spend time with maps, to play with them. Is this better done on a computer or with paper maps that can be laid out on a table? My own preference is for an array of paper maps spread out so that students can move from one of a larger area to maps of smaller regions—all visible at once. Locate specific places, talk about longitude and latitude, measure distances, learn to pronounce the names of places, don't rush. Map reading can be inspired by accounts of environmental problems, but fun with maps can, in turn, excite interest in historical and political issues. Stephen Thornton (2005) offers many examples of problems and projects that students might undertake as they become interested in maps. An interesting historical problem for students to investigate is the problem of determining longitude. Early navigators could determine latitude from the sun, moon, and stars. Why was it so difficult to determine longitude, and what invention made it possible to do so? Pause for stories and biographical accounts. Safina (2011), for example, comments on a visit to Koror (in Palau):

> The first time I came here, there were was not a single traffic light in the country. Then they tried them, but nobody paid attention when the light turned red. "It's like a machine telling people what to do," complained one person who gave me a lift. The lights came down. Now, again, the country has not one stoplight. (p. 288)

Stories such as this—irrelevant to the narrowly prescribed curriculum—help to maintain interest in the topic and arouse curiosity about the people and place under discussion.

This brief discussion of teaching geography from an ecological perspective illustrates several points central to this book. One is the need to stress interdependence. In the 21st century, we must find a way to move beyond narrow national interests and consider the future of Earth itself. That is a task for all nations to address cooperatively. Another is the vital need to connect school subjects with each other and with real life. The latter connection should encourage us to start our units of study with real problems. Sometimes, of course, even this "start" must be preceded with dialogue that uncovers the problem; problem-posing may require problem-seeking. Another point that has emerged here is that we should capitalize on incidental learning. I am not suggesting that everything can be learned incidentally; as I've said repeatedly, we have a host of methods—including direct instruction—in our pedagogical repertoire, but we use some of them too rarely, and we still seem determined to find one best way that will work for everyone on every topic. It can be rewarding to let students of any age play with the tools and objects related to a unit of study. To play with maps, to measure distances, to imagine journeys can contribute substantially to learning, and wise teachers can build on the interests that arise in such informal settings, making links to literature, mathematics, economics, and politics.

Although it is clearly necessary to put the well-being of Earth above national interests, we must find a way in our schools to treat the topics so familiar to American adults without arousing antagonism. How, then, should we approach topics such as patriotism, military heroes, pacifism, and American exceptionalism?

TOWARD PEACE ON EARTH

It is feasible to introduce and emphasize ecological problems in our schools, but the traditional curriculum is not going to disappear overnight. The social studies curriculum has—with periodic attempts at something more meaningful—long been organized around wars and economic development. With a new concentration on the well-being of Earth and its inhabitants, we might emphasize the power of nations to make treaties that will advance that project. E. O. Wilson, for example, discusses the possibility of converting the demilitarized zone (DMZ) in Korea to a wildlife sanctuary. Sponsored by the DMZ Forum, such thinking is still active, and the hope is that it will acquire enough support to accomplish its goal.

It is more difficult to help students understand the forces that manipulate their thinking on patriotism and national pride. In recent work, I have suggested a move toward *ecological cosmopolitanism* that might soften the belligerency often associated with national patriotism:

> If we love a particular place, we know that its welfare is intimately connected to the health of the Earth on which it exists. . . . Because I love *this* place, I want a healthy Earth to sustain it. . . . If the well-being of my loved place depends on

the well-being of Earth, I have a good reason for supporting the well-being of *your* loved place. I have selfish as well as cosmopolitan reasons for preserving the home-places of all human beings. (Noddings, 2012a, p. 66)

Cosmopolitanism—a perspective that regards the whole world as a focus for citizenship—has never been enthusiastically embraced in American schools or, for that matter, in the country at large. (But see the useful discussion in Hansen, 2010, 2011.) We might start by informing students that Thomas Paine declared himself a citizen of the world and was roundly castigated for it. Students will have heard of Paine and *Common Sense*, his work widely admired in promoting the American Revolution, but they may have heard little or nothing about *The Age of Reason* in which he wrote of world citizenship, "My country is the world; to do good is my religion." Indeed, his support of cosmopolitanism earned him the later condemnation of Theodore Roosevelt, who referred to him as a "filthy little atheist" (True, 1995, p. 14).

Drawing on ecological cosmopolitanism, it may be somewhat easier to discuss world citizenship without arousing the anger of those who cling to a traditional idea of national patriotism. *Ecological* patriotism also adds some urgency to the expression. A difficulty with cosmopolitanism, one pointed out by several writers, is the "thinness" of the concept (see, for example, Barber, 1996). It simply does not "grab" us emotionally as does national patriotism with its multiple supports in rousing music, flags, parades, uniforms, heroic stories, and celebrations. The possibility of destroying Earth through neglect and selfish exploitation might well have some emotional impact.

Without scorning or ignoring the usual displays of patriotism, schools should help students understand how the various ceremonies and celebrations affect them emotionally. To understand how we are influenced by the customs and expectations of our culture is a large factor in self-understanding.

If we are serious about critical thinking as a major aim of 21st-century thinking, we have to be willing to admit our nation's failings as well it as its accomplishments. It would be unwise (and almost certainly forbidden) to launch into unit after unit documenting such failures. Our aim is to produce critical thinkers, not cynics. That means raising a finger of caution now and then, reminding students that not everyone agrees. Our memories as well as our evaluations may differ, and living memories are a significant part of history (Wood, 2011b). It is important to make these differences part of the curriculum. For example: Was it right to use an atomic bomb on Hiroshima? How has the decision been defended? How many people is it acceptable to kill in a military bombing? At what point can such acts be prevented?

It is possible to plan reading and discussions that will advance the aims of peace education, but it is demanding work. I have already rejected the method of "righteous indoctrination" suggested by George Counts, because that method can be used—and has been used—for anti-democratic purposes. Further, the task should not fall only on social studies teachers. English courses can, for example, include poetry that glorifies war and poetry that condemns it. But it is not enough simply to include the World War I poetry of, say, Wilfred Owen. Teachers must be willing (and competent) to go beyond the techniques of poetry to the social issues addressed. Students should hear how W. B. Yeats castigated Owen and his poetry, calling it "all blood and dirt" (see Goldensohn, 2003, p. 74). The curriculum should also include literature from the countries that were once our enemies. It should induce a shiver of horror in students to hear of the hatred that once characterized our relations with people we now regard as friends.

As science teachers lead the way in ecological studies, they too can move laterally into discussions of war and its destructiveness. Reading about the bombing of London, Hamburg, Dresden, and Tokyo in World War II, students should be prodded to consider the quirks of human psychology. How is it that we humans can be horrified and thrilled by the same awful events? Why are we attracted to war as a spectacle (Noddings, 2012a)?

Through the combined efforts of teachers across the disciplines, students should become aware of a hazard rarely discussed in our schools—the possible loss of moral identity in those who participate in combat. Most high school students cannot imagine themselves committing horrible acts on other human beings. But it happens, and many veterans suffer over these events for a lifetime, asking, Why did I do that? Why did I do that? again and again (Shay, 1994). As teachers, we bear some responsibility for failing to prepare our young people for such possibilities. A major element in critical thinking is self-understanding.

In this chapter, we have considered how love of our particular places should lead to concern for the well-being of Earth, our universal home. That consideration can be encouraged by a study of local ecology and ecological problems. We looked at just a few such problems as examples: water pollution, garbage removal, and overconsumption. Moving beyond the local environment, we explored the possibility that schools might develop a spirit of ecological cosmopolitanism, and then we very briefly discussed how this spirit might be used in educating for world peace.

Throughout this chapter, we have been primarily concerned with the large domain of civic responsibility, but the material also contributes strongly to the self-understanding that underlies critical thinking. In the next chapter, the emphasis will be on educating for well-being in occupational life.

8

Vocational Education

Vocational education in the United States today is in a state of neglect. This neglect is due in part to the well-intentioned but faulty view of equality discussed earlier and in part to an unwillingness to spend the considerable amount of money required to build a really fine vocational program. A third factor working against vocational education at the secondary level is the constantly repeated claim that the country needs more engineers, scientists, and mathematicians. This claim can be challenged. The "engineers" in short supply are not all graduate engineers—people with BAs or graduate degrees. Rather, they are often people who can be well prepared with a year or 2 of sound post-secondary education. A good start on this preparation can be made at the secondary level.

In this chapter, we'll look briefly at the history of vocational education in the United States, at current problems, and then at possibilities for the future. Finally, we'll consider how the middle school years might be used for a wide and rich exploration of occupational possibilities.

VOCATIONAL EDUCATION: THE PAST

On vocational education, John Dewey left us a legacy of both wisdom and confusion. The confusion arises from his ambiguous use of language, particularly with the word _occupation_. "An occupation," Dewey (1916) writes, "is a continuous activity having a purpose" (p. 309). But on the next page, he says, "The only adequate training _for_ occupations is training _through_ occupations" (p. 310). Here, his first use of _occupation_ seems to be the one familiar to all of us—a useful mode of earning a living—and preparation for this activity must itself be conducted through continuous activities (the second sense of _occupation_) that have purpose. We encountered a similar problem earlier in his discussion of aims, where he counsels that the aim of education does not lie beyond itself, that it is simply continued capacity for growth. That claim leads to questions about the meaning of _growth_. Although it can be rewarding to spend time unraveling Dewey's language, I will use _occupation_ in the common sense—a mode of making a living—and move onto the wisdom in Dewey's account.

Speaking of an occupation, Dewey (1916) writes:

> To find out what one is fitted to do and to secure an opportunity to do it is the
> key to happiness. Nothing is more tragic than failure to discover one's true busi-
> ness in life, or to find that one has drifted or been forced by circumstances into
> an uncongenial calling. (p. 308)

Dewey deplores work that requires only machine-like responses from a
worker, and he argues strongly against forms of vocational education tai-
lored to the regime that exploits this sort of work. Work, he insists, should
be meaningful:

> Sentimentally, it may seem harsh to say that the greatest evil of the present
> regime is not found in poverty and in the suffering which it entails, but in the
> fact that so many persons have callings which make no appeal to them. (p. 317)

But there will always be unattractive work that needs doing, and that
fact in itself is a good reason to include aims other than occupational in the
school curriculum. To work at a job one dislikes or is indifferent to is, to
be sure, unfortunate, but there is more to life than one's occupation, and
schools should take the aims directed at personal and civic life seriously.
Still, Dewey was right that the schools should not be complicit in *preparing*
students for jobs that require no thought, jobs that require no continuity
of purpose—the only purpose being the product designed by others. The
schools should direct their efforts toward producing people who can act
purposefully and morally in every domain of life. When people are forced
to work at meaningless jobs, they need even more to find meaning in their
personal and civic lives.

We must be careful here. When we accept the fact that there will always
be unpleasant work that must be done, we need not glorify that work by
talking thoughtlessly of the "dignity" of all work. Herbert Kliebard (1999),
reflecting on the misery his father experienced doing "piece-work," writes:

> Undoubtedly, satisfaction may be derived from the work of the hands, but I
> sometimes think that the conviction that all work has dignity regardless of the
> circumstances has served to inhibit attempts to improve conditions in the work-
> place and to stave off efforts somehow to humanize it. When all work, even
> under the most degrading conditions, is declared to be ennobling, the need to
> reform the workplace somehow seems much less urgent. (p. xv)

This is an important warning. All students—especially teachers in training—should read some of the best-known utopian writers who have tackled
the problem of what to do about degrading work, for example, Edward

Bellamy's *Looking Backward* and B. F. Skinner's *Walden Two*. Is there a way to share society's hardest, dirtiest, most boring work?

Dewey (1916) hoped that schools could restore a sense of the intellectual possibilities in manual work. The following paragraph, written 100 years ago, might have been written yesterday:

> Industry has ceased to be essentially an empirical, rule-of-thumb procedure, handed down by custom. Its technique is now technological: that is to say, based upon machinery resulting from discoveries in mathematics, physics, chemistry, bacteriology, etc. . . . As a consequence, industrial occupations have infinitely larger cultural possibilities than they used to possess. The demand for such education as will acquaint workers with the scientific and social bases and bearings of their pursuits becomes imperative . . . (p. 314)

Dewey recognized the paradoxical nature of the new industrialism. On the one hand, the intellectual requirements underlying the new industries were enormous; on the other hand, technological advances made it unnecessary for many workers to understand the underlying science and, thus, increased their subservience to machines. (We might think here of Charlie Chaplin in *Modern Times*.) We are caught in something of the same difficulty today. Some argue that, to give more young people chances at well-paying jobs, we must increase educational participation in science, technology, engineering, and mathematics (STEM courses). But as technology grows, more can be produced by fewer people. I'll return to this very difficult problem in the next section.

Here, we can agree with Dewey that an adequate vocational education should not consist of mere preparation for a routine job. In addition to the loss in intellectual possibilities for individuals, such a program would perpetuate a class system supported by both business and education. Dewey rightly objected to talk of "probable destinies" and the "sorting" function of schools. But as the 20th century progressed, the schools did indeed engage in such sorting. We might argue that, instead of cooperating in the sorting process, schools should be active in informing students about the continued social pressure to accomplish such sorting. Inevitably, some students will find themselves in jobs that many of us would reject. The democratic hope is, first, that the society will insist that such workers receive a livable wage (so there is some dignity in the pay, if not in the work) and, second, that people who cannot obtain satisfaction in their occupation will be able to find satisfaction in one of the other great domains of life.

It is hard to evaluate the performance of vocational education in the first half of the 20th century. Studies seemed to show little economic advantage for graduates of vocational programs over those who did not participate in such programs. However, high school attendance and graduation over that period grew dramatically—from less than 9% in 1910 to almost 60% in 1950. Students apparently found that schools were offering something of practical value. There is contention even on this claim. More students may have remained in school because there were so few jobs for many years, but the increase continued during years of high employment. Another factor adding to confusion over the value of vocational education is the difficulty of clearly separating the various programs available in comprehensive high schools. A typical list would include college preparatory, commercial, general, and vocational. But the "commercial" program was clearly vocational; most of its students were girls, and it was almost certainly the most successful vocational program offered.

The reputation of vocational education was also damaged by the proliferation of poor courses in the "general" track, which were sometimes mislabeled as "vocational." These courses, often poorly designed and poorly taught, have rightly been attacked by critics who object to tracking (Oakes, 1985, 1990). However, I have argued—and will argue further here—that the solution to this long-standing discrimination and neglect is *not* to force a college preparatory curriculum on everyone. Indeed, that solution to program tracking increases the problems inherent in another form of tracking—organizing courses such as algebra into sections designated "remedial," "advanced," "honors," and so on. Predictably, and shamefully, some pseudo-courses called "algebra" are every bit as bad as the dead-end courses criticized by reformers. I'll suggest a direction toward one possible solution using democratic choice in a later section of this chapter.

Let's summarize what has been touched upon so far. (Readers interested in the history of vocational education in the United States might consult, in addition to references already mentioned, W. Norton Grubb and Marvin Lazerson, eds., *American Education and Vocationalism: Documents in Vocational Education*, 1974; and Harvey Kantor and David Tyack, eds., *Work, Youth, and Schooling: Historical Perspectives on Vocationalism in American Education*, 1982.) Dewey (1916) argued strongly that everything taught in our schools should evoke a sense of purpose in students, that subject matters should be connected to each other and to the present life of students. But his ambiguous use of the term *occupation* caused confusion, and his rejection of education as *preparation* should be questioned. If we read Dewey carefully, we see that he did not entirely reject the notion of education as preparation. Rather, he urges caution on the issue:

> Now "preparation" is a treacherous idea. In a certain sense every experience should do something to prepare a person for later experiences of a deeper and more expansive quality. That is the very meaning of growth, continuity, reconstruction of experience. (1938/1963, p. 47)

What he rejects as counterproductive is the controlling use of preparation where the value of everything taught is put onto some future—"suppositious" or fictitious—date. But, even here—largely agreeing with Dewey—we should acknowledge that teachers must sometimes introduce skills and information whose usefulness will not be immediately apparent. Good teachers learn to do this in a way that increases their students' anticipation.

In what follows, I will use *occupation* in the familiar sense of work by which one earns a living, and I will argue that education should be thought of as *both* a mode of continuous growth *and* preparation for success and satisfaction in all three great domains of human life: personal, civic, and occupational.

In addition to hearty agreement with Dewey on the basic measure of quality in the courses we offer, I share his aversion to using schools to sort students arbitrarily according to their probable destinies. I will insist that students should make the choice of program. But, inevitably, they will be sorted by their own interests and abilities and by the value our society puts on those factors. Dewey and his colleagues in Progressive Education believed that the schools could, and should, effect significant changes in a society. I believe, with the critical theorists, that the society, far more powerful, exerts more influence on the schools. Still, tapping into the best instincts of our society, schools can make at least a small difference in changing society for the better.

VOCATIONAL EDUCATION: THE PRESENT

When we look at vocational education today, we immediately encounter another area of significant confusion. There are still comprehensive high schools that include vocational programs in their offerings, and there are some separate vocational schools to which students can apply, but these programs are not always well organized around the industrial/commercial needs of their communities, and they are not generally held in high esteem. Teachers and counselors, rightly rejecting the old "sorting" function of schools, rarely guide students into these programs.

The most popular, highly admired "vocational" schools are actually high-powered academies organized around categories of professional interest. These "vocational" schools follow Dewey implicitly by offering education *through* occupations rather than education *for* occupations. Their programs are organized around such themes as marine sciences, medical sciences, aerospace sciences, and so forth. They are elite schools aimed at the best college preparation; they accept students on the basis of test scores, and they are highly competitive. In most counties or regions, these schools regularly post the highest test scores in their states. But these are *not* vocational schools in the sense that interests us here.

Schools that provide programs in cosmetology, construction trades, automotive service, culinary arts, and other vocational programs are still available, but admission can be difficult. Students cannot choose a vocational program as easily as they can a standard academic program. As mentioned in Chapter 3, the United States does not have the sort of vocational programs offered in Europe. Such programs require close coordination among educators, employers, unions, and government agencies. One payoff in countries with strong VET programs is a low unemployment rate; a second is that skilled manual work is more highly valued.

Although there are few signs that European-style vocational education will become popular in the United States, there are some signs of renewed respect for manual work. Mike Rose (2005) does not call directly for an increase in attention to vocational education, but he makes an eloquent plea for renewed respect for the full range of talents and work interests. Indeed, he writes, this respect is at the foundation of democracy and required for its maintenance:

> To affirm our capacity as a people is not to deny the obvious variability among us. . . . To acknowledge our collective capacity is to take the concept of variability seriously. . . . To affirm this conception of mind and work is to be vigilant for the intelligence not only in the boardroom but on the shop floor; in the laboratory and alongside the frame house; in the classroom, the garage, the busy restaurant. . . . This is a model of mind that befits the democratic imagination. (p. 216)

Matthew Crawford (2009) also makes a case for increased attention to manual arts. Noting that more than half of the shop classes in California have disappeared since 1980, he also notes that attempts to reinstate these courses are handicapped by the shortage of people who might teach them. Probably government action—something like the re-education of math teachers sponsored by the National Science Foundation in the 1960s—will be required. Both Kliebard (1999) and Crawford discuss the Smith-Hughes Act (1917) that endorsed greater support for vocational education but also aggravated status differences between academic and vocational education. Instead of inaugurating an era in which the "mind at work" celebrated by Dewey, Rose, and Crawford would receive higher recognition, it promoted a system in which academic education is revered and those "too dumb" for academics would be shunted into vocational programs.

The Smith-Hughes Act did recognize the value of shop classes in general education (a sort of "gentleman's manual training"), and in those classes some attention was given to critical thinking and learning through doing. Dewey's idea of "education through occupations" (see also W. Norton Grubb, 1995) was honored in academic programs but largely ignored in the vocational courses where it was most needed.

The promise remains: Vocational education could enrich general education for students concentrating on either college or job preparation. Kliebard (1999), however, raises an important warning:

> If vocational education is to build on its symbolic success and help redress the injustices inflicted on a neglected segment of the school population as well as revivifying education for all, it will not be by concentrating obsessively on rewards to be reaped at some indeterminate point in the future, or by isolating itself from the rest of education, and certainly not by converting the entire educational system to the narrow end of economic gain, as important as that may be. (p. 235)

As I argue throughout this book, education is not a single-aim enterprise. Vocational education can and must contribute to future satisfaction in personal, occupational, and civic life.

An important set of questions nags at us as we try to decide how to guide students in their choices for secondary and post-secondary education. We are bombarded by articles and speeches that urge us to increase our efforts at STEM (science, technology, engineering, and mathematics) education. It is said that we need more college graduates in these areas. But if we look at predictions supplied by the U.S. Bureau of Labor Statistics, we see that many of the occupations likely to hire the most people in the next decade do not require a college education. Why, then, are we insisting that everyone should go to college? If we—sadly but courageously—apply critical theory, we may fear that a well-intentioned movement to increase upward mobility is once again serving the purposes of the already well educated. Many young people will go to college but fail to attain a degree. Others will finish with an accumulated debt that will hold them back for years. More than a few will not find work that requires the college degree they obtained at such a high cost. For example, those of us safely employed in academia know many talented young people with higher degrees who may never gain full employment in the areas for which they are prepared. Who benefits from this movement? The salaries of tenured professors at prestigious institutions have increased greatly, and there has been an enormous increase in administrative managers and assistants. Although it does seem to be true that college graduates are less likely than high school graduates to be unemployed, this may be simply because they are now often employed in work that does not require a college degree.

There is another source of confusion for those who would guide the young wisely. When the need for more "engineers" is relentlessly pushed, advocates often point to the increasing number of engineers produced in Asia. But this, too, can be misleading. China, for example, is suffering from an overload of college graduates, and "engineer" in Asian countries does not always imply a graduate with a 4-year degree. It often refers to someone who has a year or 2 beyond secondary school specializing in the technology required for a special industry. The same is true in the United States, although we seldom admit it. Adam Davidson (2012) has described the dilemma of a tech-factory worker, Maddie, who effectively uses the machines with which she works. Maddie cannot, however, move up to the next level because she does not understand, among other things, the computer language needed to direct the machines. Probably a 1- or 2-year course at a good community college would qualify her as an "engineer" for the work done at her factory. But now we run into another dilemma. We do need some engineers of this sort, but the technology is so advanced that we actually need fewer such people than were once needed. A very few people, adequately trained, can supervise machines that make many other human workers superfluous.

VOCATIONAL EDUCATION: THE FUTURE

Thinking about vocational education in the near future, we can agree with Dewey that everything the schools offer should have educational purpose and meaning; it should not be mere job training. However, we should be willing to put somewhat greater emphasis than Dewey did on *preparation*. Much of what we do in teaching is necessarily preparation for something in the future. Sometimes the preparation is aimed at the acquisition of skills needed to work on an important problem or concept; sometimes it is aimed at an occupation—a way of making a living. As I argued earlier, this kind of preparation should be preceded by an introductory exploration of the big picture—job, project, or concept. On this, I agree with E. O. Wilson that we should teach from the top down and with Dewey that our efforts at preparation should not be aimed at usefulness delayed to some "supposititious" future.

In vocational education, a practical vision of excellence—sometimes aesthetic excellence—should be integral to the educational effort. There is something beautiful about a smoothly running machine, a well-built cabinet, a well-prepared meal, a hairdo perfectly suited to its wearer.

We can agree with Dewey again in objecting to using the school as a sorting instrument. Schools should not decide arbitrarily on the basis of their students' "probable destinies" what programs they should pursue. Students must be allowed to choose, but their choice should be continually guided. Can things go wrong here? Of course. Counselors and/or teachers can be heavy-handed and short-sighted in their guidance. Real talents may be overlooked. Such errors of judgment cannot be entirely eliminated. However, if we insist that all teachers take part in program and occupational guidance, if we refuse to leave the job exclusively to professional counselors, we can do a better, more personal job at guidance. Teachers may be in a better position than counselors to understand students' motives, dreams, directed energies, strengths, and weaknesses. This should not be taken as a criticism of counselors but as a reminder of the weaknesses of bureaucracy. Guidance is not merely a job for specialists.

The present determination to send everyone to college should be rethought. Not all students are cut out for the academic study that should be central to college work (Arum & Roksa, 2011; Murray, 2008). The lack of aptitude for academic work need not be considered a deficiency. The job of good schools is to help students find out what they are good at and would like to do. They should be able to choose a vocational program with pride.

President Obama has recently urged community colleges to work more closely with industrial and commercial leaders in their local areas. The idea is to analyze employment needs and prepare adequate numbers of graduates for available positions—along the lines described in European VET programs. But why not push these programs into our high schools where they might well encourage kids to stay in school and graduate? We should greatly expand access to vocational and magnet schools and make it possible for students to change from one concentration to another when there is good reason to do so.

It should be clear that I do not recommend "consigning" some young people to a second-class education. That is, in fact, what we are doing now in a misguided commitment to preparing everyone for traditional college. There are many generous, good-hearted people who insist that, if they are taught well, all children can succeed at academic mathematics. Having taught the full range of high school mathematics courses, I can say with some confidence that this is not true. So what? Our task is to help students develop their talents and interests. If they need mathematics to do this, we should help them satisfy what is required for that purpose. If not, we should allow them to choose courses that will be useful for them and at which they can succeed.

Are there things that all students *should* know? There is, of course, much that all students should learn in all three of life's great domains. In our curriculum planning, we recognize these as assumed needs, but many of our assumptions should be reexamined. There are skills such as basic reading that everyone needs. There are also almost certainly some mathematical skills needed by everyone, but these probably do not include formal algebra and geometry. In addition to basically necessary skills, we might point to the vast volume of material included in school curricula as somehow contributing to what it means to be an educated person—someone possessing cultural literacy. I am not suggesting that we blithely scrap all or even most of this material as unnecessary. Rather, I am suggesting that we review it closely and evaluate its worth in preparing people for work, civic responsibility, and personal fulfillment. We should also ask what the material offered and its mode of presentation may contribute to the present life of our students.

In vocational education, one universal need that we should take seriously is the need to learn standard English. One of the few things schools can do to shake up the society's class system is to bring all students to standard language proficiency. It is a mistake to assume that this is accomplished through formal instruction in English and the liberal arts. If there is a causal relation, it is in the opposite direction; that is, children who have already learned standard grammar and pronunciation are generally ready for further instruction in English. Those who are not so prepared often gain nothing from formal instruction, and so we have high school graduates who say, "He don't care," "You shoulda saw it," "She didn't do nothing," and "I seen it with my own eyes."

Should we "respect" this poor language, or should we correct it? Students need to understand that, rightly or wrongly, people are judged by the language they use. It accomplishes nothing to say that "we" should not engage in such judgment. *We do.* Because so much in adult life depends on standard language proficiency, every teacher must be a language teacher. Vocational *teachers* do not simply teach manual skills. In our public schools, they—like all teachers—should gently correct grammatical errors and encourage students to correct each other. For this kind of genuine vocational education, we need well-prepared educators who can act as masters in the shop and as models of educated persons in the classroom.

It should be clear also that vocational schools should provide opportunities for students to engage in music, art, sports, and drama. All of the activities associated with the usual public schools should be offered—student government, service activities, exhibits, visiting artists, and the like.

Vocational and academic education have much to offer one another. Just as vocational students will profit from learning to use standard English, academic students will profit from learning to use their hands. Crawford (2009) quotes the director of the California Agriculture Teachers' Association as saying, "We have a generation of students that can answer questions on standardized tests, know factoids, but they can't do anything" (p. 12). The same point was made in an article in *The Chronicle of Higher Education* that reported on the lack of hands-on skills in college students (Carlson, 2012). Many of the students interviewed could not cook a meal or do anything useful with their hands. It can be argued that learning to make minor repairs, build things, plan and prepare meals, and plant gardens is good in itself, but it should also increase appreciation for the work of others.

It would be good if vocational and academic students could take some courses together, especially in social studies. We have already noted the need to reduce time spent on wars and give more attention to the history of homes, parenting, transportation, and agriculture. Following this line of thought, the history of labor should have high priority. It is not enough to include a bland paragraph here and there in texts that otherwise emphasize war and the doings of presidents and Congress. Students need to hear about the real struggles, heroic persistence, mistakes, and victories of working people.

Certainly, both groups should hear about Paulo Freire and read at least parts of *Pedagogy of the Oppressed* (1970), and they should discuss a question that has nagged at many of us: As we urge the oppressed to climb out of poverty and claim justice for themselves, how can we ensure that, once free, they will not themselves become oppressors? Do we need a pedagogy of the oppressor as well as one for the oppressed?

Social studies and English teachers can work together to guide students in reading the story of Myles Horton (1998) and Highlander Folk School. In that remarkable story, students will meet Rosa Parks, Pete Seeger, Fannie Lou Hamer, Eleanor Roosevelt, Paulo Freire, and Lilian Johnson, among others. They will hear about cooperative work on peace, civil rights, and labor unions. They will read stories of harrowing efforts—some really dangerous—to change the lot of working people. They will encounter socialism and Christian Socialists working for social justice. Working through this book, encouraging students to make excursions along biographical lines and campaigns for justice, should be a mind opening experience.

Doing this sort of work should remind us that education is not a matter of cramming unrelated facts into students' bewildered heads. We should take some time and explore matters in some depth and breadth, as suggested by Egan. Reading Horton, for example, students might want to follow up by reading more about Pete Seeger. Music teachers might pitch in, too. In the introduction to an essay on Seeger in *It Did Happen Here*, the author-interviewers write:

> For more than four decades, Pete Seeger's songs have given inspiration to protest. He has sung with Woody Guthrie in a union hall ringed by company thugs; from the flatbed truck made into a stage at Peekskill, New York; on the civil rights march from Selma to Montgomery; at a New England benefit for demonstrators arrested at a nuclear power plant; and to 750,000 peace marchers packed into Central Park. He has found audiences in hobo jungles, on picket lines, in school auditoriums, on the deck of the Hudson River sloop the Clearwater, and in Carnegie Hall. (B. Schultz & A. Schultz, 1989, p. 13)

Students might also have fun singing "If I Had a Hammer" and "Give Peace a Chance."

The story of Scott Nearing is another that students might find inspiring—a story of intellectual prowess, vigorous manual labor, and unflagging work for social justice. Nearing (2000) was a graduate of Central Manual Training High School of Philadelphia,

> which I chose in preference to the more academic Central High School because it linked practice with theory and seemed to me to give a more useful education—(p. 30)

Schultz and Schultz (1989) introduce their interview with Nearing when he was 99 years old, pushing a wheel barrow load of firewood:

> An assurance in the rightness of his beliefs and a fierce self-sufficiency of thought and living had held him on his radical course for nearly a century, as debater of Clarence Darrow, author of fifty books, grower of his own food, brewer of maple syrup, and guru to a later age then taken by homesteading. (p. 5)

And if we are interested in cultural literacy, we might encourage students to learn a bit more about those whom Nearing (2000) credited with influencing him:

> Socrates and his rule of reason; Buddha and his doctrine of harmlessness; Lao Tzu and Gandhi and their philosophy of nonviolence; Jesus and his example of social service; Confucius and the middle way; Thoreau and the simple life; Whitman and the naturists; Marx, Engels, and Lenin on exploitation and revolution; Victor Hugo and humanitarianism; Bellamy and the utopians; Olive Schreiner and the allegorists, Bucke's cosmic consciousness, and Romain Rolland's Jean Christophe. (p. 29)

Stories and biographical accounts such as these give real substance to the study of history, inspire interest in political/social action, and encourage a spirit of interdependence and appreciation for the full range of human talents. The pedagogical approach also closely resembles that recommended by the founders of the middle school movement (National Middle School Association, 2003), and we turn next to an exploration of how the ideas discussed so far might be employed at that level.

MIDDLE SCHOOL: A TIME TO EXPLORE

So far in this chapter, we have been talking about vocational education at the high school level. However, if we want to help students find out what they are interested in doing, middle school might be the ideal setting for an open exploration of possibilities. There is a second reason to give thought to the middle school. The sad failure of middle schools to fulfill the hopes of idealistic, early advocates illustrates a major theme of this book: The culture controls the schools, and those who would like to make changes in schools must do so within a stubbornly entrenched structure. With care and persistence, some changes may yet be made. It is a heartache that so many of our children effectively quit school during the middle school years, unable to succeed at what is required and foreseeing only more of the same if they hang on into high school.

The first middle schools (so labeled) appeared in the 1960s. Before that, schools moved from a standard 8-4 structure to a 6-2-4 structure with the introduction of junior high schools. It is often said that the middle school was created when the failure of junior high schools became too obvious to be ignored. But, despite the inspirational thinking of educators who saw a real opportunity to create a humane center of education (Lounsbury & Vars, 1978), the main change was one of name only. Even the slight variations—6-3-3, 5-3-4—arose more often from logistical needs in communities than from cogent educational analysis.

John Lounsbury (2009), a strong advocate of the middle school, asks us to see that "the valid middle school concept . . . has not been practiced and found wanting; rather, it has been found difficult to implement fully, and practiced then only partially" (p. 3). Much of what was recommended for the middle school built upon what was accomplished in 30 Progressive experimental schools in the 1930s and reported in the Eight-Year Study (see Kahne, 1996). That very fact—the similarity of practices recommended by middle school advocates and earlier Progressives—should have warned middle school educators about what they were up against. The aims and practices recommended for the middle school in the 1970s were similar to those now advocated for the 21st century: development of problem-solving skills, reflective thinking, individualized instruction, integration of the disciplines. The actual result, however, is that the middle school too often remains a pathetic subsidiary of the high school. Lounsbury (2009) admits that practice has not followed the concept and suffers from arrested development. Worse, "since No Child Left Behind (NCLB) has been in force, mere arrested development has regretfully given way to regression" (p. 3).

Given that the structure of our schools—courses in the disciplines, periods, classes—is not likely to change, it may still be possible to use the middle school as a portal to expanded options for students. Some of the best theoretical thinking on middle schools suggested forms of organizing the school day that simply will not work and will not be allowed given the inflexibility of dominant structures. (See, for example, the interesting chart in Oliva, 1988, p. 360, in which the day was to be divided into core, continuous progress nongraded skills, and "variables" such as music, typing, home economics, and industrial arts.) School buildings, classrooms, administrative structure, and daily schedules are firmly established. Where can we intervene to give appropriate attention to future vocations and personal life? In the two previous chapters, I've suggested some possibilities for engagement with home and civic life. Can we do something similar for vocational life at the middle school level?

First, we could give allegiance to the idea that schooling should help students find out what they would like to do as a vocation. Following that pledge, we would abolish grades in the middle school—no A's, B's, and F's. The idea would be to provide 2 wonderful years of exploration with no grades or high-stakes testing. Faculty would provide written evaluations completed in consultation with students to give parents a useful picture of their children's interests and aptitudes and what they might do with them.

Science classes might concentrate on issues of health, nutrition, and meal planning and preparation. Social studies, in coordination with science, would concentrate on ecological problems, the design of homes and backyards, and gardens. In mathematics, students would be introduced to algebra, and those who show aptitude would continue studying it. Other students might be engaged in studies of personal finance, gambling, basic statistics, games, and/or the mathematics of testing (e.g., when it makes sense to guess). English classes would act to integrate the disciplines by providing literature relevant to the topics presented in each of them *and* by concentrating on the mastery of oral language. In the larger schedule, there would be no electives, but within each subject—as described above for mathematics—there would be many choices in addition to units in which all students would be required to "try it." With the elimination of high-stakes testing and grades, more students might feel less anxiety in "trying" various studies.

Industrial/commercial arts would join the traditional subjects as a requirement. Those schools already possessing shops, studios, and kitchens can easily make this addition. For other schools, some expense would be involved to provide appropriate space and equipment, and it would be necessary to find well-prepared teachers. In schools ill-equipped for work in manual arts, field trips can be arranged for students to observe a wide variety of work, and representatives of various occupations can be invited to speak to the classes and answer students' questions.

Throughout their 2-year adventure in middle school, students should be organized into cohorts guided by a permanent faculty advisor who will provide continuous support and encourage students to share their experiences and support one another. The role of the teacher-advisor is vital to ensure that every student feels cared for. Instead of serving as a pre-dropout factory, the middle school should be both a wonderful experience in itself and a prelude to further genuine education.

In concluding this chapter, we might notice that, while we continue to force all children into academic studies for which many are not suited, Finland, a country whose schools we admire for their high test scores, offers 9 years of broad, common education to all of its students, after which they may choose to continue their education at either a vocational or academic high school (Ravitch, 2012; Sahlberg, 2012). Almost half of Finnish students choose a vocational school. Without *copying* the Finns or any other group, we can learn from them and adapt promising ideas for our own conditions and purposes. It is time to renew our efforts and our respect for vocational education.

9

Educating the Whole Person

Throughout this book, I have emphasized the three great domains in which people seek success and satisfaction. We should keep in mind, however, that it is *persons*—human individuals—who live and work in these domains, and education must be concerned with the moral, personal, and spiritual development of these persons. Human personality and character are significantly involved in all three domains. Consistent with earlier emphases, I will argue that education in these areas should not be separated from the education we offer in the standard disciplines.

MORAL EDUCATION

Philosophers, teachers, and parents have always been concerned about the moral education of children. For many centuries, the moral evaluation of persons was based primarily on their character, their possession of virtues. Even today, character educators and virtue ethicists put greater emphasis on the intentions of moral agents than on the consequences of their acts. But what is virtue, and how is it acquired? This is a question that vexed Socrates in the *Meno* (Cahn, 1997) where he seemed to decide on the basis of evidence that the virtues cannot be taught. Later, in *Protagoras*, he argued that, although the virtues cannot be taught directly, teaching must have *something* to do with their development.

Despite the evidence that shook Socrates's confidence in teaching the virtues, character education (which relies on the inculcation of virtues) has been the main approach to moral education for centuries. The biblical injunction to "train up a child in the way he should go" has been the guiding principle. The conclusion of that passage, however—"and when he is old, he will not depart from it"—presages Socrates's worry. People *do* depart from what they have been taught. We might still decide that, although there is no guarantee of lasting success, direct teaching of the virtues is our best bet.

In the United States, character education came under fire in a study conducted by Hugh Hartshorne and Mark May in the late 1920s (Hartshorne & May, 1928–1930). Their studies seemed to show convincingly that children subjected to direct instruction in the virtues behaved well while adults were watching them but frequently failed to conform when there was no adult supervision. The Hartshorne and May studies, among other works, persuaded Lawrence Kohlberg (1981) to criticize character education as a "bag of virtues" approach; his criticism rested on two important grounds: First, it does not seem to work and, second, it is a form of indoctrination. The second objection is very important because, depending on the virtues posited, we might thoughtfully hope that the method of character education would *not* work. Here, of course, we have in mind the sort of virtues taught under totalitarian regimes. The fact that the method does so often work, as indoctrination, suggests that character education cannot be summarily dismissed. Perhaps we simply need to be sure that what we are teaching is morally sound and worthy. Recall our earlier discussion of George Counts and his advocacy of what amounts to indoctrination in the name of social justice.

Thoughtful character educators from Aristotle to the present day have been aware of these two criticisms. Most recommend beginning with the control of behavior in the young to secure the desired conduct; then, at an age deemed appropriate, the initial indoctrination is followed by critical reasoning on the virtues. Aristotle, for example, advised that we should first ensure the right behaviors and then discuss the "whys." Similarly, a popular program sponsored by the Character Development League in the early 1900s named *obedience* as the first virtue to be taught (White, 1909). In that program, the 31 virtues taught were to culminate in number 32: character.

Character education as the primary method of moral education gave way to other approaches in the later part of the 20th century. Kohlberg's cognitive developmentalism emphasized moral reasoning and the commitment to act on principles of justice. This trend in moral education was compatible with changes in moral philosophy that began in the late 18th century and continued to develop throughout the 20th century. The new approaches emphasized big general principles and described moral conduct with reference to identification of the appropriate principle and the moral agent's rational decision to act on it. From Kant's categorical imperative to John Rawls's *Theory of Justice* (1971), the trend in moral philosophy has been away from a concentration on virtues and toward a commitment to reasoning and universal principles of justice.

The move just mentioned might also be described as a move from communitarianism toward liberalism. Virtue ethics with its emphasis on character is deeply anchored in a sense of community. It is the community that defines and describes the virtues, just as it decides which everyday customs and manners will be accepted and which frowned upon. Recognition of the fundamental role of the community in character education underscores the worry about indoctrination. What if the community goes somehow wrong?

When we look at the rise of totalitarianism in the 20th century, we see that virtues and character were heavily stressed in fascism and Nazism: Honesty, courage, self-sacrifice, comradeship, loyalty, and patriotism were taught vigorously (Noddings, 1996), but the virtues were badly misdirected. The community itself must be constantly observed and critiqued with respect to its moral goodness; it, like its individual members, can go wrong. We should feel a good deal of sympathy for the youngsters who experienced moral/social education under Hitler's regime. Those of us who were children in the United States during that era—those of us who are reflective—wonder with a shudder what we would have been like had we suffered the same indoctrination.

Liberals committed to a theory of universal justice try to avoid this perceived weakness in communitarian character education by reaching beyond the community to universal principles accessible to reason. But problems arise here as well. First, we have learned that there does not seem to be a *universal* definition of justice. Concepts of justice differ over time and place. Second, and perhaps more important, the concept of universal justice—like that of cosmopolitanism—does not have the emotional appeal of community solidarity and patriotism. It is for that reason, among others, that many of us have taken the warning of Martin Buber seriously. When thinking of moral life, Buber (1965) said, we should start with neither the collective nor the individual but with the *relation*. This recognizes that we become individuals largely through the relations to which we belong and that the strength and nature of these relations will affect our allegiance to or rejection of collectives. Care ethics posits relation as ontologically basic and the caring relation as morally fundamental. Our attention is on the *relation*, not solely or principally on the moral agent.

Recognizing weaknesses in character education and cognitive approaches does not imply that both should be discarded. Again, schools and teachers should analyze these programs and their own needs for promising strategies. The much favored use of biographical accounts in character education may prove widely useful. Similarly, the critical reasoning required in studying moral dilemmas or problems such as those posed in *Philosophy for Children* (Lipman, 1991) can contribute to moral growth.

In today's schools, too much emphasis is placed on rules and penalties. Zero-tolerance rules are especially harmful, and their use has made educators look foolish. Punishing a kindergarten boy for kissing a classmate and suspending a 4th-grade girl for accidentally bringing a knife to school by mistakenly picking up her mother's lunchbox instead of her own are silly responses that make a mockery of justice. Teachers and parents should promote a zero-tolerance *attitude* toward harmful acts and language, but they should reject zero-tolerance rules backed by prescribed penalties. It is right and important to remind students who verbally abuse classmates firmly that "we do not talk to others like that," and students who toss things across the room that "we don't throw things in here." When a nasty, antisocial comment is made, everything else should come to a stop. Forget the arithmetic lesson for the moment. "We do *not* talk like that in here—not ever." There need be no rule-prescribed penalty for the offense. Indeed, when teacher and students have established relations of care and trust, the verbal reminder should be effective. Treating one another with respect and care establishes the environment of safety required for learning. Exacting a penalty for every infraction may well have a counterproductive effect. The offender undergoes a penalty that may anger him or cause him to shrug it off—penalty paid. This is not the result we should seek.

A BETTER WAY

Our objective in moral education is to establish a climate in which natural caring flourishes. By "natural caring," I mean a decent, respectful way of meeting and treating one another that is maintained by inclination, not by rules. We treat one another with care because we want to do so—because we value a climate of care and trust within which to do our work. Life in happy families and friendly communities is characterized by natural caring, and it is the condition we cherish. When natural caring fails—under stress or antisocial behaviors of some community members—we turn to ethical caring, in which we rely on a repertoire of caring behaviors built up through years of caring and being cared for. In essence, we ask ourselves how we would behave if we were at our caring best or if this other were not so difficult. It is a main task of teachers—all teachers—to help students develop this repertoire of caring and being cared for. It is an attainable ideal to which we turn repeatedly throughout our lives.

Our first task is to model caring. We must show in our daily actions what it means to care. At the most basic level, we must do this because we *do* care; our behavior must be a genuine reflection of our moral selves. We do not put on an act because the "kids are watching," and we relate to them as we hope they will relate to each other. Some time ago, I talked with a school principal who bragged that he was tough on his teachers because he "cared about the kids." I gently warned him that his teachers might very well treat their students as he was treating them. When our emphasis is on accountability, rules, assessment, and penalties, we are likely to encourage self-protective conduct—behavior that will stave off criticism and keep those in authority off our backs. In contrast, when we emphasize *responsibility*, we pledge ourselves to respond with care to the needs of those for whom we are responsible and to encourage them to respond with care to their peers.

Accountability triggers a self-protective mechanism. Responsibility, a beautiful concept, puts emphasis on the response, acknowledgment of another's existence and needs. Martin Buber wrote, "All actual life is encounter" (1970, p. 62) and we "practice responsibility for that realm of life allotted and entrusted to us, . . . for which we have a relation of deeds which may count . . . as a proper response" (1966, p. 19). Eye contact, a smile, a raised finger of caution, a gentle reminder, a disappointed frown . . . are all responses that recognize the student as a special, particular human being. The relation thus established sets the stage for effective instruction as well as further social interaction.

Dialogue is the second component of moral education from the care perspective. Dialogue involves both talking and listening, and it is characterized by openness. Often, as Paulo Freire suggested, the end is open; the participants are exploring a topic or question and neither knows exactly where the dialogue will take them. Other times, one or both are aware of a desired end—solving a problem or understanding a concept—but neither is certain how to get there. Both are on the watch for signposts along the way.

Dialogue consonant with care ethics is properly open to distraction. The partner in dialogue is more important than the topic. If either partner shows signs of discomfort, the other will digress to provide reassurance, have a good laugh, or reminisce. Short pauses also offer an opportunity for self-reflection. A teacher may suspect she is going too fast or too deep for her student, or she may realize that the language she uses is not helpful to this student.

In my years as a math teacher, I often taught as part of a team or with a partner. I have told the story of how I sometimes asked my partner to explain something to a student with whom I seemed unable to connect. Her explanations were often successful—the student would complete the next few exercises correctly—but the explanations were mathematically weak. We talked about this, and even today I have dialogues with myself about the difference in language that was used. As a mathematics teacher, can I justify language that says, "put this here, subtract, put that over there"? But can I justify continuing to use precise mathematical language with a student to whom it is just a boring mystery? An idealistic teacher joining the dialogue might insist that I should have persisted in trying to make the rigorous language clear. Perhaps. But when should the commitment to rigorous language give way to the expressed needs of the student? Which response accomplishes the most for the teacher-student relation? One can see that this dialogue might continue well into the future.

I am now almost convinced that my colleague was right. It was our job to get students through a subject they would not have chosen to study and, with conscientious effort, we could get almost every student to learn some basic required skills—learn them well enough to do passably well on a standardized test. In an earlier chapter, I described how we did this in an Algebra 2 course. Given the demands of current schooling, the intellectually destructive insistence on everyone's "mastering" material that most will never use, we did the right thing. But I would not claim that all of these students learned *mathematics*.

Dialogue is intellectually stimulating, and it should enhance our relations with dialogue partners. At bottom, the teacher engaged in dialogue with a student implicitly asks Simone Weil's question again and again: What are you going through? And the student's response helps establish the direction of the ensuing dialogue.

There is another outcome we seek through dialogue with our students. We hope that they will learn how to engage in genuine dialogue and resist the party-line stubbornness described by Sunstein (2009). We want them to reject what might be called the "war model" of dialogue. The main point is not to win an argument but to find the truth or a workable compromise. Sometimes in social/political situations, we have to decide, as we do in one-to-one personal dialogue, to put a major point of difference aside and work on something less contentious. When we are sure that our relation is securely established as a *caring* relation, we may be able to tackle the contentious issue again. In our teaching, we show that it is safe and productive to engage in genuine dialogue.

Dialogue is basic to critical thinking, an important aim posited for 21st-century education. It is through dialogue—sometimes with ourselves—that we explore ideas, argue points, raise questions, and decide to pursue further investigation. Learning to engage in civil dialogue with others should make us less afraid to reflect on our own beliefs and actions. As we make it safe for others to raise questions, we also make it safer for ourselves.

In addition to modeling care and engaging in dialogue to strengthen caring relations, we should provide students with opportunities to practice caring. Students should be encouraged to work with partners and in small groups. The groups need not be formally organized unless the purpose is to teach students how to fill a particular role in group work. When students choose their own working groups, teachers have an opportunity to observe how they work together and who is left out. A competent, caring teacher can find unobtrusive ways to be sure all students have someone to work with, and she can use the group time to advance both intellectual interest and social competence. If she hears a nasty remark, she can raise that warning finger and remind the culprit that "we don't talk like that in here." With practice and, even, humor, she may soon have the students speaking with her: "Hey, man, we don't talk like that in here." . . . They will also join her in watching for kids who might be left out and make sure that doesn't happen.

Dialogue and practice in caring should help reduce the current epidemic of bullying. Too often—today is no exception—we suppose that the remedy is stronger laws and stiffer penalties, but while these may occasionally help a bit, they may also drive the impulse to take different, sneakier forms, and almost certainly they strengthen peer sanctions against snitching. We need to build caring communities in our schools—a climate in which kids will join their teachers in raising that finger of caution before bullying gets out of hand. It is easier and more effective to say "cool it" when the first questionable remarks are made than after real hurt has been inflicted. Supervised group activities provide a setting in which caring behaviors are monitored and maintained.

Educators have long endorsed pro-social goals. In the last several decades, many schools have introduced service learning programs in which students participate in activities that provide for various needs in the school or community. Like so many ideas in our schools, however, service learning is susceptible to corruption. Should it be required? Should students be given formal credit for it? Some have argued that, if it is to be taken as seriously as math and English, it should be *graded*. When that happens, the purpose is twisted inward. Instead of thinking about those who need help, students may strive for an "A" and keep a careful eye on how their service learning looks on their transcript.

As we talk about these things, we might begin to challenge many long-held assumptions about requirements and grading. Are there ways to allow more student choices in the curriculum without risking the quality of individual student programs? When attractive ideas such as service learning enter the curriculum, what can we learn from them? Instead of allowing them to be corrupted by the established curriculum, we should ask how they, implemented with integrity, can help resuscitate intellectual and social wholeness in the larger curriculum. Instead of assigning grades in service learning, for example, we might ask what other courses could be offered without formal grading. Perhaps many "honors" and AP courses could be offered pass/no credit. That would reduce the emphasis on GPAs and might even encourage some learning for its own sake.

A fourth component in moral education is *confirmation*. When we confirm a person, we help bring out the best in him or her. When a student commits an uncaring or unethical act, we respond by attributing to the actor the best possible motive consonant with reality. To a boy who cheats on a math test, we might say, "I know you want to please your father with good grades," and then go on to remind him that *this* way of doing it is beneath him. We may assure him that he is a better person than his act suggests. Notice that to do this, we need to know the boy reasonably well. Confirmation is not a mere strategy. We should have reason to believe that the boy really is a better person. This supplies one argument, among several others, for keeping students and teachers together for several years. It takes time to develop strong caring relations.

It should be understood also that confirmation does not provide justification for a reprehensible act. It recognizes the badness of the act and that such an act is unworthy of this person. It contrasts the unworthy act to the best in the actor. It may even increase the person's sense of guilt; he has betrayed himself as well as others. But it grants the guilty student assurance that this observant, caring teacher sees something better in him. It confirms *him*, not his act.

In endorsing confirmation, we share some of the problems faced by character education. Confirmation itself is motivated by our dedicated care for the one who is confirmed. But our judgment of acts is heavily influenced by the community to which we belong. How well do we understand and share the moral commitments of our community? Have we made the ideals to which we are committed clear to our students? We differ from character education in our use of dialogue and confirmation in preference to rules and penalties, but we share the need to reflect continually on our community and its values. We should bear in mind that a high level of formal education does not in itself guarantee a high moral standard. Unfortunately, it is a fact that members of the medical profession were among the strongest supporters of Hitler and the Nazi party (Kater, 1989; Watson, 2010). Members of the legal profession and academics in general were not far behind. In part, such deplorable moral outcomes stem from our habit of separating disciplines—making medical and legal ethics into separate subjects instead of incorporating them into everything we teach and investigate. It happens also because we too easily come to accept the authority of leaders in both political and intellectual life.

Consider as an example how we treat plagiarism and dishonesty in academic life. We condemn and penalize them. But it is rare for a science or math professor to interrupt a lecture on some scientific point to remind students that the whole enterprise depends on intellectual honesty. We are intellectually interdependent, and a breach of honesty threatens the whole scientific community. Members should understand that dishonesty betrays not just themselves but the whole community to which they have pledged allegiance.

In turn, that community must be studied and morally evaluated continuously. How is it that intellectual communities can come to endorse racism, sexism, or militarism? Some of us worry that the current revival of enthusiasm for American exceptionalism may lead to moral corruption. When we confirm an individual or group, we urge an examination of and recommitment to the identifiable best in that individual or group. And we stand ready to ask ourselves and others in what way this trait, attitude, or way of behaving is "best." We do not confirm an individual or group in the belief that they are better than others but, rather, that they have given evidence that they are better than their current acts suggest.

SELF-KNOWLEDGE

In *Critical Lessons* (2006), I devoted a chapter to learning and self-understanding. In that chapter, I suggested that biographical accounts of how people work, manage their time, and generally structure their lives may be useful for teachers who want to encourage self-understanding in their students. Whether or not students study the work habits of others, however, it is essential that they study their own. Do they do their best work in the morning or at night? With or without music? With or without food and drink? Before or after exercise? On their own volition or only under orders from teachers or parents? There may be no area of life in which critical thinking is more important than in acquiring and reflecting on self-knowledge. The motto of Socrates is good for all time: Know thyself.

Are there subjects they look forward to studying? One of the saddest things about today's schooling is that so few students claim to be excited by anything they study. As Wendell Berry and Wes Jackson have noted, schools seem to encourage a single major in upward mobility. Even at prestigious colleges, many students think primarily of the good jobs they hope to get when they graduate. Few talk enthusiastically about what they are studying. At the high school level, the "best" students—those with the highest GPAs—often devote equal effort to all subjects—whatever it takes to get that "A" (Pope, 2001). The phenomenon is not new, but it seems to have worsened in the last decade or so. An impressive case was described in *A Separate Peace* by John Knowles (1960). The narrator of the story, Gene, detected a way to surpass Chet, his only rival for academic honors:

> I began to see that Chet was weakened by the very genuineness of his interest in learning. . . . When we read *Candide* it opened up a new way of looking at the world to Chet, and he continued hungrily reading Voltaire, in French, while the class went on to other people. He was vulnerable there, because to me they were all pretty much alike—Voltaire and Moliere and the laws of motion and the Magna Carta and the Pathetic Fallacy and Tess of the D'Urbervilles—and I worked indiscriminately on all of them. (p. 46)

Gene's attitude is common today, and it is encouraged by the grim insistence on the same curriculum for everyone. Teachers are expected to have a learning objective for every lesson and some reasonable way of testing to see that the learning has occurred. Unless that objective is simple and straightforward, it is unlikely that all students will master it and, even if they do, they might not be able to do anything with it. Reflect for a bit on the kids who can fill in the right bubble on a question that asks them to choose between "don't" and "doesn't" in a sentence and yet go on saying, "Jim don't," in their everyday conversation.

It isn't only that we concentrate too heavily on material that can be easily tested. I have already acknowledged that some such material is necessary; it provides the knowledge and skill to get started on material of real substance. But what of all the wonderful ideas that might interest only some students—ideas from which they might construct their own learning objectives? Must everything a teacher introduces be aimed at an objective everyone will master? This is such an impoverished notion of teaching that one wonders why anyone with intellectual vitality would enter the profession. Teachers—real teachers—offer much wonderful material that will be received differentially, used eagerly by some students and largely ignored by others. Offering such material is basic to teaching because, with Dewey, we believe that the function of education is to help students find out what they are "fitted to do." It is *not* to force exactly the same curriculum on all students with the promise that, if they obey and learn, they will have a successful future doing something or other.

Students should study their own energy levels. When we are deeply interested in something, our energy is easily directed at that topic or task. How can we use that knowledge to accomplish tasks about which we are not enthusiastic? Some of us find it effective to self-motivate with the promise of time to be spent on a loved activity. Let's say that, like Knowles's Chet, we are fascinated by Voltaire. A good energy manager might bargain with herself—I'll do half of the math assignment, and then I'll read some Voltaire. Later I'll do the other half and then read more Voltaire. The promise of indulgence in the loved activity provides motivation to complete less-loved, required activities.

A word of caution should be noted here. When we are compelled to do something like math homework and feel guilty about hating it, we sometimes push ourselves too hard at it, telling ourselves that we should appreciate its importance, that we really like it. The result is often what Carl Jung (1969) called *enantiodromia*; the false desire to like something and do well at it is converted to the opposite, and we hate it even more. Worse, we can kill a genuine interest by forcing ourselves to engage in it when we are just not in the mood. Writers are sometimes guilty of this mistaken choice. Love and interest are converted into their opposites. That is why many of us have cultivated several interests. If one flags, we let it rest a bit and turn to another. Obviously, there are tasks that simply must be done, and we do them by exercising methods of self-motivation that do not involve guilt or any other emotion that might block the restoration of energy for the temporarily arrested interest.

Parents and teachers often believe that it is their duty to schedule children's work and study time, but learning to manage their own time is a task more important than any daily homework assignment. As early as possible, children should learn to schedule and manage their own work-time. It is especially sad and dispiriting for kids to be forced to do homework as soon as they come home from school. The energy available to genuine interest is likely to flow in a torrent toward the opposite pole. Clearly, I am not suggesting that students just leave their homework undone—although I do believe that they are given too much of it today. (On this, see also Kohn, 2006.) Rather, I am suggesting that they be encouraged to study their own motivational energies to find the best way of doing what must be done without losing intellectual interest in an idea or subject they have chosen. This process should start informally in elementary school in the form of conversations about their interest and work habits. No preaching! It should continue a bit more formally in high school, perhaps with written logs and commentaries.

SPIRITUAL EDUCATION

In the 21st-century Western world there is a well-documented shift of emphasis away from formal religion toward "spirituality." What is meant by spirituality? Discussing the increasing interest in spirituality, Robert Wuthnow (1998) notes that it is accompanied by a deplorable ignorance about religion. Thus, it would seem that schools have two more tasks generally neglected—imparting some knowledge of religions and their role in human affairs, and helping students explore what they might mean if they claim to be "spiritual but not religious" (Smith, 2005).

Let's consider first what we might reasonably teach about religion in our public schools. This is a potentially huge topic, and I have written more extensively about it elsewhere (Noddings, 1993, 2003, 2006). Some schools already offer courses in world religions that introduce students to some of the great religious literature, festivals, and personages. Usually, these courses avoid theological questions and keep debate on differences to a minimum but, at least, students who take the courses should be considerably less ignorant about Bible stories and major figures in Judeo-Christian history. Both atheists and believers can support the teaching of biblical literature as part of our culture. Richard Dawkins (2006), a militant atheist, has argued

> that an atheistic world-view provides no justification for cutting the Bible, and other sacred books, out of our education. . . .We can give up belief in God while not losing touch with a treasured heritage. (p. 344)

Indeed, Dawkins (2006) offers two full pages of biblical expressions with which educated people should be familiar, and he refers to a tally of more than 1,300 biblical references in the works of Shakespeare. He offers some humor, too, with this bit of rhyme by Lord Justice Bowen:

The rain it raineth on the just,
And also on the unjust fella.
But chiefly on the just, because
The unjust hath the just's umbrella. (p. 343)

Although critical thinking is obviously needed in religious education, it is rarely encouraged. In the United States today, it is widely believed that a confessed atheist could not (indeed, should not) be elected to the presidency, and one can only imagine what might happen if a teacher asked students to read Bertrand Russell's *Why I Am Not a Christian* (1957). Yet more and more people are questioning religious teachings and even the existence of God, and surely young people need opportunities to discuss such matters in safety and a climate of mutual respect. As we discussed in an earlier chapter, the liberal arts at the college level have long provided a venue for the discussion of such questions, but the sharply separated subjects we present at the high school level do not deserve the title "liberal arts." At that level, without digging deeply into technical theological questions, we might do at least three things: introduce students to the fundamental ideas of the major religions and atheism, discuss what each has to say about some great existential questions, and encourage respectful critical thinking on all of the views presented.

It is probably best, however, to include existential, moral, and religious questions wherever possible in *all* of our subjects. Including them in this way recognizes their importance and may reduce the objections that arise so easily when they are collected in a single course on religion. Katherine Simon (2001) comments on this:

Despite my appreciation for many aspects of the religion courses I observed, however, I found nothing to support the notion that "morality," "ethics," or "character education" should be added as a separate course of study in public schools. The strengths of the religion courses could readily be integrated into any of the subjects where an attempt was being made to include discussion of moral and existential issues. The ubiquity of morally charged questions in *all* subject areas, indeed, suggests the possibility of conceptualizing the teaching of *each* subject as "moral education." (p. 227)

Teachers of every subject can collect and share material relevant to religion and existential questions. For example, when math teachers mention the work of Leibniz (one of the inventors of calculus), they can discuss briefly his notion of the world's creation by God. Leibniz held that our world is the "best of all possible worlds." What does this mean? Leibniz suggested that God had explored and considered all logical possibilities for the world he would create and, from that array, he chose the *best* of all *possible* worlds. Does this mean that the laws of logic precede God, that even God is constrained by logic? Some critics objected strongly to this possibility and insisted that God could have established a different logic if he wished to do so. Each of the great characteristics attributed to God (omnipotence, omniscience, and all-goodness) can be challenged in this way. If God must obey the laws of logic, he is not omnipotent. If human beings have free will, God cannot be omniscient; he does not know with certainty what any human being will do. If he is all good, why is there so much suffering in the world? And why, if they believe in an all-good God, would any Christian believe that this God would allow any soul to suffer eternal damnation? These are logical questions that do not require dedication to any one set of religious beliefs. Such discussion may also help students learn that questions of this sort arise *within* belief communities and do not necessitate a turn to atheism or agnosticism.

Every subject in the school curriculum is loaded with possibilities for discussion of moral, existential, and religious questions. To activate these possibilities, however, will require a major change in teacher education, especially in the way we prepare "specialists."

Let's turn now to the idea of *spirituality*. Those who claim to be spiritual but not religious may or may not believe in God. Most do. They simply do not believe that formal religious institutions are necessary to establish a connection with God. Some even find that these institutions stand in the way of such connection by emphasizing rituals and stories that separate them from genuine spiritual experience. They seek God but not in church, temple, or mosque.

Acknowledging a spiritual aspect of life need not involve the idea of God. The human spirit may be equated with an immortal soul, but it need not be. That spirit may be thought of as a capacity for deep emotional response—a soaring feeling that carries us above routine, daily life. Or, in contrast, the response—still deeply spiritual—may be a pervasive feeling of calm, of contented peace at the end of a satisfying day. Such experiences are at least in part aesthetic. We are moved by a Beethoven symphony, a painting by Monet, a poem by Hardy, a passage from Shakespeare, or an aesthetic feeling of completion in peace and quiet. Many of us experience the spiritual in connection with nature: a mountain peak emerging from the clouds, the roar of the ocean, sunrise, the sight of a lovely garden covered with dew in the morning. Holding an infant or the hand of a dying parent may induce a spiritual feeling. The boom of an organ in a cathedral may do it. Life would be dull and drab without the capacity of spirit to connect, to be moved. Indeed, the dictionary defines *spirit* as the principle of conscious life, that which connects the physical body to something felt beyond it.

It is not the job of educators to *tell* students what should bring forth a spiritual response. We should provide opportunities and possibilities, not indoctrination. This is work that requires sensitivity and critical thinking on the part of teachers. C. S. Lewis (1955) argued powerfully that educators should inculcate the "right" sentiments; he deplored the phenomenon of "men without chests"—that is, human beings with heads and guts but no hearts. Listen to his persuasive words:

> The right defense against false sentiments is to inculcate just sentiments. By starving the sensibility of our pupils we only make them easier prey to the propagandist when he comes. The famished nature will be avenged and a hard heart is no infallible protection against a soft head. (p. 24)

But when "just sentiments" are implanted by indoctrination, students may still be easy prey for the propagandist. Consider what happened to youth under fascist and Nazi education. The language used under both ideologies was inspiring, and it often sounded *just*. We can agree with Lewis that the sensibility of our students should not be starved, but if we prescribe it, the result may simply be a rigid adherence to whatever they are told by authorities. It can be a tremendous relief not to suffer the agonies of critical thinking. A Nazi concentration camp commander expressed this view:

> I was full of gratitude to the SS for the intellectual guidance it gave me. We were all thankful. Many of us had been so bewildered before joining the organization. We did not understand what was happening around us, everything was so mixed up. The SS offered us a series of simple ideas that we could understand, and we believed in them. (quoted in Glover, 2000, pp. 361–362)

Is there, then, nothing that we should inculcate? I have already said that teachers should take a zero-tolerance attitude toward hurtful deeds and language. "We do not treat each other that way in here." We remind students regularly about rules and manners, but we also *discuss* these matters and encourage a critical attitude toward them. Why do we accept these rules? Which are morally important and which simply matters of custom? What we inculcate must pass a continually reviewed and renewed devotion to caring: It must not allow the deliberate infliction of pain, separation, or helplessness. It encourages connections and interdependent efficacy. And we ask ourselves regularly whether the sentiments we inculcate need revision or extension.

Students should be encouraged to think about their spiritual life and examine the encounters that produce spiritual highs. They should not be compelled to share these experiences, but voluntary disclosure should be allowed. Why are we moved by patriotic music and ceremonies? Why does the solemnity of a religious service move us? And, looking back over the material on home life and ecology, we should remind students that one can find spiritual satisfaction in everyday life. A "perfect" day described by Anne Morrow Lindbergh is a lovely example of spiritual satisfaction: "physical work, conversation, intellectual work, play on the beach, sipping sherry by the fireside, lying on the beach under bright stars, and silent communion with her companion" (quoted in Noddings, 2006, p. 279). Students should watch for such moments in their own lives and in the accounts of others in literature—especially poetry—and biography.

It is a responsibility of educators to introduce the idea of spirit to students and to get them thinking about it. Ordinary life, considered boring by so many, can be deeply inspirited. To become sensitive to the sounds, touches, and sights that call forth a spiritual response is to live life more fully. Surely, this is what a genuine education seeks.

[handwritten margin notes] ways to show care in subjects
math - woodwork cooking w/ to products give
community.

10

Problems in Today's Education For Citizenship

In an important sense, because it is impossible to separate the three domains of human life, this entire book is about educating citizens. It is necessary, however, to say more about some problems and topics on citizenship that are regularly treated or neglected in today's schools. So far, in agreement with John Dewey, I have argued that democracy should be thought of as a mode of associated living and, in that spirit, I have discussed the need to maintain and extend relations of care and trust in our schools, in parenting, in global concerns, in attention to the Earth, in occupations, and in moral education. The emphasis throughout has been on balance and connections—working from big ideas to the knowledge and skills required to identify and solve related problems. As we have seen, critical thinking is necessary in every subject, and receptive attention (listening) and cooperation are needed in every area of life.

In the earlier chapter on democracy, I discussed participatory democracy as it has been described by John Dewey, Ralph Waldo Emerson, and Walt Whitman. I also noted the desirability of *deliberative* democracy, and it is a major task of education to involve students as participants in democratic settings and move them toward deliberative engagement. I have argued that competent deliberation is best learned through participation and dialogue, not through the mere acquisition of facts. Because participation in democratic activities is essential, I have suggested that educators should resist the abolition or reduction of extracurricular activities. Participation in well-supervised, democratically organized activities is as important—perhaps more important—than structured classes in developing deliberative citizens. This is not easy work, however, and we encounter numerous barriers. It is also tempting to think that our citizens, supposedly schooled in democracy, possess the capacity to address local and global problems rationally. This is a mistake that Dewey made in assessing the ability of his fellow citizens to engage rationally in the "war to make the world safe for democracy," World War I. We may be no closer today than we were in 1916 to producing rational, critical thinkers. Indeed, many thoughtful critics believe that the exercise of critical thinking and deliberation has deteriorated badly over the last 2 or 3 decades.

Traditionally, education for citizenship in America (and in most other countries) has concentrated on the nation's history, government structures and documents, and economic development. In the 21st century, as we begin to think seriously about global democracy, we must consider how to treat some traditional topics in a way that will diminish their influence without disrespecting them. One way to do this is to emphasize the best in these ideas and show how they might be extended beyond the confines of narrow nationalism. With that hope in mind, we'll discuss patriotism, race and multiculturalism, military service, and political education.

PATRIOTISM

In our earlier discussion of cosmopolitanism, we noted the "thinness" of the idea—that is, its lack of emotional impact on citizens compared to that of national patriotism. Cosmopolitanism, in contrast to patriotism, packs little emotional wallop; there are no uniforms, bands, parades, memorials, or rituals to support it. It is, in part, why I have suggested starting with *ecological* cosmopolitanism, a cooperative enterprise directed at concern for Earth, our common home. The need to protect the Earth and the life it supports should have some emotional appeal.

American schoolchildren are introduced in the earliest grades to the rituals of patriotism. We need not abandon these rituals, but we can demythologize them by informing students about their origins and purposes. Little children are taught to sing "The Star-Spangled Banner," for example, but few ever learn that its tune came from an old English drinking song, nor do many know that, although its words were written in 1814, it was not officially made the national anthem until 1931. I'm not suggesting that we teach this material to very young children, but it should be taught somewhere in the school curriculum. Similarly, many citizens seem to think that the Pledge of Allegiance was "there from the start" when, in fact, it was written in 1892 by a Christian Socialist, Francis Bellamy, at the request of the National Education Association. In this time of bitter partisanship, it should invite reflection to recognize the contributions of a teachers' union to national unity and the fact that there was once a respectable Christian Socialist movement in the United States. Students should hear, too, that the phrase "under God" was added to the pledge during Eisenhower's presidency at a time when Americans were eager to differentiate the American state from "Godless communism." These stories tend to humanize our rituals and, perhaps, to encourage greater openness to the possibility of modifying them.

Aristotle described a good friend as one who points his friends upward. A good friend does not "cover" for us or ignore our less exemplary acts. He or she reminds us of our best selves and works with us to actualize our ideals. Similarly, patriots should acknowledge the wrongdoings of their country and criticize failures to live up to our written ideals. It is not only necessary to admit and correct mistakes where possible, it is also increasingly necessary to adopt a more modest attitude in the 21st-century global community. Just as we dislike hearing individuals brag about their wealth, strength, and achievements, so global neighbors tire of hearing Americans brag about being "number one" on countless measures. And will we love our country less if it is no longer "number one"? As positions shift globally, it is likely that our status will be challenged in many areas. While retaining our love of country, devotion to the Earth should supplant the earlier, overly competitive pride in our nation.

Nationalistic pride has gotten in the way of building a truly deliberative democracy. The revival of American exceptionalism tends to make talk of deliberative democracy just that—empty talk. Cynthia Dunbar, a former member of the Texas school board and strong advocate of teaching exceptionalism in our schools, has claimed: "We as a nation were intended by God to be a light on a hill to serve as a beacon of hope and Christian charity to a lost and dying world" (quoted in Shorto, 2010, p. 39). She is also quoted as saying that sending our children to public schools is like "throwing them into the enemy's flames, even as the children of Israel threw their children to Moloch" (quoted in Collins, 2012, p. 115). Writing about the influence of Texas on school policies and textbooks, Collins (2012) notes that objections to environmental science books expressed the worry that these books "were teaching children to be more loyal to their planet than their country" (p. 112). Such worries raise real concerns about the success of efforts at ecological cosmopolitanism. Perhaps we can win over some listeners by pointing out that the well-being of our beloved country does in the long run depend on the health of Earth.

Our intention should not be to condemn or eliminate patriotic rituals but to help students understand the context in which they have been established and the psychological effects they induce. Our aim is not to produce cynics or revolutionaries but, through dialogue and persistent questioning, to encourage critical thinking. Jean Bethke Elshtain (1987) has recommended a *chastened* patriotism:

> But it is a *chastened* patriot I have in mind, men and women who have learned from the past. Rejecting counsels of cynicism, they modulate the rhetoric of high patriotic purpose by keeping alive the distancing voice of ironic remembrance and recognition of the way patriotism can shade into the excesses of nationalism. . . . (pp. 252–253)

One way to endorse a chastened patriotism is to organize our history and social studies courses around issues instead of "facts" (Noddings, 2012a).

If we want students to think critically, we must give them time to explore events and opinions in some depth. It is predictable that they will forget most of what they read and hear in courses that consist of long lists of facts. Instead of memorizing the names of labor unions and events in which they participated, for example, students would be invited into dialogue about the origin and purposes of unions, the benefits for which they worked, the mistakes they have made, and the corruption that has sometimes infected them. As mentioned in the chapter on vocational education, there are many stories to be told in this context, and they provide insight into our nation's history. Were the founders and leaders of labor unions democratic patriots or subversives? How about those who claimed to be pacifists in our wars?

RACE AND MULTICULTURALISM

The United States has struggled throughout its existence to achieve a defensible way to treat its minority populations. There have been horrible, morally unjustifiable practices—the slavery of Black Americans, the near-genocide of American Indians. The civil rights movements of the 1960s and 1970s constituted a real revolution, one in which the injured parties stood up for their rights, and did so for the most part nonviolently, whereas the offenders often used violence to maintain their advantage. It is a remarkable story.

Despite dramatic success in securing voting rights, access to public facilities, and reduced discrimination in hiring and housing, many problems persist. Schools in the north are more segregated than ever, and achievement gaps have been only slightly reduced. Black youngsters are more likely than Whites to drop out of school, and Black adults suffer a higher rate of unemployment than Whites. People of goodwill recognize these problems and seek a way to surmount them.

As we have seen with so many of the problems addressed in this book, a lack of critical thinking often handicaps discussion of the issues. Those of us who want to do "the right thing" find ourselves polarized, afraid to talk openly about problems lest we be misunderstood or, worse, stand accused of racism. For example: Should we enthusiastically endorse multicultural education or should we raise questions about its purposes and effects? Should we continue to put emphasis on the disaggregation of test scores or should we give more attention to areas in which minority students are doing well? As critical thinkers, educators should be able to talk about these things.

Consider the reactions to Arthur Schlesinger's (1992) "reflections" on a multicultural society. He was heckled and booed on college campuses; his message was condemned before he spoke. Granted, we might have serious objections to his argument, but we might also learn something from discussing his points. His main worry—that emphasis on group (ethnic) identity might undermine the unity of our nation—is one that should be discussed. However, his language tends to anger us; it does not sound like an invitation to dialogue:

> The new ethnic gospel rejects the unifying vision of individuals from all nations melted into a new race. Its underlying philosophy is that America is not a nation of individuals at all but a nation of groups, that ethnicity is the defining experience for most Americans, that ethnic ties are permanent and indelible, and that division into ethnic communities establishes the basic structure of American society and the basic meaning of American history. (p. 16)

Even I—an advocate of receptive listening and open dialogue—get angry when I read this. A nation of individuals? Remember when—in America—a Black "individual" constituted only a fraction of a person? Who labeled Native Americans "savages"? Did people withdraw into ethnic communities or were they forced into them? We could devote many pages to the underlying causes of our outrage at these remarks.

Schlesinger writes eloquently of American unity and allegiance to the idea of assimilation, an idea that has been identified by many minorities with destruction of their identity, not inclusion. Language on the issues of multicultural education has become polarized. At a meeting some years ago, I listened to graduate students discussing the issues. One student angrily brushed aside a comment about the contributions of Jane Addams on the grounds that Addams was "an assimilationist." As a longtime admirer of Addams, I intervened to remind the students that "assimilation" should not be regarded as a pejorative. Addams did indeed work to help immigrants assimilate into American society and succeed in their new national home. But she also encouraged them to retain and share their original cultures. She even established the Hull-House Labor Museum in which various tools and artifacts of their original cultures were displayed (Lagemann, 1985). Every teacher today might profit from reading Addams's beautiful essay on "The Public School and the Immigrant Child" (National Education Association, 1908). In that essay, she wrote:

> Can we not say, perhaps, that the schools ought to do more to connect these children with the best things of the past, to make them realize something of the beauty and charm of the language, the history, and the traditions which their parents represent. (p. 100)

Her position fits well with the one I've taken on global democracy. I, too, advocate assimilation—especially in the vital mastery of standard

English—but with Addams, I want cultural understanding that goes beyond assimilation. Addams wanted students to learn not only about the culture of their parents but also about the universal sense of culture:

> In short, it is the business of the school to give to each child the beginnings of a culture so wide and deep and universal that he can interpret his own parents and countrymen by a standard which is world-wide and not provincial. (p. 100)

Assimilation to American culture, attachment to an original culture, and a move toward universal culture need not be mutually exclusive. Schlesinger (1992) is right, however, to warn that a polarized emphasis on ethnicity could lead to a form of separation that "nourishes prejudices, magnifies differences and stirs antagonisms" (p. 17). This danger could be very real if a multicultural class concentrates on the evils and failings of the majority group. As discussed in earlier chapters, educators should not want to produce cynics but generous, critical thinkers.

There is another matter that worries some advocates of multicultural education. Sonia Nieto (1999) has written convincingly about multicultural learning communities, and she has acknowledged the power of multicultural education in "improving students' self-esteem, incorporating cultural content into the curriculum, and fostering interethnic friendship" (p. 174). However, she confesses that "the question, *But can they do math?* has gnawed at me for years because it underscores the lack of access of bicultural students to high levels of learning and thus to expanded options for the future" (p. 175). She notes that both the funding supplied by society and the policies established by school administrators have a strong effect on the provision of such access. But individual teachers exercise an even greater effect:

> Tightening institutional norms that grant unearned privileges to some students over others, challenging ideologies that insist that some children are inherently superior to others, and uniting with other activists both inside and outside of school who believe that all children are capable of high levels of achievement and therefore deserve the very best, these educators make a significant difference in the lives of the children they teach. (p. 175)

Many of us are inclined to agree with Nieto enthusiastically and join her set of activists. But just as I had to put aside an angry reaction to Schlesinger and admit, with important reservations, that he has made points that demand our attention, here I must put aside my general agreement with Nieto and suggest that we bring critical thinking to her remarks. First, the claim that "all children are capable of high levels of achievement and *therefore* (my italics) deserve the very best" is highly questionable. I do not believe that all children are capable of high levels of academic achievement, but I do believe that all children deserve the very best. The best we can offer should not depend on the capacity of a child to achieve a high level of academic competence. The task of educators, I have argued, is to help children find out what they are good at and to develop those capacities with respect, enthusiasm, and competence.

I understand why Nieto has been nagged by the question, *But can they do math?* We live in a society that puts inordinate emphasis on academic prowess. But if we are going to maintain—or restore—the democracy dreamed of by Dewey, Emerson, and Whitman, we should expand the list of talents recognized and promoted in our schools.

We should reject polarization over multicultural education and commit ourselves to genuine dialogue on topics related to race and ethnicity. Lawrence Blum (2013) has given us a powerful account of young people studying and talking together about race and ethnicity across racial and ethnic lines. Guided by a sensitive and highly competent teacher, a high school class of mixed race and ethnicity discussed racism, identity, the history of slavery, the language of racial conflict, and the status of racial/ethnic minorities in America today. Blum's account is a model of using critical thinking in classroom discussion of racial issues.

One of the most challenging and sensitive topics tackled by Blum's class was that of the alleged mental inferiority of Blacks. Several students expressed disappointment, even disillusionment, when they read accounts of Thomas Jefferson's views on Black intelligence and slavery. Today, although most people are aware that the full range of intelligence occurs in all races, there are still influential writers, accepted in the scientific community, who claim that Blacks, on average, are less intelligent than Whites and Asians. This claim, based on the results of standard IQ tests, has given rise to the experience of "stereotype threat" among Blacks, the fear that they cannot match the achievement of White students in mathematics and logic (Steele, 2011). How many of us could continue to study a subject energetically if we were told repeatedly that we were part of a group that simply could not do well in it?

This question raises a whole set of questions for educators. Should we respond by telling students that they *can* "do it"? Should we remind them that lots of adequately intelligent, creative people are not good at math— that, if they are having trouble with it, they are not alone? Probably the best answer to easing this threat is to dismiss the racial claim and respond to each individual in a way that addresses that individual's needs. Some students should be urged to keep trying for excellence; others should be assured that there are different talents to be developed.

At present, we may be inadvertently aggravating the problem by insisting on the disaggregation of test scores. The intention here may be admirable; we want Black and Hispanic students to do as well as Whites. But the result, year after year, is like rubbing salt in wounds. The gap between races remains, and the publicity on it almost certainly adds to the fears and worries described as stereotype threat. We might do better to drop the practice and turn our attention to expanding the curriculum and encouraging the development of a full range of talents for all students. For youngsters—Black or White, male or female—who choose to study academic mathematics, we should work hard and enthusiastically to help them succeed, but we should stop forcing everyone to study it.

MILITARY SERVICE

Schools today concentrate almost entirely on preparing students for college and, as we have seen, little is done to prepare them for competent home life and parenting, full personal life, or occupations. We do almost nothing to prepare those students who choose to enter the military right out of high school. We do express concern that many high school graduates cannot pass the basic mental test and/or test of physical fitness, and it is right that such failures should worry us.

However, what of the young people who will enroll successfully in the military? Do we help them to understand what they may experience? During wars, even wars that drag on for many years, young people in the military are referred to as "heroes," but in nonwar times, public opinion has not been so kind. The most successful high school students rarely join the military, and it is also rare for young people today to regard such participation as a patriotic duty. More than 100 years ago, Rudyard Kipling (1956) wrote of the scorn with which the public looked upon enlisted men ("Tommies" in Britain)—until there was a war:

> For it's Tommy this, an' Tommy that, an' "Chuck him out, the brute!" But it's "Savior of 'is country" when the guns begin to shoot. (pp. 491–492)

Students should learn something about the hypocrisy of public attitudes toward the military. They should also hear about the current rash of suicides among military personnel and veterans. At this time, we do not have a definitive explanation for these tragedies, but we can explore a few possibilities with our students.

Adjustment to military life is hard for many young people, but readjusting to civilian life can be even harder for some. If you join the military, you give over control of your daily life to superiors. You no longer decide when and where to sleep, when and what to eat, when and how to exercise, when and how to speak, how to dress, what sort of haircut you'll have, and what work you will do. While some of us abhor such regimentation, others find it something of a relief to turn these decisions over to those officially in charge. The transition from military to civilian life can be very difficult; it requires accepting responsibility for a host of decisions in everyday life, and some veterans find this hard.

The change from one social yardstick to another is hard, but the change of *moral* yardstick can be ruinous. In everyday life, young people are taught to believe that killing is wrong. In military life, they may be forced to march and chant, "Kill, kill, kill!" The great danger here, of course, is that people in combat may lose their moral identity. There is so much evidence that this danger is real and devastating to personal lives that ignoring it in our schools should be regarded as a moral failure. Jonathan Shay (1994), a psychiatrist and writer, has written about his work with Vietnam veterans, some of whom will never completely recover. We are beginning to realize that post-traumatic illnesses are more frequent and more severe in wars where there are no well-defined battlefields and enemies in uniform.

Soldiers suffer, however, not only from what has been done to them. They suffer even more, it seems, from what they have done. Combat introduces a whole new moral world. Lorrie Goldensohn (2003), in her study of soldiers' poetry remarks, writes: "War's worst murder is the destruction—dulling, blunting—of our capacity to care" (p. 81). And J. G. Gray (1970), a philosopher who served in a counterespionage unit in World War II, has also written about the psychological suffering induced by feelings of guilt and, paradoxically, lack of guilt. Gray points out that modern warfare—from World War II on—has involved the killing of civilians as well as enemy soldiers. It is especially traumatic for sensitive young soldiers to see the bodies of children and other innocent nonparticipants and realize that they have had a part in causing this destruction. In his wartime journal, Gray (1970) wrote:

> My conscience seems to become little by little sooted. . . . If I can soon get out of this war and back on soil where the clean earth will wash away these stains! (p. 175)

Gray then goes on to tell the story of an old German man accused of being a Gestapo agent. Under Gray's investigation, the old man and his wife both committed suicide. Gray (1970) comments: "I hope it will not rest too hard on my conscience, and yet if it does not I shall be disturbed also" (p. 176).

The reading and discussion of such accounts—including the poetry of soldiers from World War I through Vietnam—should be part of every high school student's education (Noddings, 2012a). It is morally irresponsible to neglect this material. It is not that such preparation will prevent psychological and moral injury, but it may reduce its occurrence. More important, it may contribute to an enhanced civilian sensitivity that will come to abhor war and work to prevent it.

POLITICAL EDUCATION

Political education in the United States consists primarily of American history and some civics. Students are taught something about the great events in their country's past and something about the institutions and laws by which they are governed. They rarely hear anything about the philosophical differences that characterize political life beyond the barest outline of what might be called *liberalism* and *conservatism*. One widely used textbook I examined has just one citation under *socialism* in its index. It mentions Eugene Debs and the strong showing of the Socialist Party in the 1912 presidential election, and there is a very brief paragraph mentioning the fact that Debs was sentenced to 10 years in prison under the Espionage and Sedition Acts for discussing the economic causes of World War I in a speech. (He served 3 of the 10 years before being pardoned by President Harding.) But the great conflicts inspiring socialism and arising *within* socialism are not discussed.

It is reasonable to object that precollege education cannot provide courses in political philosophy and, even if there were time and available expertise to do this, public reactions would almost certainly not allow the sort of open political discussion encouraged at the university level. However, a discussion of democracy is badly incomplete—indeed misleading—if it does not include a range of recognized meanings of democracy. Educators must stand up against critics who prevent the sort of critical teaching addressed to the production of deliberative thinkers.

Without incurring political wrath, we can continue, even expand, the extracurricular activities that introduce students to the workings of participatory democracy. Such activities were a great strength of our schools until the last decades of the 20th century. In the last 30 years or so, the emphasis on academic study and achievement has squeezed out many of these activities. Even when they are offered, the emphasis has shifted from democratic apprenticeship to the significance of each activity in enhancing a participant's individual transcript. Everything is aimed at eventual economic success.

Teachers, well educated in the social sciences and philosophy, might be able to soften this economic emphasis and help students understand that human beings are not mere economic machines. As we saw earlier, it has been among the great strengths of the liberal arts to emphasize learning for its own sake, encourage the immortal conversation, and sustain the human pursuit of aesthetic appreciation, sound moral character, and spiritual meaning. Students should be made aware of sociological studies showing that, beyond an income necessary for a reasonably secure life, there is little correlation between increased wealth and happiness (Lane, 2000).

It worried Dewey that socialism—the political philosophy he favored—put so much emphasis on the economic. On one level, this emphasis is understandable. A socialist society *is* concerned with the economic welfare of all its citizens, but it must be interested in more than this. Dewey spoke with great admiration of Karl Polanyi, who affirmed Aristotle's view that humans are *social* beings, not merely economic units. He agreed with Polanyi's statement that an economy is "submerged in social relations" (quoted in Westbrook, 1991, p. 460). Dewey rejected both communist and fascist versions of socialism, insisting on *democratic* socialism. As he commented favorably on the work of Daniel Bell on industrial sociology and on Polanyi's *Great Transformation* (see Westbrook, 1991), he searched conscientiously for a "humanistic socialism." He never succeeded in describing such a socialism in detail, but that incompleteness is actually consonant with his lifelong commitment to openness—to experimenting, analyzing, revising, transforming. His search was for a politics of human life considered over all of the great domains of life.

In many of our high schools today, there is no discussion of socialism at all, and in some—when it is mentioned—the word itself, a pejorative, condemns the ideas without argument. It should be admitted that many American citizens view socialism as a slippery slope to communism. But it should also be noted that many thoughtful people regard democratic socialism as our strongest bulwark *against* communism. Emphasizing that possibility, we might be able to discuss the topic without raising objections from perennial textbook critics.

In this chapter, I have considered briefly topics that present problems for citizenship education in today's schools. Each of these topics might fill a volume or more of discussion. In keeping with a main theme of this book, I have concentrated on matters involving critical thinking. In every topic, the need for critical thinking is clear, and the difficulties in encouraging such thinking are equally clear. Dare we apply critical thinking to patriotism, multiculturalism, military service, and political education? With Dewey, I have rejected indoctrination, but even to broach some of these topics is considered by some to be indoctrination of sorts—a rejection of American exceptionalism. Somehow, we have to move beyond the group polarization described by Sunstein (2009) and so familiar in today's political talk. We have to learn how to *listen* to arguments before making conclusions; our conclusions should not be made solely on the basis of a speaker's affiliations but on the logic and strength of the argument. Surely, an education for critical thinking must include efforts to produce open-minded listeners who will deliberate on the merits of an argument.

11

Critical Thinking
On 21st-Century Education

In earlier chapters I have offered some suggestions for creative thinking on the topics and methods we might use under the guidance of 21st-century aims in the three great domains of life. Now I want to return to the problems noted in Chapter 1 and bring some critical thinking to bear on them. If we are to have any realistic hope of teaching students to think critically, surely policymakers and educators must exercise critical thinking in assessing what we are doing and planning for the future. The first question we might ask is whether the current emphasis on standards and core knowledge will make a positive contribution. If so, what might that contribution be? If not, we are wasting huge amounts of money, time, and effort.

STANDARDS AND CORE KNOWLEDGE

A major objection to the standards laid out in the description of core knowledge has been that states and school districts should not be told what to teach by the federal government. This is not in itself a criticism of content standards but merely an argument over who should establish them. As noted earlier, however, the public attitude toward a national curriculum has changed drastically over the last 30 years. What was nearly unthinkable in the 1970s is now widely accepted; most states have formally signed on to the Common Core Standards. But how useful are these standards?

Teachers should bring some critical thinking to bear on the "new" content standards for mathematics. Look carefully, for example, at the outline of content for algebra. Those of us who taught math during the "new math" era will find *nothing* new in the core standards for algebra. Indeed, if there is any detectable change, the current material is a bit less demanding. For example, work on matrices and vectors is optional under the Core. Why are we making such a fuss about material that has been with us for 40 years?

Most students could not handle the curriculum suggested by SMSG (the School Mathematics Study Group) and other new math projects in the 1960s and 1970s, and unless the current Core Standards bring with them some magical methods, most students will experience difficulty with this barely restated version. We can credit the Core with simpler, more straight-forward language. The problem facing teachers now, however, is enormously complicated by the insistence that *all* children should participate in the college preparatory curriculum. Think about this. The college preparatory curriculum in mathematics (and probably every subject) has long been informally standardized with respect to content. Go to the library and look at the texts used for many years. In any given decade (except for the wildly creative years of the 1960s), texts varied very little in content. I am not arguing against the regular, careful review of content by content experts; indeed, I have argued for such reviews throughout this book. My objections are twofold: First, it is simply not true that the material is new; second, by pretending that equality will be advanced by forcing this material on all students, we actually put our democracy at risk. I will not repeat my earlier arguments here, but I urge readers—especially teachers—to consider the billions of dollars spent on texts, tests, and supporting material for old content when we should be asking serious questions about new content and how to provide a variety of programs aimed at meeting the needs of different interests and talents.

[handwritten margin note: Texts must be frequently updated to account for the knowledge that is new]

If we look beyond the topics specified for the mathematics curriculum to the set of "standards for mathematical practice" stated in the Core, we may be even more worried. The first standard on the list is this: Make sense of problems and persevere in solving them. The idea apparently is to bring *meaning* to problems and their solution. But mathematics educators have emphasized *meaning* for decades. William Brownell wrote an essay entitled "The Place of Meaning in the Teaching of Arithmetic" in 1947; the essay is read today by students in math education. But we still have not figured out how to get all students to make sense of problems. Students still react to "word problems" with dread. One of my favorite old cartoons, entitled "Hell's Library," shows the sad inhabitants of hell gazing forlornly around a library composed entirely of mathematical word problems. There was even a period in math education during which text writers were advised to formulate word problems with as few words as possible. Words complicate mathematical thinking! From the perspective taken in this book, reading difficulties in mathematics offer another argument for making connections across the disciplines. Every teacher is, at some level, a reading teacher.

The second standard for practice recommends that students learn to "reason abstractly and quantitatively." What's new about this? Perhaps a clause should be added to the recommendation: "and now we really, really mean it." Yes, we should encourage students to engage in the practices listed, and we should provide many opportunities for them to do so. What we cannot do is reduce these activities to exercises that can be taught directly by establishing specific learning objectives. Often, they are better developed by playing games, experimenting, and engaging in conversation. Even then, mathematical problem-solving will remain a mystery to some students. This does not mean that they will be unable to formulate and solve problems of any kind. In an area of keen interest, most students can exercise the intelligence required to solve problems. Again, just as every teacher must be a moral educator and guide to standard oral English, so must every teacher help students develop their capacity for critical thinking and problem-solving in the arena of everyday life.

There is, oddly, no mention in the list of standards for mathematical practice of the orderly and accurate use of mathematical symbols and procedures. We are so captivated by the importance of "higher" cognitive processes that we have come to avoid discussion of dull and rote procedures—even though, paradoxically, we so often reduce the "higher cognitive" material to exactly that. I, too, hope to encourage clear and creative mathematical reasoning, but the relation between thinking and orderly written work needs some analysis. Good teachers spot signs of trouble early when they see students scribbling sideways and illegibly, when their written work is so messy that we (and they) cannot tell a plus sign from a times sign, when they inconsistently jumble A's and a's. Order and accuracy in procedures are not antithetical to higher-order thinking; they facilitate it. We should build on that facilitative relation.

Why do we continue to spend so much time and money on the writing and distribution of content standards? I've objected so far that there is little new in the Core, but perhaps it is important to repeat and endorse old material. This time, some of us believe, getting it all together and well publicized will have an impact. The evidence so far suggests that this belief is misplaced. Citing studies that look carefully at the acceptance and implementation of the standards in many states, Tom Loveless (2012) concludes:

> States have tried numerous ways to better their schools through standards. And yet, good and bad standards and all of those in between, along with all of the implementation tools currently known to policymakers, have produced outcomes that indicate one thing: Standards do not matter much. (p.32)

Advocates of standards argue that schools simply do not use the standards effectively. But apparently, they never have. Textbooks have long provided fairly uniform standards—certainly in mathematics. The behavioral objectives movement and the competencies movement following it were narrowly specific but had little effect. It is not that teachers do not know what they are expected to teach; rather, they simply cannot find a way to teach the required material to *everyone*. Sometimes, as in the new math era, many teachers do not know the material well enough to teach it to anyone. I don't think this is the problem today, because there really is nothing new in the standards. However, it might invigorate the teaching of mathematics if we restored the kinds of courses and funded degree programs that were once provided by the National Science Foundation.

Citizens should be outraged at the unjustified expenditure of money on standards, high-stakes testing, and counterproductive (but expensive) schemes to evaluate teachers. For-profit educational groups have made billions in just the past decade, and there is no end in sight. "New" standards require new tests with all the complex operations of design, trying out, monitoring, scoring, sophisticated efforts to detect and prevent cheating, followed by the demand for "alignment." The curriculum—which should be a varied, rich, relevant body of material continually open to creative and responsible change—the *curriculum* must be aligned with the tests. Talk about putting the cart before the horse! Consider what happens when the alignment is nearly perfect. Teachers, then, are fully justified in "teaching to the test," because the test really has become the curriculum. Suppose teachers succeed in this teaching, and the students do well on the tests. This happened a few years ago in New York City. Was there a celebration? No. Policymakers decided that, because so many kids passed, the tests must be too easy, and therefore they should be made harder.

As I was writing this section, an article appeared in the local paper (in New Jersey) announcing that high school students in the near future will have to pass much more demanding exit tests to get their high school diplomas. Why? Apparently, many of our high school graduates require remedial courses in math and language arts when they enter college. We can agree that this *may* be a problem, but we should know from past experience and present research that the problem will not yield to the demand that students pass a more difficult high school exit exam. Several states—neighboring New York, for example—have long had such tests. Do they have fewer students who need remedial instruction at the college level? Have New Jersey policymakers looked at the deplorably low level of "passing" scores allowed on some of these tests? What makes them think that students will learn more if such tests are instituted? Have they considered how many more young people might simply drop out of high school?

CONSTRUCTING CURRICULUM

Construed rightly, the construction of curriculum is a wonderfully challenging, creative, multistep task. It should begin with a discussion of the large aims posited for each of the three great domains of human life: home and personal life, occupational life, and civic life. Well-informed policymakers, interested citizens, and educators should be involved at this stage, and they should spend time considering the questions raised in this book. How can we provide for the variety of interests and talents of our children? When and how should their school experience be universal in order to establish a foundation for further learning? When should their educational programs diverge and in what ways? This sort of exploration and discussion rarely take place today. Instead, we are forced to begin with the rigid disciplinary structure already in place and work from there. We can ask, however, how each of the existing subjects can be guided by the aims and whether we can introduce new programs—such as vocational education—that make use of the current subjects.

Are there things that everyone should know and be able to do? We should proceed with both caution and imagination. Too often, we start reasonably with something like "command of the fundamental processes," and swiftly find ourselves insisting that everyone should know the difference between a definite and indefinite integral. Universal aims must be translated into attainable goals at each stage in each program. At the universal level, they should be stated vaguely. All children should acquire some facility in communicating: reading, speaking, listening, writing, and using basic technological processes. These basic communication skills should be interwoven with the attitudes and values we believe should be universally developed: recognition of human interdependence and respect for the variety of talents and interests, a growing dedication to the health of Earth, aesthetic sensibility, willingness to listen and respond with critical respect, a commitment to gain self-knowledge and moral integrity.

As we begin to put together written curricula in the various subjects, we keep our universal 21st-century aims in mind. Any topic or skill *required* of all students should pass a test suggested by Jerome Bruner (1960):

> We might ask, as a criterion for any subject taught in primary school, whether, when fully developed, it is worth an adult's knowing, and whether having known it as a child makes a person a better adult. If the answer to both questions is negative or ambiguous, then the material is cluttering the curriculum. (p. 52)

This is, however, a hard test to apply. It invites endless arguments over what might be useful together with impassioned testimony about how important knowing the date of the Battle of Hastings was in someone's life. It is helpful, however, as advice against over-specification of the curriculum in terms of facts and minor skills that do indeed clutter the curriculum. Interpreted this way, it also reminds policymakers and subject-matter experts that it is not their province to prescribe exactly what should be taught at every grade level in every class to every student. It is the job of teachers, working daily with students, to build the actual curriculum based on the broad initial outline provided. Many wonderful bits of curriculum will be offered as free gifts for students to build upon or ignore as their interests dictate. At every stage of development, as the prescribed curriculum is filled out interactively, much new material will be added as teacher and students discuss the initial material. (For background on such distinctions as pre-active and interactive curriculum, see Jackson, 1992.)

Recognizing the legitimacy of the interactive curriculum—material that is added by teachers in response to needs and interests expressed by students—invites another devastating criticism of the current move to convert curriculum *content* into content *standards*. Highly effective, creative teachers are too often criticized—even reprimanded—when they deviate from a prescribed lesson objective to address ideas that arise in interaction with their students. The result can be a grim, stultifying series of lessons devoid of the connections we've been discussing throughout this book.

The only payoff possibly gained from such lessons is high test scores for students and acceptable evaluations for teachers, but so far we have made little progress toward them. In any case, these may be poor measures by which to judge the worth of what we are doing. A recent poll, like so many in the past, reported that only about 21% of native-born American citizens know that Woodrow Wilson was president during World War I. New immigrant citizens, in contrast, were much more likely to know this fact; it was something they learned in preparation for their citizenship test. No doubt they, too, will soon forget it. Looking critically at our curriculum and at the aims suggested for the 21st century, we might speculate that people would be more likely to remember that Wilson was president during World War I if classroom discussion concentrated on the destruction of that war, on the stupidity and arrogance of leaders in the Battle of the Somme, the search for peace through the League of Nations, the reading of World War I poetry, the vow of Oxford students never again to fight for "king and country," the moral courage of Representative Jeannette Rankin who voted in Congress against the war, and the rise of conscientious objection. Big ideas and concepts provide a receptacle for the facts we so often cherish.

Analyzing and reflecting on aims for 21st-century education with attention to all three domains of life, we provide a broad foundation for the next step in curriculum construction—deciding on a variety of programs to meet the needs of a diverse population in a worldwide democracy. There should be room, as discussed above, for enrichment of the written curriculum at every level, but opportunities to explore and build upon individual interests and abilities should be somewhat more formalized in middle and secondary schools. At this stage, we face the dual task of *differentiating* courses and programs and also of *integrating* our efforts to be guided by the universal aims already identified. I have suggested, for example, that the richest ideas of liberal education be incorporated in all of the courses offered by our schools. We should be able to offer practical vocational courses that invite students to engage in the immortal conversation, and we should make a continuous effort to make connections across the disciplines and to life itself.

In this book, I have not embraced any one theoretical approach to curriculum making in its entirety. (For discussion of several such approaches, see Schubert, 1986.) Rather, I have suggested that we may learn much from all of them. It is not a matter of throwing them together willy-nilly but of employing a thoughtful, critically eclectic analysis that considers the needs of students, the nature of the subject matter, and the needs of the larger society. We cannot engage in a full discussion of curriculum development here, but both aspiring teachers and teachers in service should spend some time reviewing the thought of curriculum theorists and reflecting on how it might contribute to their own work. (See, for example, Eisner, 1979; Pinar, 1975; Pinar, Reynolds, Slattery, & Taubman, 1995.) When the broad work of establishing programs and outlines for subject development has been done, teachers take over the work of elaborating and guiding the interactive curriculum. They should not be told how to teach. Rather, they should be encouraged to explore the treasure chest of material on pedagogy already available.

PEDAGOGICAL TREASURE

When the written curriculum and goals are established, we may begin to plan lessons. There are two cautions to be observed here. First, teachers must be open to "teachable moments," those classroom events that invite a spontaneous change of plans; second, they should not restrict themselves to one theoretical framework on which to build. In psychological theory, for example, much can be learned from both behaviorists and constructivists. Many lessons—those aimed at teaching specific, well-defined skills—properly begin with a well-stated learning objective, followed by explanation and examples, a practice session, and short quiz to be sure that students have achieved the objective. Committed constructivists sometimes reject such lessons and, especially, anything that calls for *drill*; "drill and kill" is to be avoided. But there is a rich psychological literature describing the judicious use of practice and, used wisely, drill will not kill interest; on the contrary, it should free students to work more confidently and creatively on matters that make a higher cognitive demand.

Such lessons should not dominate our lesson plans, however. They should be preceded by the "big picture" introduction suggested by E. O. Wilson and endorsed throughout this book, and they should be judiciously spaced to provide opportunities for discovery. After the publication of

Jerome Bruner's *The Process of Education* in 1960, there followed a decade or so of keen interest in discovery learning. Discovery lessons can be exciting and rewarding. When students are confronted by a set of examples and draw a significant generalization from them, it can be a memorable experience. In teaching geometry, for example, I asked students to work in pairs to measure the angles of various triangles and compute the sums. The resulting answers led to a tentative generalization, discussion of the difference between empirical evidence and mathematical proof, and even some discussion about measurement error. Experimentation, discussion, and conjecture set us up nicely for an attempt at proof.

But not everything in the curriculum can be learned through discovery. This exciting, useful approach has been nearly lost because teachers and researchers pushed it too far (Shulman & Keislar, 1966). Some years ago, I worked with a group of teachers who were trying to get their students to "discover" the names of several heavenly constellations. It might indeed be fun to show students pictures of the constellations and spend a few minutes making guesses on their names, but the lessons had dragged on, and the kids were simply not "discovering." I asked the teachers, "Why don't you just tell them?" These teachers, committed to constructivism, were aghast. So was I. A good idea was being pushed to an early death by asking too much of it.

Learning by discovery is still a wonderful idea. Bruner's valuable suggestions were anticipated years before by Dewey in his broader discussion of the role of inquiry in learning. He identified *inquiry* or *finding out* as one of the fourfold interests of children (Noddings, 2012b). Wise teachers capitalize on this basic interest by building on the particular, topical interests of students or by arousing interest in the topic prescribed in the curriculum. Notice that it doesn't have to be all one way or the other. We can encourage students to inquire into problems or topics in which they express interest or we can arouse their interest in a problem that we introduce (Cuffaro, 1995; Fishman & McCarthy, 1998). It is a great mistake to suppose that, as followers of Dewey, we must wait for students to say what they want to do. The idea, Dewey (1938/1963) said, is to secure their *participation* "in construction of the purposes which direct [their] activities in the learning process" (p. 67).

Dewey identified the desire to express themselves artistically as another of the fourfold interests of children. The best elementary school teachers have always encouraged this interest both for its own sake and to motivate all sorts of learning. In an earlier chapter, I described a language arts lesson that departed from the stated learning objective to allow students to write poetry and sing about snow and sledding. The teacher was reprimanded when she should have been commended. Teachers should watch for opportunities to connect logical and aesthetic interests (Garrison, 1997).

It has always seemed harder to combine aesthetic and logical or mathematical interests at the high school level, but this is a failure of both imagination and teacher education. It is easy to get caught up in the routine exercises laid out in textbooks, and today teachers are ordered to pursue a stated objective, encourage diligent practice, give lots of homework, and test, test, test. Dare mathematics teachers take time out to discuss mathematics as "the poetry of the universe" or talk about Edwin Abbott's *Flatland*, a mathematical fantasy that challenges sexism, classism, and religious pretension? As we look reflectively at Dewey, Bruner, and other early arguments for an emphasis on inquiry, we must remember to look ahead: Toward what aims should we now direct student efforts at inquiry? How does what we are teaching connect to home life, civic life, or vocational life?

We do have a treasure chest to choose from when we consider pedagogical methods. Where might we use Pestalozzian object lessons, Socratic questioning, role playing, mock courts or a model United Nations, games, and varieties of group work? How might we include stories, art, poetry, and music in science and mathematics classes?

I want to say a bit more here about another item in the treasure chest— mastery learning and its possible adaptations. I've mentioned several times the Algebra 2 course in which I was involved years ago. One might brush off mastery learning because we disagree with Bloom (1981) on the claim that, with patience and expert teaching, we can bring all students to mastery. In fact, I *do* disagree with him on this. However, we can analyze his suggestions and adapt them to strive honestly toward *limited* mastery. To accomplish this, we need to engage in task analysis, work for which teachers are often unprepared (Cronbach, 1977). The assumption may be that textbooks are so organized that teachers need not engage further in task analysis; unit x prepares students for unit x+1. But even when texts are well organized with graded exercises and the like, teachers of sequential subjects still need to investigate more deeply the question of what students need to know before proceeding to the next topic, and there really is no point in moving on if this limited mastery has not been achieved. If we insist on this limited mastery, can we cover the entire prescribed curriculum? Probably not. But we can raise questions about that curriculum and urge modifications and alternatives better matched to the talents and interests of students. A significant purpose of education as stated by Dewey and endorsed in this book is to help students find out what they are good at and what they would like to do. We do not advance our democracy by insisting that everyone is equal (or even nearly equal) in the ability to succeed at whatever we decide to teach.

A powerful way to build on individual interests and to make the vital connections demanded by 21st-century aims is to have students undertake projects. We need not make projects the pedagogical center of our instruction as suggested years ago by William Heard Kilpatrick, nor need we insist that students pursue one project through all of their elementary schooling as suggested by Kieran Egan. But we can learn much from both Kilpatrick and Egan as we help our students to select and carry out projects. The *activity* emphasized by Kilpatrick is vital; we want students to be engaged, to believe that their interests can be connected to material the school imposes on them. With Egan, we endorse the idea of learning in depth, and well-chosen projects should promote such learning.

Finally, in this brief examination of the contents of our pedagogical treasure chest, I want to consider diagnostic methods. There are now powerful computerized programs designed to diagnose student difficulties with various concepts and techniques. One such program promises to give math teachers —"at the click of a button"—information on how many students completed an assignment, how long each one spent on it, and which exercises caused the most difficulty. Such programs are part of a current effort to press teachers into "data-driven" instruction. We should look critically and appreciatively at these programs. Almost certainly, more and more instruction in the future will be done online. But we need to know what to look for, and we need to acknowledge what we may sacrifice as we rely more heavily on electronic methods.

We already have human-centered methods by which to diagnose problems. A math teacher might begin a review of the homework by asking students whether there are any problems they would like to see done at the board. The computer program above will tell us that many students had problems with, say, numbers 5 and 6. Face-to-face, we may learn that some students also had problems with numbers 3, 10, and 13, and we will review and discuss each of these. As student volunteers work the requested problems at the board, the teacher may walk around the room, glancing at the work in front of each student. The computer can tell us that some students did not do the homework, but our walk about can do the same thing. Better, more directly, we can stop beside a student and ask quietly, "No homework?" The student's answer may trigger a sympathetic response for last night's headache, a worried reminder that this is happening too often, or even a joke about the proverbial activity of the family dog.

As we employ critical thinking on the recommendation for data-driven instruction, we want to remain receptive to new possibilities but also reflect on what should drive us and on what occasions. When should our instruction be data-driven and when should it be student-driven?

A computerized curriculum should be very useful when we want students to be able to move at their own pace through a set of required exercises. But when the material under consideration is homework for the whole class, we should be more cautious. In this case, it is probably better to operate as described in the paragraph above. The idea is to discuss, share solutions, and make direct face-to-face contact. We want students to learn the prescribed academic material but, just as important, we want to give them opportunities to grow morally, socially, and emotionally. We need that direct contact in order to establish relations of care and trust.

There may be no more powerful diagnostic tool than the method of overt thinking that Piaget used in his research. The idea is to ask the student, "Let me hear you think." Clearly, the success of this method depends on a level of trust maintained between teacher and student. The student must be comfortable talking with the teacher, confident that he will not be mocked or treated as a hopeless case. Again, it is respectful human interaction and the responses thus obtained that drive instruction—not data in the form of numbers. The method is powerful one-to-one, but it can be extended to whole-class instruction when students are asked to share their thoughts, arguments, and solutions. And it can be used implicitly as a teacher moves about the room listening to students as they work together. Hearing the same error or misunderstanding repeatedly may lead the teacher to interrupt a practice session in order to make a point clear to the whole class. On hearing something creative, the teacher may again interrupt the session, commenting, "Just listen to what Barb and Nick have discovered. This is terrific!"

Professional teachers are rightly in charge of lessons, just as physicians are in charge of treatments. Both are in positions of enormous responsibility.

THE STATUS OF TEACHERS AND TESTS

Teachers are under relentless attack today and, if we value education and the democracy it supports, we should protest this attack and put an end to it. Teachers, as professionals, should be in control of their lessons. No teachers should be told to use a scripted lesson. No teacher should be forced to state a specific learning objective for every lesson. No teacher should be evaluated solely on the basis of test scores. And, certainly, no teacher should be publicly shamed by the publication of pseudo-evaluations. Many of us who have had distinguished careers in teaching would not even consider entering the profession as it is demeaned today.

Professional teachers welcome the support of reputable organizations that provide seminars and professional development courses. In the years following Sputnik (1957), for example, the National Science Foundation offered seminars and even degree programs with stipends for teachers of math and science. Similarly, there were programs for teachers interested in open education, the new social studies, and language development.

Today, many of the programs offered to teachers come from for-profit organizations; education has become, at every level, big business. The enormous expenditure on standards and testing would be better invested in seminars and paid sabbaticals sponsored by reliable, professionally accredited organizations. It is not that everything offered by for-profit agencies is bad, but it is necessarily and properly suspect—very like the seminars offered to physicians by pharmaceutical companies. Some of the material thus offered is useful, but it would be better if it were impartially evaluated, organized, and presented by reputable, nonprofit groups.

Possibly nothing is more distressing and distracting to professional teachers than the current emphasis on standardized tests. Although many teachers see this emphasis as degrading their professional efforts, a surprising number (usually younger people who have grown up in this environment) accept the emphasis on tests as necessary. Working as a guest lecturer with a group of energetic teachers preparing to become principals, I raised questions about this emphasis. Several students defended the need for these tests, saying, "How would we know how the kids are doing if we didn't use these tests?" A slightly older student (an English teacher) responded in some amazement that she didn't need the test scores to know how her students were doing; she could predict how each of them would do on the tests. I agreed with her. I, too, always knew (with very few exceptions) how my students would do and could predict how they would score. Indeed, a teacher's inability to do this with a fair degree of accuracy may be a surer sign of incompetence than poor scores. In large part, the tests confirm what we already know.

Sadly, one can anticipate eager researchers gleefully gathering data on teacher predictions and offering the data as part of each teacher's evaluation. I am not recommending that, but I do think department meetings at which teachers discuss their predictions could be very useful.

Current efforts at value-added evaluation of teacher effectiveness are riddled with errors. Recent attempts to use such methods in New York City verged on the bizarre. Reading accounts of the results and teachers' outraged reactions to them, I thought of the knave's trial in *Alice's Adventures in Wonderland*. The jurors listened raptly as witnesses mentioned several dates. Numbers! The jurors wrote the numbers on their slates, added them up, and reduced the answer to shillings and pence. What we are doing with the numbers we gather to evaluate teachers may not be quite this crazy, but it has far more dire consequences.

The question is not how to perfect a numerical system of teacher evaluation. The fundamental question to ask even before we work on a method of evaluation is what the consequences will be if we employ it. Will we be pressed to publish the results? Teachers must be able to exercise authority in their classrooms. Part of that authority is conveyed by the position itself, and part of it is earned by the way in which teachers interact with their students. Now suppose a teacher has been judged ineffective, and that information is published. Will parents stand for their child's assignment to an ineffective

teacher? Will the kids accept direction from this teacher? Resented and dis-
trusted by parents, scorned by their students, will the teacher have a real
chance to improve?

The idea, of course, is to find a way to dismiss ineffective teachers. But
publishing numerical ratings will not achieve this end. It will more likely
lead administrators to limit arbitrarily the number of teachers so labeled in
much the same way that the number of student failures have been artificially
limited under various competency projects. In the case of student failures,
planning committees have often started their work by asking how many
failures their community will tolerate. Keeping a careful eye on that limit,
they set standards to stay within it, and they can then point to an acceptably
high failure rate as proof that their district maintains high standards. Any
such system should be soundly rejected.

There are some ineffective teachers, and they should be given help to
improve. If they will not accept such help, they should be counseled into
another line of work. Administrators and unions should work together on
this and, if there are incentives for successful teachers to work as guides
and mentors, cooperative arrangements should be attractive to both sides.
Teachers should be treated as we hope they will treat their students; those
who are having difficulties should be helped. Penalties, shame, and threats
rarely work to improve student performance, and it is illogical to suppose
that they will improve teacher performance. Just as we have a treasure
chest of pedagogical methods to draw on, we also have volumes of material
that can guide us on in-service teacher education (Darling-Hammond &
Bransford, 2005; Holmes Group, 1995). It is not a matter of adopting the
methods in these volumes wholesale but of getting ideas, thinking, reflecting, imagining, and committing ourselves to methods that are both morally
justifiable and practically reasonable. Despite the richness of sources we
possess to draw upon, we will be unlikely to move toward plans that are
genuinely *educational* and that incorporate well-chosen aims for the 21st
century if we do not analyze and transform the language we are now using
to direct education.

THE LANGUAGE OF EDUCATION CRITICALLY APPRAISED

A critical examination of the language of educational policy is likely to gen-
erate concern, if not outright dismay. Policymakers and too many educators
have adopted the language of business, and its use has corrupted public
education. *Business* has become the main metaphor in education, and we
constantly hear talk of competition, accountability, scaling-up, rankings,
effectiveness, zero-tolerance, and "what works." These concepts are not

'employ-
ability'

useless in education but, when they dominate educational language, they are deeply troubling. Indeed, if we allow them to control educational language, they may actually destroy public schooling.

If we must choose a metaphor to guide our discussion of schools, it should be *home.* The words and slogans associated with *home* invite us to think of schools as places of safety and support, companionship, fun, intellectual stimulation, cooperation, food, plants and animals, conversation. "Home is where the heart is," and as Bachelard wrote, the house shelters the dreamer. We do not have to go overboard in our use of "home" language, nor need we abandon the language of business entirely. Even the most poetically lovely homes require their inhabitants to use sound financial thinking. But the language that *characterizes* educational policy today is dominantly business talk, and it is antithetical to genuine education.

Businesses emphasize the idea of a *bottom line*, and that bottom line is profit for owners and stockholders. In education, people also talk of a bottom line—student achievement, measured by test scores. Thoughtful critics object strenuously to the evaluation of achievement entirely by test scores. They rightly insist that achievement cannot be adequately described by numbers alone. Their objections, sound as they are, do not probe deeply enough. We should want more from our efforts at schooling than achievement. Surely, we also want healthy, happy, caring children who will become competent, caring, thoughtful, moral, well-balanced . . . adults. The dots in this last sentence are meant as an invitation to readers to consider and insert still more adjectives. As I have emphasized throughout this book, education is an enterprise with many aims, and it requires us to abandon bureaucratic thinking, to cross disciplinary lines, and to employ language that encourages dialogue and creativity.

Consider *accountability*, a word adopted without modification from business. When people are held accountable, they must answer to someone for what they have done or failed to do. Usually, workers are accountable for the quality and quantity of their work; they must report to superiors who judge both quality and quantity. Accountability induces an increase in defensiveness, the natural desire to preserve oneself from criticism and penalties. In an impersonal, business situation where people are competing for higher wages and recognition, we expect to find a hierarchy of power, each layer accountable to the one above it. The system is meant to ensure that everyone is doing the job to which he or she has been assigned.

Accountability is rarely used, however, in homes or home-like settings. The far stronger, more fitting word is *responsibility*. Parents are responsible for the welfare of their children. Teachers are responsible for the healthy growth (intellectual, moral, aesthetic, . . .) of their students. Parents do not report to their children; teachers do not report to their students.

Responsibility digs deeper and carries further than accountability. When we are moved by accountability, we are concerned with what may happen to us, what penalties we may suffer, what rewards we may gain. In contrast, when we are moved by responsibility, our concern is with *others*; it is not focused on ourselves. Probably most people who choose teaching as a profession feel their responsibility keenly. The current emphasis on accountability may actually undermine the moral/emotional state of mind that supports the best in teaching.

The demand for accountability has led to an increase in "exit" tests. It is argued that, if teachers are doing what they should—what they are properly held accountable for—students should pass yearly standardized tests and a high school exit test. (We can guess that something is wrong when we can't figure out how to define "passing.") Why should it be necessary to pass a test in order to receive a diploma? Why is it not sufficient to pass the courses required by the program in which one has been enrolled? If these courses are inadequate, why do we not revise them and make them stronger? The business-corrupted approach is shot through with distrust. We do not trust teachers to act responsibly, and so we insist that they must be held accountable. How? For what exactly? We are using language that belongs to another game.

Consistent with the corrupting influence of bottom lines and accountability, we constantly hear talk of "what works." The supposition seems to be that there is one task—or, at least, a way to take on one at a time—and someone has found "what works" for that one task. Exercising Dewey's method of intelligence and a well-developed sense of responsibility, we should ask: "Works" for what? For whom? Under what conditions? And if we succeed at this (whatever works), might other important aims or goals be sacrificed or undermined as a result?

The language of education is both beautiful and complex. It is not a collection of slogans and keywords. We should listen carefully to recommendations and ask respectfully: What do you mean? What is meant by "All children can learn"? *What* can all children learn, and why should they learn it? When someone tells us that instruction should be "data-driven," what does he mean? How far and for what tasks should we depend on data? And what exactly do we mean by *data*? Must data be quantitative? Can a set of stories be data? Is good teaching sometimes driven by feeling?

Rigorous is another word heard ad nauseam. When people demand that a course or program be made "more rigorous," what do they mean? Harder? Stiffer? More boring? One that fewer people will pass? More faithful to the subject being taught? This last is worth talking about in some depth. In an earlier chapter, I confessed my ambivalence about teaching algebra in a way that made it possible for more students to pass the course but somehow compromised mathematics itself. Such discussions are important, indeed vital, to the educational enterprise, even though they may not be resolvable in a universally accepted way. They will always be with us and, approached intelligently, they should enrich our conversation.

An important theme in this book has been *ecology*—not directed solely at the natural world but, more universally, at a search for balance in our thinking on education and democracy. Rejecting the notion that schooling should concentrate on intellectual development academically conceived, we should design programs that support satisfying ways of life for whole persons in all three of the great domains. Rejecting the search for panaceas, as educators we should not force the same educational program on all students or the same methods on all teachers for all purposes. As Americans, we should stop trying to force our form of democracy on everyone else. If we value our democracy, we will remember that it is perpetually a cooperative work under construction. So is education. We have much to gain from a critical and appreciative appraisal of the past and, perhaps even more, from a cooperative and imaginative exploration of the future.

References

Adler, M. J. (1982). *The paideia proposal*. New York: Macmillan.

Anderson, R. N. L. (1999). *Managing the environment, managing ourselves: A history of American environmental policy*. New Haven: Yale University Press.

Apple, M. W. (1996). *Cultural politics and education*. New York: Teachers College Press.

Aries, P. (1962). *Centuries of childhood* (R. Baldwick, Trans.). New York: Vintage Books.

Arum, R., & Roksa, J. (2011). *Academically adrift: Limited learning on college campuses*. Chicago: University of Chicago Press.

Bachelard, G. (1964). *The poetics of space* (Maria Jolas, Trans.). New York: Orion Press.

Barber, B. (1996). Constitutional faith. In M. Nussbaum, *For love of country?* Boston: Beacon Press.

Beecher, C. E., & Stowe, H. B. (1869). *The American woman's house*. New York: J. B. Ford.

Bellamy, E. (1960). *Looking backward*. New York: New American Library. (Original work published 1897)

Berry, W. (1995). *Another turn of the crank*. Washington, DC: Counterpoint.

Bestor, A. Jr. (1953). *Educational wastelands: The retreat from learning in our public schools*. Urbana: University of Illinois Press.

Bettelheim, B. (1976). *The uses of enchantment: The meaning and importance of fairy tales*. New York: Alfred A. Knopf.

Bloom, B. S. (1981). *All our children learning*. New York: McGraw-Hill.

Blum, L. (2013). *High schools, race, and America's future*. Cambridge: Harvard Education Press.

Booth, W. C. (1988). *The vocation of a teacher*. Chicago: University of Chicago Press.

Bowles, S., & Gintis, H. (1976). *Schooling in capitalist America*. New York: Basic Books.

Brownell, W. (1947). The place of meaning in the teaching of arithmetic. *Elementary School Journal, 47*, 256–265.

Bruner, J. (1960). *The process of education*. Cambridge: Harvard University Press.

Bryson, B. (2010). *At home*. New York: Anchor Books.

Buber, M. (1965). *Between man and man*. New York: Macmillan.

Buber, M. (1966). *The way of response*. (Nahum Glatzer, Ed.). New York: Schocken Books.

Buber, M. (1970). *I and thou*. (Walter Kaufmann, Trans.). New York: Charles Scribner's Sons.

Cahn, S. M. (Ed.). (1997). *Classic and contemporary readings in the philosophy of education*. New York: McGraw-Hill.

Callan, E. (1997). *Creating citizens: Political education and liberal democracy*. Oxford: Oxford University Press.

Carlson, S. (2012, February 10). The future of American colleges may lie, literally, in students' hands. *Chronicle Review, The Chronicle of Higher Education*, B, 6–9.

Carson, R. (1962). *Silent spring*. Boston: Houghton Mifflin.

Casey, E. S. (1997). *The fate of place*. Berkeley: University of California Press.

Cohen, L. (2003). *A consumers' republic*. New York: Vintage Books.

Collins, G. (2012). *As Texas goes . . . How the lone star state hijacked the American agenda*. New York: Liveright.

Counts, G. S. (1969). *Dare the school build a new social order?* New York: Arno Press. (Original work published 1932)

Crawford, M. B. (2009). *Shop class as soulcraft*. New York: Penguin Press.

Cronbach, L. J. (1966). The logic of experiments on discovery. In L. S. Shulman & E. R. Keislar (Eds.), *Learning by discovery* (pp. 76–92). Chicago: Rand McNally.

Cronbach, L. J. (1977). *Educational psychology*. New York: Harcourt Brace Jovanovich.

Cuffaro, H. K. (1995). *Experimenting with the world: John Dewey and the early childhood classroom*. New York: Teachers College Press.

Darling-Hammond, L., & Bransford, J. (Eds.). (2005). *Preparing teachers for a changing world*. San Francisco: Jossey-Bass.

Davidson, A. (2012, January/February). Making it in America. *The Atlantic*, 58–70.

Dawkins, R. (2006). *The God delusion*. Boston: Houghton Mifflin.

De Nicola, D. R. (2011). Friends, foes, and Nel Noddings on liberal education. In Rob Kunzman (Ed.), *Philosophy of Education*. Urbana, IL: Philosophy of Education Society.

Dewey, J. (1900). *The school and society*. Chicago: University of Chicago Press.

Dewey, J. (1916). *Democracy and education*. New York: Macmillan.

Dewey, J. (1929). *The quest for certainty*. New York: G. P. Putnam's Sons.

Dewey, J. (1963). *Experience and education*. New York: Macmillan. (Original work published 1938)

Dewey, J. (1927). *The public and its problems*. New York: Henry Holt.

Dewey, J. (1988). *Individualism, old and new*. In J. Boydston (Ed.), *The later works*, Vol. 5 (pp. 45–123). Carbondale and Edwardsville: Southern Illinois Press. (Original work published 1929–30)

Douglas, M. S. (1997). *The everglades: River of grass*. Sarasota, FL: Pineapple Press.

Egan, K. (2010). *Learning in depth*. Chicago: University of Chicago Press.

Eisner, E. (1979). *The educational imagination: On the design and evaluation of school programs.* New York: Macmillan.

Eliot, C. W. (1908). Industrial education as an essential factor in our national prosperity. National Society for the Promotion of Industrial Education, *Bulletin,* no. 2, 12–13.

Elshtain, J. B. (1987). *Women and war.* New York: Basic Books.

Farley, J. D. (2011, September 2). Letter. *New York Times.*

Ferguson, N. (2011, September 19). Texting makes us stupid. *Newsweek,* 11.

Fineman, M. A. (2004). *The autonomy myth: A theory of dependency.* New York: New Press.

Fishman, S. M., & McCarthy, L. (1998). *John Dewey and the challenge of classroom practice.* New York: Teachers College Press.

Ford, L. R. (2000). *The spaces between buildings.* Baltimore: Johns Hopkins University Press.

Forster, E. M. (1993). *Howard's end.* New York: Barnes & Noble. (Original work published 1910)

Forster, E. M. (1995). *A room with a view.* New York: Dover. (Original work published 1908)

Freire, P. (1970). *Pedagogy of the oppressed.* (Myra Bergman Ramos, Trans.). New York: Herder & Herder.

Gardner, H. (1983). *Frames of mind.* New York: Basic Books.

Gardner, H. (2011). *Truth, beauty, and goodness reframed: Educating for the virtues in the 21st century.* New York: Basic Books.

Gardner, J. W. (1984). *Excellence.* New York: W. W. Norton. (Original work published 1961)

Garrison, J. (1997). *Dewey and eros.* New York: Teachers College Press.

Gilbreth, F. B., Jr., & Carey, E. G. (1966). *Cheaper by the dozen.* New York: Bantam. (Original work published 1948)

Glover, J. (2000). *Humanity: A moral history of the 20th century.* New Haven: Yale University Press.

Goldensohn, L. (2003). *Dismantling glory.* New York: Columbia University Press.

Gray, J. G. (1970). *The warriors: Reflections on men in battle.* Lincoln, NE: University of Nebraska Press.

Greenawalt, K. (2005). *Does God belong in public schools?* Princeton: Princeton University Press.

Grissell, E. (2001). *Insects and gardens: In pursuit of a garden ecology.* Portland, OR: Timber Press.

Grubb, W. N. (Ed.). (1995). *Education through occupations in American high schools,* Vols. 1 & 2. New York: Teachers College Press.

Grubb, W. N., & Lazerson, M. (1975). Rally 'round the workplace: Continuities and fallacies in career education. *Harvard Educational Review, 45*(4), 451-474.

Gutmann, A. (1987). *Democratic education.* Princeton: Princeton University Press.

Hacker, A., & Dreifus, C. (2010). *Higher education?* New York: Times Books.

Halberstam, D. (1992). *The best and the brightest.* New York: Ballantine Books.

Hansen, D. T. (2010). Chasing butterflies without a net: Interpreting cosmopolitanism. *Studies in Philosophy and Education, 29*(2), 151–166.

Hansen, D. T. (2011). *The teacher and the world: A study of cosmopolitanism as education.* London: Routledge.

Hardy, T. (1961). *Jude the obscure.* New York: New American Library. (Original work published 1894)

Hartshorne, H., & May, M. (1928–1930). *Studies in the nature of character*, Vols. 1 & 2. New York: Macmillan.

Hawkins, D. (1973). How to plan for spontaneity. In Charles E. Silberman (Ed.), *The open classroom reader* (pp. 486–503). New York: Vintage Books.

Hawkins, F. P. L. (1997). *Journey with children.* Niwot, CO: University Press of Colorado.

Heath, S. B. (1983). *Ways with words.* New York: Cambridge University Press.

Held, D. (2006). *Models of democracy.* Stanford, CA: Stanford University Press.

Hellman, H. (1998). *Great feuds in science.* New York: John Wiley & Sons.

Hersh, R. (1997). *What is mathematics really?* Oxford: Oxford University Press.

Hersh, R., & John-Steiner, V. (2011). *Loving and hating mathematics.* Princeton: Princeton University Press.

Hess, F. M. (2010). *The same thing over and over.* Cambridge: Harvard University Press.

Hirsch, E. D., Jr. (1987). *Cultural literacy: What every American needs to know.* Boston: Houghton Mifflin.

Hirsch, E. D., Jr. (1996). *The schools we need: Why we don't have them.* New York: Doubleday.

Hoffman, N. (2010, August 3). Learning for jobs, not "college for all": How European countries think about preparing young people for productive citizenship. *Teachers College Record* (ID#: 16096).

Hofstadter, D. R. (1985). *Metamagical themes: Questing for the essence of mind and pattern.* New York: Basic Books.

Holmes Group. (1995). *Tomorrow's schools of education.* East Lansing, MI: The Holmes Group.

Horton, M. (1998). *The long haul* (with J. Kohl & H. Kohl). New York: Teachers College Press.

Howe, K. (1997). *Understanding equal educational opportunity.* New York: Teachers College Press.

Hulbert, A. (2003). *Raising America.* New York: Alfred A. Knopf.

Hutchins, R. M. (1999). *The higher learning in America.* New Haven: Yale University Press. (Original work published 1936)

Jackson, J. B. (1994). *A sense of place, a sense of time.* New Haven: Yale University Press.

Jackson, P. W. (Ed.). (1992). *Handbook of research on curriculum.* New York: Macmillan.

John-Steiner, V. (2000). *Creative collaboration.* Oxford: Oxford University Press.

Johnston, J. S. (2011). The Dewey-Hutchins debate: A dispute over moral teleology. *Educational Theory, 61*(1), 1–16.

Jung, C. G. (1969). *Collected works,* Vol. 2. Princeton: Princeton University Press.

Kahn, P. (1999). *The human relationship with nature.* Cambridge: MIT Press.

Kahne, J. (1996). *Reframing educational policy.* New York: Teachers College Press.

Kater, M. H. (1989). *Doctors under Hitler.* Chapel Hill: University of North Carolina Press.

Kerber, L. K. (1997). *Toward an intellectual history of women.* Chapel Hill: University of North Carolina Press.

Kipling, R. (1956). In J. Beecroft (Ed.), *Kipling: A selection of his stories and poems,* vol. II. Garden City, NY: Doubleday.

Kliebard, H. (1995). *The struggle for the American curriculum 1893–1958.* New York: Routledge.

Kliebard, H. (1999). *Schooled to work: Vocationalism and the American curriculum 1876–1946.* New York: Teachers College Press.

Knowles, J. (1960). *A separate peace.* New York: Macmillan.

Kohlberg, L. (1981). *The philosophy of moral development,* Vol. 1. San Francisco: Harper & Row.

Kohn, A. (2006). *The homework myth.* Cambridge, MA: Perseus Books.

Kozol, J. (1988). *Rachel and her children.* New York: Crown.

Kozol, J. (1991). *Savage inequalities.* New York: Crown.

Kozol, J. (2005). *The shame of a nation: The restoration of apartheid schooling in America.* New York: Crown.

Labaree, D. (1997). *How to succeed in school without really learning: The credentials race in American education.* New Haven: Yale University Press.

Lagemann, E. C. (Ed.). (1985). *Jane Addams on education.* New York: Teachers College Press.

Lane, R. E. (2000). *The loss of happiness in market democracies.* New Haven: Yale University Press.

Leahey, C. R. (2010). *Whitewashing war.* New York: Teachers College Press.

Lewis, C. S. (1955). *The abolition of man: How education develops man's sense of morality.* New York: Collier Books.

Lipman, M. (1991). *Thinking in education.* Cambridge: Cambridge University Press.

Livio, M. (2002). *The golden ratio: The story of phi, the world's most astonishing number.* New York: Broadway Books.

Lounsbury, J. H. (2009, February 6). Deferred but determined: A middle school manifesto. *Middle School Journal.*

Lounsbury, J. H., & Vars, G. F. (1978). *A curriculum for the middle school years.* New York: Harper & Row.

Loveless, T. (2012, April 18). Does the common core matter? *Education Week*, 32.

Macedo, D. (1994). *Literacies of power: What Americans are not allowed to know*. Boulder, CO: Westview Press.

Martenson, C. (2011). *The crash course*. Hoboken, NJ: John Wiley & Sons.

Martin, J. R. (1985). *Reclaiming a conversation*. New Haven: Yale University Press.

Meier, D. (1995). *The power of their ideas: Lessons for America from a small school in Harlem*. Boston: Beacon Press.

Meier, D., & Wood, G. (Eds.). (2004). *Many children left behind*. Boston: Beacon Press.

Molnar, A. (1996). *Giving kids the business: The commercialization of America's schools*. Boulder, CO: Westview Press.

Morris, S. C. (2003). *Life's solution: Inevitable humans in a lonely universe*. Cambridge: Cambridge University Press.

Murray, C. (2008). *Real education*. New York: Random House.

Nabhan, G. P., & Trimble, S. (1994). *The geography of childhood: Why children need wild places*. Boston: Beacon Press.

National Education Association. (1908). *Journal of proceedings and addresses*, pp. 99–102. Washington, DC: Author

National Middle School Association. (2003). *This we believe: Developmentally responsive middle level schools*. Westerville, OH: Author.

Nearing, S. (2000). *The making of a radical: A political autobiography*. White River Junction, VT: Chelsea Green.

Newman, J. R. (Ed.). (1956). *The world of mathematics*. New York: Simon & Schuster.

Nichols, S. L., & Berliner, D. (Eds.). (2007). *Collateral damage*. Cambridge: Harvard Education Press.

Nieto, S. (1999). *The light in their eyes: Creating multicultural learning communities*. New York: Teachers College Press.

Noble, D. F. (1992). *A world without women*. Oxford: Oxford University Press.

Noddings, N. (1984). *Caring: A feminine approach to ethics and moral education*. Berkeley: University of California Press.

Noddings, N. (1993). *Educating for intelligent belief or unbelief*. New York: Teachers College Press.

Noddings, N. (1996). On community. *Educational Theory, 46*(3), 245–267.

Noddings, N. (2003). *Happiness and education*. Cambridge: Cambridge University Press.

Noddings, N. (2005). *The challenge to care in schools* (2nd. ed.). New York: Teachers College Press.

Noddings, N. (2006). *Critical lessons: What our schools should teach*. Cambridge: Cambridge University Press.

Noddings, N. (2007). *When school reform goes wrong*. New York: Teachers College Press.

Noddings, N. (2009). Responsibility. *Learning Landscapes, 2*(2), 17–23.

Noddings, N. (2012a). *Peace education: How we come to love and hate war.* Cambridge: Cambridge University Press.

Noddings, N. (2012b). *Philosophy of education.* Boulder, CO: Westview Press.

Oakes, J. (1985). *Keeping track: How schools structure inequality.* New Haven: Yale University Press.

Oakes, J. (1990). *Multiplying inequalities: The effects of race, social class, and tracking on students' opportunities to learn mathematics and science.* Santa Monica: Rand.

Oliva, P. F. (1988). *Developing the curriculum.* Glenview, IL: Scott Foresman/Little, Brown College Division.

Orme, N. (2001). *Medieval children.* New Haven: Yale University Press.

Pears, I. (1998). *An instance of the fingerpost.* New York: Riverhead Books.

Peshkin, A. (1986). *God's choice: The total world of a fundamentalist Christian school.* Chicago: University of Chicago Press.

Piaget, J. (1971). *Biology and knowledge.* Chicago: University of Chicago Press.

Pinar, W. F. (Ed.). (1975). *Curriculum theorizing: The reconceptualists.* Berkeley: McCutchan.

Pinar, W. F., Reynolds, W. M., Slattery, P., & Taubman, P. M. (1995). *Understanding curriculum.* New York: Peter Lang.

Pollan, M. (1991). *Second nature.* New York: Delta.

Pollan, M. (1997). *A place of my own: The education of an amateur builder.* New York: Delta.

Pollan, M. (2001). *The botany of desire.* New York: Random House.

Pope, D. C. (2001). *"Doing school": How we are creating a generation of stressed out, materialistic, and miseducated students.* New Haven: Yale University Press.

Posamentier, A., & Lehmann, I. (2004). *A biography of the world's most mysterious number.* New York: Prometheus Books.

Powell, M. (2011, September 20). A knack for breaking orthodoxy. *New York Times.*

Ravitch, D. (1995). *National standards in American education.* Washington, DC: Brookings Institution Press.

Ravitch, D. (2010). *The death and life of the great American school system.* New York: Perseus Books.

Ravitch, D. (2012, March 8). Schools we can envy. *New York Review of Books,* 19–20.

Rawls, J. (1971). *A theory of justice.* Cambridge: Harvard University Press.

Reisner, M. (1993). *Cadillac desert: The American west and its disappearing water.* New York: Penguin Books.

Rose, M. (1995). *Possible lives: The promise of public education in America.* Boston: Houghton Mifflin.

Rose, M. (2005). *The mind at work: Valuing the intelligence of the American worker.* New York: Penguin.

Ruddick, S. (1989). *Maternal thinking: Toward a politics of peace.* Boston: Beacon Press.

Russell, B. (1957). *Why I am not a Christian.* New York: Simon & Schuster.

Rybczynski, W. (1986). *Home: A short history of an idea.* New York: Viking.

Safina, C. (2011). *The view from lazy point.* New York: Henry Holt.

Sahlberg, P. (2012). *Finnish lessons: What can the world learn from educational change in Finland?* New York: Teachers College Press.

Schaffarzick, J., & Sykes, G. (Eds.). (1979). *Value conflicts and curriculum issues.* Berkeley: McCutchan.

Schlesinger, A. M., Jr. (1992). *The disuniting of America: Reflections on a multicultural society.* New York: W. W. Norton.

Schubert, W. H. (1986). *Curriculum: Perspective, paradigm, and possibilities.* New York: Macmillan.

Schultz, B., & Schultz, R. (1989). *It did happen here.* Berkeley: University of California Press.

Shay, J. (1994). *Achilles in Vietnam: Combat trauma and the undoing of character.* New York: Scribner.

Shorto, R. (2010, February 14). Founding father. *The New York Times Magazine,* pp. 32–39, 45–47.

Shulman, L. S., & Keislar, E. R. (Eds.). (1966). *Learning by discovery: A critical appraisal.* Chicago: Rand McNally.

Simon, K. G. (2001). *Moral questions in the classroom.* New Haven: Yale University Press.

Sizer, T. R. (1984). *Horace's compromise: The dilemma of the American high school.* Boston: Houghton Mifflin.

Skinner, B. F. (1962). *Walden two.* New York: Macmillan. (Original work published 1948)

Smith, C. (2005). *Soul searching: The religious and spiritual lives of American teenagers.* Oxford: Oxford University Press.

Smith, R. P. (1957). *"Where did you go?" "Out" "What did you do?" "Nothing".* New York: W. W. Norton.

Soder, R., Goodlad, J. I., & McMannon, T. J. (Eds.). (2001). *Developing democratic character in the young.* San Francisco: Jossey-Bass.

Sparks, S. D. (2011, June 9). Statistics shed light on costs and benefits of career paths. *Education Week,* 18–19.

Spock, B. (2001). *On parenting.* New York: Pocket Books.

Spring, J. (1997). *Political agendas for education.* Mahwah, NJ: Lawrence Erlbaum.

Steele, C. (2011). *Whistling Vivaldi: And other clues as to how stereotypes affect us.* New York: Norton.

Stein, S. (1993). *Noah's garden: Restoring the ecology of our own back yards.* Boston: Houghton Mifflin.

Steinberg, T. (2002). *Down to earth.* Oxford: Oxford University Press.

Sunstein, C. R. (2009). *Going to extremes: how like minds unite and divide us.* New York: Oxford University Press.

Thornton, S. (2005). *Teaching social studies that matters.* New York: Teachers College Press.

True, M. (1995). *An energy field more intense than war.* Syracuse: Syracuse University Press.

Upitis, R. (2010). *Raising a school.* Ontario, CA: Wintergreen Studios Press.

Walker, R. (2007). *The country in the city.* Seattle: University of Washington Press.

Wallace, J., & Louden, W. (Eds.). (2002). *Dilemmas of science teaching.* London & New York: Routledge.

Walter, E. V. (1988). *Placeways: A theory of the human environment.* Chapel Hill: University of North Carolina Press.

Ward, D. R. (2002). *Water wars: Drought, flood, folly, and the politics of thirst.* New York: Penguin Putnam.

Watson, P. (2010). *The German genius.* New York: HarperCollins.

Westbrook, R. B. (1991). *John Dewey and American democracy.* Ithaca, NY: Cornell University Press.

White, J. T. (1909). *Character lessons in American biography.* New York: The Character Development League.

Whitehead, A. N. (1967). *The aims of education.* New York: Free Press. (Original work published 1929)

Whitman, W. (1982). *Poetry and prose.* New York: Library of America.

Wilhelm, J. D., & Novak, B. (2011). *Teaching literacy for love and wisdom.* New York: Teachers College Press.

Wilson, E. O. (2002). *The future of life.* New York: Alfred A. Knopf.

Wilson, E. O. (2006). *The creation: An appeal to save life on earth.* New York: W. W. Norton.

Wood, G. S. (2011a). *The idea of America.* New York: Penguin Press.

Wood, G. S. (2011b, January 13). No thanks for the memories. *New York Review of Books,* pp. 40–42.

Woolf, V. (1966). *Collected essays,* Vol. 2. London: Hogarth Press.

Wuthnow, R. (1998). *After heaven: Spirituality in America since the 1950s.* Berkeley: University of California Press.

Zeldin, T. (1994). *An intimate history of humanity.* New York: HarperCollins.

Index

School(s)
  democracy in, 22–24
  home as metaphor for, 155
  preparing children for, 68, 77
  private versus public, 23, 37
  reform issues, 1–9
  religious, rational deliberation and, 23–24
  structural uniformity of, 85–86
  test scores and, 1–2
  vocational, 102, 105–106
School choice, 8–9, 23–24
School Mathematics Study Group (SMSG), 142–143
Schooling
  equality of opportunity for, 36–39
  primary purpose of, 25
  20th- versus 21st-century ideas on, vii–viii, 9–11
School-place, 85–86
Schubert, W. H., 148
Schultz, B., 111, 112
Schultz, R., 111, 112
Science
  projects, in local environment, 89
  popular courses, 80
Scientific observation, 89–90
Seeger, P., 111
Self-knowledge, 124–126
Self-motivation, 125–126
Self-productive conduct, 119, 120
Self-understanding, educating for, 45, 100
Sentiments, just, 129
Service learning programs, 122
Shay, J., 100, 139
Shorto, R., 133
Shulman, L. S., 149
Simon, K. G., 127
Sizer, T. R., 28
Skinner, B. F., 38, 103
Slattery, P., 148
Small home movement, 71, 74
Smith, C., 126
Smith, R. P., 70
Smith-Hughes Act (1917), 106
Snobbery
  learning and, 55

liberal arts education and, 58
Sneetches story and, 16
Social activism, child labor and, 81
Social class
  language proficiency and, 110
  liberal arts education and, 58
  perpetuating differences in, 77
Social justice
  academic and vocational students and, 111
  indoctrination and. *See* Indoctrination
  middle school movement and, 112
  parenting courses and, 77
  teaching of, 18–19, 62
Socialism, 16, 140–141
  democratic, 141
Socrates, 56–57, 85, 116, 124
Soder, R., 17
Sparks, S. D., 29
Spiritual education, 126–130
Spirituality, 126, 128–129
Spock, B., 79
Spring, J., 19, 21
Standardized tests, 46–47, 153
Standards, 2–7
  content, 5–7
  for core knowledge, 142–145
  cost of, 145
  opportunity-to-learn, 5–7
  performance, 4–5
"The Star-Spangled Banner," 132
Steele, C., 137
Stein, S., 87
Steinberg, T., 86, 87, 88, 92, 94, 96
STEM courses, 103
Stereotype threat, 137, 138
Stowe, H. B., 74
Student choice, 24–25
Student-centered learning, alternative to, 51–52
Students
  academic and vocational, shared courses for, 110–111
  enthusiasm for study, 124, 125
Subject disciplines
  breadth of knowledge in, 61–62
  lateral movement between, 42, 73
  liberal arts approach to, 60–61

About the Author

Nel Noddings is Lee Jacks Professor of Education, Emerita, at Stanford University. She is a past president of the National Academy of Education, the Philosophy of Education Society, and the John Dewey Society. In addition to 19 books, she is the author of more than 200 hundred articles and chapters on various topics ranging from the ethics of care to mathematical problem-solving. Her latest books are *The Maternal Factor: Two Paths to Morality* (2010) and *Peace Education: How We Come to Love and Hate War* (2012). Her work has so far been translated into 12 languages.

Professor Noddings also spent 15 years as a teacher and administrator in public schools. She served as a mathematics department chairperson in New Jersey and as director of the Laboratory Schools at the University of Chicago. At Stanford, where she received the Award for Teaching Excellence three times, she served as associate dean and acting dean for 4 years.